ISLES OF ILLUSION

First published in 1923, the identity of the author of this fascinating collection of letters was preserved by their recipient, Bohun Lynch, who nicknamed his friend Asterisk. The letters come from an outspoken and unusually honest Englishman, who, enchanted by Stevenson's accounts of the South Pacific, had left England before the First World War to escape the boredom of schoolmastering.

Gavin Young, the internationally respected travel writer, paid tribute to the letters in his *Slow Boats Home*, and *Isles of Illusion* is reprinted for the first time in paperback with a new introduction by Young, in which he describes the background of the author—Robert James Addison Gerard Fletcher—in detail.

Traveller, author and correspondent for the *Observer*, Gavin Young described in his first book, *Return to the Marshes*, his adventures in Iraq with the Marsh Arabs, and this was the basis of a BBC film in 1979. But it was with *Slow Boats to China* and its sequel, *Slow Boats Home*, that Gavin Young established himself as one of the most original and appealing of present day travel writers.

The cover shows 'Nevermore' by Paul Gauguin in the Courtauld
Institute Galleries

ISLES OF ILLUSION

Letters from the South Seas

Edited by Bohun Lynch
With an Introduction by Gavin Young

Century
London Melbourne Auckland Johannesburg

First published by Constable & Co. Ltd in 1923

© Century Hutchinson 1986
© Introduction Gavin Young 1986

This edition first published in
1986 by Century, an imprint of Century Hutchinson Ltd,
Brookmount House, 62–65 Chandos Place, London, WC2N 4NW

Century Hutchinson Publishing Group (Australia) Pty Ltd
PO Box 496, 16–22 Church Street, Hawthorn, Melbourne, Victoria 3122

Century Hutchinson Group (NZ) Ltd
PO Box 40–086, 32–34 View Road, Glenfield, Auckland 10

Century Hutchinson Group (SA) Pty Ltd
PO Box 337, Berglvei 2012, South Africa

ISBN 0 7126 9468 4

Printed in Great Britain by
Richard Clay (The Chaucer Press) Ltd, Bungay, Suffolk

Introduction

'Who is Asterisk?' I stood in the offices of the China Navigation Company in Hong Kong with a dog-eared second- or even third-hand copy of *Isles of Illusion: Letters From the South Seas* in my hand and asked the obvious question.

Tim Bridgeman, the company's shipping manager, who a moment before had picked the book up from his desk and handed it to me, said, 'God knows. I found it in a bookstall in Charing Cross Road. Borrow it. If you promise to give it back.' That was brave of him, because next day I was boarding a freighter called the *Chengtu* on a slow ship-hop across the South Seas, round the Horn and back to England, and I had no idea when I would see Hong Kong again. 'Go on, take it,' he said. 'He's an unusual chap, I'll tell you that.'

By the time I returned *Isles* – not much damaged – to Tim Bridgeman a year or more had gone by and Asterisk (that was still the only name I knew him by) had come to seem like an old friend about whom I felt considerable anxiety. I had sailed in a variety of vessels, most of them as tired and dog-eared as that ancient copy of *Isles of Illusion*, with its wryly amusing or tormented pages open before me on my knee or a ship's rail while those sombre, sunlit islands of Asterisk's closed in around me. Blackbirding, the murder of black men, the degradation of whites – and above all the death of a dream of paradise on earth: that was what Asterisk with a gritty and self-flagellating honesty had recorded in letters to his friend Bohun Lynch. It is that honesty that makes *Isles of Illusion*, once read, extremely difficult to forget.

We know now that poor Asterisk was not at all happy when he learned that Lynch had edited his personal letters and had them published. All the same, *Isles of Illusion* sold well and was translated into several languages. And since then we have learned – thanks largely to the strenuous and invaluable investigations of Mr Will Stober of Birmingham University – a good deal about the identity and life of Asterisk.

Introduction

Born in 1877, he was baptised Robert James Addison Gerard Fletcher. His father was 'something in the City' (a not very successful something, it seems), and after his death in 1896, Fletcher got a job, first as a bank clerk, and then for a short time as junior master at various prep schools. Later, he went to Oxford University where, in between boxing and roof-climbing, he managed to take a degree in chemistry and – most important for us and for him – made friends with Bohun Lynch, an aspiring writer and boxing enthusiast.

Fletcher was thirty-three in 1910 when he impatiently threw up schoolmastering ('bum-brushing', he picturesquely called it) and charged off to South America (where he taught once again!) and later to the South Pacific – to the 'enchanted seas' that had called to him, siren-like, from the published letters of Robert Louis Stevenson to his friend Sidney Colvin. For no particular reason, he landed up in 1912 in the New Hebrides (the independent state of Vanuatu since 1980) which was then an Anglo-French Condominium. We can read what happened next in *Isles of Illusion*. For a complex, bookish man the brutal life of the plantations proved intolerable, and a deep, dark disillusionment slowly overwhelmed his soul like a creeping paralysis. Increasingly comforted by whisky, he stuck life in his Pacific purgatory for seven years, moving eastwards at last from the plantations of the New Hebrides to Tahiti where in 1923 he seemed to have found semi-contentment as a secretary-meteorologist with a French phosphate company. Then he was fired for some trivial misdemeanour ('an awkward customer', his successor sneered). And that might have been the end of him. Luckily, this outcast of the islands had the sense to go home.

The success of *Isles of Illusion* had been largely due to a rare quality in autobiographical books then – the author's willingness to come clean, to be frank about personal failure and despair in a region of the world that was generally supposed to be a lotus-land of blue lagoons and grass skirts. The letters were the 'confidential whimperings' (Fletcher said later) of a sensitive Englishman foundering in an insupportable world of heat, disease, ignorance – white and black – and the appalling cruelty of

white colonists to native islanders. Nor did Asterisk make any
bones about his own sexual gratification with the Melanesian
servant-girl who bore him a son. Raw stuff, this, for the 1920s.
From the leather-upholstered armchairs in England came out-
raged cries of 'I say, look here!'. Cries, too, no doubt, of 'the
chap's a bounder', because Fletcher, convention-breaker and
cynic, had made no effort whatever to return home to do his bit
for Britain in the Great War.

Yet the book sold well, and Constable, its publishers, asked
Fletcher to write them a novel of the South Seas. *Gone Native*
(1924), obviously autobiographical, is about an English settler
who had a child by a woman of the islands. The *Times Literary
Supplement* found it 'a moving and convincing story'; and it too
did quite well. Back in England, Fletcher followed it with two
mediocre thrillers. His friend Lynch died aged forty-four in
1928. Fletcher's literary career came to an end.

For some time after this the lines of Robert Fletcher's life and
my own ran strangely close. Indeed, those lines, starting in a
might-have-been sort of way, terminated in something very real:
in fact, the present reissue – the first in England for sixty-two
years – of *Isles of Illusion*. For although, as I have related, I first
became acquainted with the work of Fletcher/Asterisk by pure
chance in a shipping office in Hong Kong in 1982, I may well
have run into him in the flesh several decades before that. Quite
without knowing it; because then he would have been a school-
master in his fifties and I a nipper of less than twelve. And I was
not one of his pupils.

Let me explain. Fletcher, back in England from the South
Seas, was obliged, for want of any other occupation, to take up
once more the teaching career he had dropped in disgust twenty
years before. And of all the schools in Britain that might have
accepted him it was at St Petroc's, a prep school at Bude, a
remote beach-resort in Cornwall, that he ended up. He remained at St Petroc's – a mysterious personality, his past unre-
vealed – until his retirement in 1950.

Now, it happens that my father grew up in Bude in my
grandmother's large, ugly house only a hundred and fifty yards

up Ocean View Road from St Petroc's school. I spent most of my childhood's summer holidays in the tall, red brick house which she called Flexbury Lodge (and which is now an hotel). I wish I could say that I remember meeting a short, powerfully built, though decidedly plump, man with aquiline features, a monocle on a black ribbon and a precise way of speaking (this is the description of him by a former pupil and erstwhile colleague) as I carried my surfboard twice daily past the school gate on my way from my grandmother's front door to Crooklets beach. Unfortunately, I cannot. Whether or not I ever set eyes on Fletcher then, or later, during the short time he struggled in vain to make a go of a photographic salon in Queen Street, I shall never know. He left Bude after that and died at Deal, Kent in 1965, aged eighty-seven.

It is odd, come to think of it, that neither my father nor my grandmother ever spoke of Fletcher. Both of them were enthusiastic buyers of books. My father, in particular, liked books of adventure and the sea. So *Isles of Illusion*, a bestseller in the 1920s, might easily have been lying around the house in the thirties and forties. If it had been, it is inconceivable that I would not have met Fletcher for it would not have taken my grandmother – who knew everything that went on in Bude – long to discover that he was working just down the road in highly respectable St Petroc's, and he would have been invited to the house without delay. As it is, neither the book nor 'Bertie' Fletcher himself – his niece, Penelope Mortimer, calls him Uncle Bertie in her autobiography *About Time* – ever crossed the threshold of Flexbury Lodge. More's the pity.

But coincidence does not stop at the mere fact that, though unaware of each other's existence, Asterisk/Fletcher and I happened for a brief period of our lives to be near-neighbours in a rather small, Edwardian resort called Bude. The fates were even then working away to bring us together in quite a different place and manner. For my grandmother's attic at Flexbury Lodge was full of dusty, exciting books of adventure and travel, and it was my reading of these books by Captain Marryat, G. A. Henty, Stevenson, Melville and Conrad – coupled with the proximity of the Atlantic at the bottom of the road – that inspired in me a dream of one day Running Away to Sea. Many years passed before I answered this call of the wild, wild ocean, but finally I did so – and hence I found myself in the Hong Kong shipping office, poised like a diver on the verge of the South Pacific, with *Isles of Illusion* in my hand and Tim Bridgeman's voice in my ear, saying, 'Unusual book by an unusual chap . . . God knows who he was. . . .' The precise origins of this new edition lay in his next words: 'Borrow it'.

Through the isles of Melanesia, Asterisk was with me. I only skirted the New Hebrides because I chose to spend more time in the other Melanesian islands of New Britain, Bougainville and the Solomons. But even so, Past overlaps Present everywhere – the western Pacific is no exception – and despite the fact that Asterisk was describing events that had taken place fifty or sixty years earlier, his world was very much with me. Sardonic, enigmatic, his phantom seemed to be standing at my elbow. So when I came to write of my own experiences in the islands I quoted *Isles of Illusion* here and there to serve as a kind of backcloth, and those fragments of Asterisk read so pungently that Century Hutchinson, impressed by them, decided to re-print the whole volume. Here and now, then, the slender lines of coincidence binding Fletcher and myself come together.

One last point. I have said that Fletcher was encouraged to flee to the South Seas from the stuffiness of Edwardian England by the writings of Robert Louis Stevenson. Later, grievously disillusioned, he disparages Stevenson to Lynch, referring to the author of the *Vailima Letters* and *In The South Seas* as 'a rather amiable tripper'. He adds, bitterly, that as far as tropical islands are concerned, the wisest advice is, 'Keep your distance and you will keep your enchantment.'

He is wrong about Stevenson who by no stretch of the imagination can be called a tripper. On the contrary, R.L.S. was deeply involved in the life of the Samoan chiefs and warriors he lived among as a friend not a master, and whose language he spoke. Fletcher does not seem to have realised that, unlike R.L.S., his employment put him in a false position *vis-à-vis* his environment: he was a plantation manager, a 'boss-man' regarded askance by his native employees. He was a certain sort of 'man of his time'. Always honest, Fletcher admitted his distaste for black islanders; to him they were 'Kanakas' and 'niggers'; they stank. On the other hand, he certainly showed a great compassion for them, and positively hated white planters or traders who maltreated or cheated them. There is a world of difference between Fletcher's colonial style of life and that of R.L.S. on Samoa. Stevenson found his paradise and never lost it. He loved Samoans as he loved his own family. Vailima was open house to them. In return they built him their 'Road of Loving Hearts' and on the day he died they came to kiss his dead cheek and carried his coffin up the slope of Mount Vaea to his grave. R.L.S. never thought of 'keeping his distance', yet his enchantment survived to the end.

Comparisons with Stevenson go hard with Fletcher; and it is unfair to compare two such different men. Could it be that Fletcher simply went to the wrong islands? I have a hunch that had he, a well-read, decent, clever, compassionate middle-class Englishman, sought his new life in the more graceful 'aristocratic' world of Western Samoa rather than among the French and roughneck Australian colonists of the New Hebrides, his visions of nirvana might never have been shattered.

But then, of course, we would not have had *Isles of Illusion* by Asterisk.

Gavin Young
1986

Foreword

The following letters were addressed to me by a friend during the years 1912 to 1920. They form part of a correspondence which began in the early spring of 1910, and continues to the present day. My friend is, it seems necessary to say, a real person; though as he desires to remain anonymous I will for convenience' sake here call him Asterisk.

It is not very usual to publish the private letters of a living man, and (as will be appreciated by the reader) it would not be seemly were his identity published with them. It may also be thought that the editor, too (and especially in these circumstances), should remain decently hidden, and should not, with whatever diffidence, stand forth to take a share of any credit that may be forthcoming. Asterisk has, ever since I said good-bye to him at Euston thirteen years ago, written wonderful letters to me by almost every mail. With his leave I publish extracts from these letters and put my name to a note about them: while he (by his own wish – though that is not to the point) remains – Asterisk. It seems very unfair and very ungracious, and I have to apologise about it. At the same time, it has been thought that some name should appear upon the title-page.

Asterisk is an unusual man. I haven't the impudence to say that I understand him; but I can put down certain facts about him and let these, with the letters, speak for themselves. If the spirit of the enthusiastic showman peeps out now and again, I hope that he will forgive me.

'Though I say it as should,' he wrote once, 'I was a precociously clever child. My papa (God rest his soul – he was the product of an old-time Grammar School) taught me Latinity when I was five years old. . . . After leaving forcibly a Wesleyan school I was sent to a local "preparatory school for the sons of gentlemen." There I was stuffed with Latin verses and little else. At fourteen I was transferred to another school – I won't bore you with details. There I temporarily "found salvation." My house-master was a Yorkshire parson of the old school. He knew Wisden by heart, scribbled a sermon on Saturday night with an eye on the "Extra Special," caned us for dropped catches or missed shots at goal, and was generally charming in the English pedagogic style. I owe a great deal to him. Unfortunately I left school at sixteen and a half to be enrolled as medical student. Fancy a boy of sixteen and a half in London. I still played games violently and enthusiastically. . . .'

You have to fancy not only a boy of sixteen and a half alone in London, but one who had been given (at that age) a considerable lump sum which was to have kept him and paid his fees until he was qualified.

The lump sum disappeared rather quickly. His father died, and 'my last restraining influence of fear is gone.' In another autobiographical moment he refers to 'artistic pleasures such as my shrunken non-conformist soul had never dreamed.' He developed a pretty taste in all sorts of directions. At the same time he had not been entirely idle at 'Bart's' and had laid the groundwork of a medical knowledge which, as will be seen, was to serve him very usefully in after years.

He was a bank clerk for a short time, and then at about the age of nineteen began a long period of teaching by acting as a junior master in a preparatory school. Quite obviously, he must have taught well. For a man who had himself been educated at 'no-particular-sort-of' school or university, he got comparatively good jobs. (We most of us know – and I, for one, know from personal experience – that what is known as the hall-mark of the usual public school and university together with some tuppenny athletic distinction will bring excellent scholastic 'openings' to the large feet of the veriest dunce. They say it isn't quite as bad as that now-a-days. I don't know. I hope not. I know it used to be for ten years on either side of 1900).

Ushering, as he always calls it, predicates long holidays and many opportunities for gladness and for folly. 'Fortunately,' he writes, 'a terribly strong return of Anglo-Catholicism kept me away long enough for normal Philistinic ideas to recover their vigour. For three years I prayed and fasted and trained my body among the Westmorland Fells. Then came Oxford, at first as a neo-catholic Cowleyite – (did you ever suspect that? – it was over when I first met you) – [I did not suspect it], and then as a normal young-old undergraduate.'

A legacy enabled Asterisk, at the age of twenty-nine, to pay the necessary fees for the 'hall-mark' essential for a mastership at a public school. That had been, I think, the pinnacle of his ambition for a long time. He went up to Oxford.

'Just think,' he says, 'how at Oxford I was no older than boys seven or eight years my junior. I blush sometimes when I think of myself, with the physical appearance of sober maturity, walking about arm-in-arm with people like—.'

He came one day in his second year to the little room in Friar's Entry, which was at that time the headquarters of the Boxing Club, and in which I was, as he put it later, the 'presiding bully.' He wanted to join the club and told me that he weighed twelve stone. He was short for that weight and I contradicted him rudely. We mutually thought each other insufferable and subsequently became friends. I was two years 'senior' to him, in the university sense, and it wasn't until the last week or so of my last term that I let him initiate me into the very real delights of college roof-climbing. Up to then I had despised this occupation as a school-boy prank. Properly done (and Asterisk was a really skilled rock-climber) it is far and away the best, if most dangerous, sport that Oxford has to offer. We used an Alpine Club rope and Asterisk led two or three of us. We had implicit confidence in him, and he took us for some really sensational climbs. The arête formed by a gable of my own college was bad enough: the route from his bedroom window up a waterpipe, and so over a crumbling chimney-stack which overlooked the High makes me shudder now. I think it was Asterisk who inverted an earthenware vessel upon the head of Queen Anne on the opposite side of the road. Nobody would climb up again to take it down, and eventually it had to be broken from below by a rifle bullet. I owe him thanks for that, and for my introduction to the work of Arthur Machen, and for many other things.

Then money ran short again, and Asterisk had to teach in Cairo in order to pay the rest of his way. After a year he returned to Oxford, made up as far as possible for lost time, and finally took a tolerable place in the chemistry school. And so to the pinnacle of his ambition at last – a mastership at a public school. But all the while the South Seas called to him, chiefly through the writings of Stevenson – blessed islands of warmth and free living and beautiful indolence.

And then he found, as people of intelligence are prone to find, that the pinnacle of his ambition, once won, was not so high as he had supposed. You read his letters and you wonder less that he stuck to that job for two years than that the other masters didn't strangle him – which is not meant for a compliment to the other masters.

He knew his job, however. He was thoroughly competent and enormously trustworthy. He was something of a crank: he held ridiculous ideals about teaching. And heuristic methods were forbidden, and 'you must teach always with a view to getting boys through their examinations' he was told. ... Two years, then a few months at an Army crammer's (better fun, that) and then – freedom.

It is worth thinking about. All that pain and all that trouble, hardship, self-denial for a career – the high-hall-water-mark of respectability. For Asterisk was a bit of a snob once and the accredited respectabilities were very dear to him. Many years later he wrote: 'I am almost certain that I am not a snob now; I do not respect merely social position as such. It is unfortunate that the people who please me are invariably a long way above me in the social scale; but I cannot help that. Of course, here, in Australia, there are practically no social scales. Some folk are richer, and, consequently, more objectionable than others. That is all.'

And he had won through, not by the sensational route which leads through scholarships from Bethnal Green; but by that really more arduous route which begins by 'good' education, in circumstances that are only comparatively humble, and an instinctive discontent with 'that station in life.'

It is worth thinking 'furiously' about, especially by those of us who have perhaps gratefully accepted the chains of a comfortable slavery. Think of the pious horror, the uplifted hands! 'My boy, you have had splendid opportunities, and abilities above the average.' Though his father was long dead, there must have been someone to say that: there always is. His retort might justly have been: 'I have largely made my own opportunities: my ability is my present salvation.' Perhaps he had not yet learned what gold was like, but he had at last recognised for what it was some very pretty tinsel, and had not been afraid to say so. The 'splendid opportunities,' the 'honourable career,' were thrown away like an old hat; and he went off, not without misgivings, not without regrets, to seek no fortune, but to find the substance of a dream.

First there were two more years of 'ushering' in South America, with a view – somewhat pathetic in the light of what happened – to saving money against the great day of final deliverance. Once again he made himself valuable: and he was, from his employer's standpoint, thoroughly successful. Once again he despised his success. And then one day he found that he could stand it no longer: the transition period came to an abrupt end, and, as the letters will tell you, he sailed away.

Then followed the seven and a half years in the New Hebrides. What he found there the letters tell. But to appreciate them it has to be borne in mind what sort of man it was who lived this life of hardship with people who, in all senses of the phrase, spoke a different language. His outlook may be found often too bitter, too intolerant: he not merely lacked the insensibility of the average Colonist, – a well-read man amongst men who could scarcely read their own names – but his tastes were cultivated. He had been educated in all the 'extras.' It is worth mentioning that he hung Beardsley's drawings for Salomé upon the walls of his hut, and that *Poems and Ballads* seldom remained for long upon its shelf. These things may be superficial, but he was that sort of man.

More than once during the last few years the question of the publication of these letters has arisen between us. (A few of them, giving accounts of adventurous experiences, appeared in *Land and Water*.) But Asterisk never thought anything of them. It was not modesty on his part – that is not the point. He was unable to perceive that anything he had written could be of interest to anyone except me, and of me he was not always sure. 'Fired by sudden energy,' he said once, 'I determined to write a sort of autobiographical novel of the New Hebrides. I wrote the first chapter. Then I tried to draw up a scheme. That finished me, because my doings and seeings seemed such small beer. I put the thing away and forgot all about it. Here it is. You may say that I am too close to my events to see them properly.' Perhaps. But I prefer the letters. No more than that first chapter was ever written. The conscious 'switch over' to writing for print was plain, and the result disastrous. That first chapter, instead of telling the reader, as the letters did, what he wanted to tell, told what he thought the reader wanted.

The writing of letters is one thing: the give-and-take of correspondence quite another. During the time that Asterisk was in the New Hebrides at least six months elapsed before either of us got an answer to any particular question. 'We won't correspond,' he wrote. 'It would be too muddlesome. Never forget that I write for the moment. The fact that your moment is three months later than mine is scarcely my fault. And I have such hazy ideas of what my letters are about. I really must learn to 'concentrate upon' what I write. Wouldn't it be silly if I did?'

As a fact we did 'correspond.' We answered questions asked three months before. We commented upon each other's letters: and in this as in other ways Asterisk was, and is, a much better 'correspondent' than I. But it must be remembered always that his letters were not real letters, but the outlet of a man who has no one to talk to. I was the safety-valve. A man who has the power to put his thoughts into words, written or spoken, must communicate them to somebody. Thus it is that the reader will find in these letters of his the most absurd contradictions, not only in the change of opinions – and Asterisk's opinions were always changing – but in plain set terms. 'I am a crank,' he says more than once. 'I am not a crank,' he repeats on other occasions. It matters very little. The reader judges for himself.

The correspondence was naturally a frank one. If Asterisk felt an impulse to say something – anything – he said it, generally in the first words that occurred to him. Once I asked him if he were lying about something. I entirely forgot what. This was his reply:

'You really do set me some posers. Just think for a moment how from Plato to Pontious Pilate, from Pilate to Professor James, there has been no satisfactory definition of "truth." And you ask me whether I tell it! I know quite well what Sir Franklyn Hunter-Hodge would say: "Of course the fellow knows whether he's telling the truth or not. A thing's either true or not true, isn't it? Tell me that. I'm a plain man . . ." But you cannot hold quite such blessedly simple views. You – with me – surely

look upon "truth" somewhat from a pragmatistic standpoint.
Truth is what is best for us to believe – or words to that effect.
Furthermore we must not forget the question of subjective
idealism. What is, isn't always. What is for A. is not necessarily
for B. If you want me to descend to the Hunter-Hodge level and
talk of the dull, bare supraliminal, I will do so. I always have
been, and always shall be, a liar. I don't mean that in or about
the ordinary dealings of life I make untrue statements with in-
tent to deceive. I dare say I did as a boy. I dare say that I do so
occasionally now, when I consider that the ends justify the
means. That is tact. What I wish you to understand is that I do
often get hopelessly mixed up between what happens to my
"waking" and what to my "subconscious" self. Of course, from
the practical, the Hunter-Hodge, point of view such confusion is
lamentable and most blameworthy. But how can I help it? Can I
help being short and having blue eyes? So-called moralists of the
tell-it-to-God-and-the-curate type would bid me strive against
the tendency. Why should I? It interests me. I can subdue, or
control, the condition so that it doesn't injure my material self over
much. Further than that I refuse to go. In my bourgeois moments
I lament. I curse my inherited tendency. If my forebears had had
less "religion" and more knowledge they would have had me
properly tackled when I was young. Then I should perhaps have
been a novelist, perhaps a "local preacher." '

Once again the reader must judge for himself, though he may
safely accept statements about objective events from what Asterisk calls the 'Hunter-Hodge' standpoint.

Whilst discussing this matter of 'truth' I cannot avoid some
reference to matters in the following letters which to some
readers will be extremely distasteful. We know that to many
people naked truth and reality (we are not discussing the 'real-
ism' of modern fiction) are quite unbearable, unless they display
the pleasanter things of life. How often do we hear people say:
'We all know that there are horrid things in life: why should we
read about them?' To which the reply might be – if horrid
things were wisely written about, we should understand them
(and see, incidently, that they were not really quite so horrid as
we thought), and that then we should not be afraid of reading
about them, and the horrid things would fall into their right

place in the perspective of all things, good and bad. At present, however, the whole and horrid truth (Hunter-Hodge definition) remains a matter of individual taste, and its exposure must be governed by the exigencies of what is called public morality. So, as it has been necessary to say before in prefaces and introductions, though nothing will be found here to titilate the salacious, the book is not recommended for the nursery shelf. There are horrid truths that ought to be known. One cannot make people read if they don't want to; one can give them the opportunity or withhold it, and that last I refuse to do for the sake of 'drawing-room manners.'

In editing and, in trivial and unessential matters, expurgating these letters, I have been guided by the principles contained in – 'This should be known' – 'That is well said.' (The latter applies chiefly to those passages which might just as well have been written from New Orleans or Edinburgh as from the South Seas.) I have not tampered with the originals, nor altered them, save for an occasional change of ephithet, and a fairly general change of proper names, nor have I extracted sentences from their context in such a way as to obscure the writer's intention.

By far the greater part of the letters dealt with matters of a purely personal and domestic interest to me, and as such have been excluded. Knowing, however, that Asterisk carries the shield of anonymity – I do not exclude much that is of signally personal interest to him, because I conceive it to be of personal interest to others.

When he burned his boats and went to the South Seas, he let himself in for more than he could have guessed – sickness, hardship of every description, pain. 'There are few real tragedies in the world,' my friend wrote once. 'People either can't live them or live up to them.'

I am not so sure.

BOHUN LYNCH.

LONDON, *September* 1922.

1912

At Sea 40° S. 40° W.
March 24th, 1912.

. . .

AN ordinary diary of each day's events would be
dull, because, once given the necessary details
as to surroundings, things happen much the same
as they do on a passenger steamer. You know all
that. Take a ship ; denude it of its beastly engines
and beastlier passengers ; substitute picturesque
(if somewhat unsatisfactory) sails and loneliness and
you can well imagine what an ideal opportunity one
has for reading, thinking, and more especially for
day-dreaming. The sun is still hot, though in the
late afternoon one is glad of a jacket when sitting
on deck. The weather so far has been nearly
perfect from my point of view, though not quite
what the Skipper wants. We have cloudless days,
hot sun and what is known technically as an 8-knot
breeze ; that is, enough breeze to keep the sea
beautifully sparkling and to bowl us along merrily
without making life a burden. It's true that
occasionally one's deck chair moves with one
violently down a steep place, but this is the exception.
I am told that when in a few days we shall be nearly
in the roaring forties, such occurrences will be the
rule, but sufficient is the evil.

You will gather from the mention of day-dreaming and deck chairs that we have shipped as passengers, or rather as doctor and purser. I am not enamoured of dirty hands and lousy beds, and going aloft in snow storms. Our fares are £12 for 12,000 miles, which is reasonably cheap travelling. The accommodation is infinitely superior to anything one could get at the price on a mail boat. We have a large airy cabin apiece, and the run of the poop deck, and no ruddy idiots to bother us to play deck quoits. The food is excellent. The old Captain is a bon viveur of the best and knocks up tasty little dishes out of sharks and porpoises and other huge fish (which we catch daily) in order to vary the monotony. We are carrying quite a farmyard of animals and birds. . . . On Thursdays we get vermouth and absinthe, and every day excellent Bordeaux wine. I am feeling enormously fit, and have already grown quite a nice beard.

The life on this old hooker charms me. For the sake of practising French we mess with the Captain and three mates. I wouldn't have missed this part for worlds. The manners are entirely of the natural variety. That is, all artificial aids to eating are used only when necessary. Any function of the body which tends to give more ease to the eater is performed unblushingly and without remark. The whole ship's company of animals and birds drop casually in for snacks, and the combined smell would defy analysis. But I love it. There is an absence of convention which is really charming, and there is nothing done that is really vulgar. The Captain having filled his capacious paunch and drunk mighty draughts of the Bordeaux, calls for coffee and rum, and then launches witticisms at the officers which would make a soldier blush. The cook and the cook's boy peer round the door to join in the bellows of laughter and we keep up each meal for at least two hours, utterly regardless of the business of sailing. I spent two days translating a certain sea ballad which you wot of into passable argot and then recited it after dinner last Sunday. The Captain was charmed and immediately found a good French tune and trolled it out in a mighty bass, and ever since it has been like " The King " at dinner, the prelude to the old man's ingenious pornography. I must keep in this vein on board or I could not stand the interminable voyage. Of the South Seas and what I am to do there I will not try and think. Brookes pesters me with elaborate figures concerning plantations and I pretend to be interested. I suppose we shall be successful, but I don't seem to care. Sometimes I wish that I had waited and gone in my own way to do what I wanted. But then I think that perhaps the time might never have come. This way is a certain road to independence and I shall at least be near Aitutaki. I am not expecting much from New Caledonia itself : it will serve as a place to work in and is within nice easy reach of all the groups, and in any case the life of a planter is rather better than that of an usher. But the real time, the retirement, the forest life, is not for now.

Brookes reckons that in ten years we ought to be making about £2,000 a year. Then he is going to retire and live comfortably in England. Shall I have lost my faculty of appreciation by then ? I don't think so. I am going to treat my inner self most carefully all the time, so as to husband all my strength, all my longing and love of beauty, and I really hope that instead of having deteriorated it will have increased tremendously.

42° S. 18° W.
March 31*st.*

. . .

I HAVE had my first experience of a gale in mid-Atlantic in a sailing ship, and I don't care if I never see another. If this is adventure, then God grant me a humdrum life. It wasn't that the thing frightened me. I suppose my land lubber's ignorance kept me from appreciating how uncommonly near we were to going to the bottom. It was the beastly discomfort that annoyed me. For five mortal days we were shaken about like peas in a box. Eating, sleeping, washing were impossible. For five days I had the same clothes on. For five days they were soaked in sea water. There were two feet of water in the cabins, and a stink such as I never want to smell again. All the time the ship rolled and wallowed like a dropsical pig. Out of mere curiosity I asked the Captain how much the ship could roll without capsizing. He told me about 35 degrees on either side of the vertical. I then asked him how much we were doing. "Oh, about 33°—not more." Cheery wasn't it ? I went on deck several times by day and night, partly to escape from the stench below and partly to see if I could gather anything in the way of impressions. I assure you I gathered very little. I was not in a receptive mood, being fearfully angry and very sore. The only thing that struck me was the utter lack of good sense on the part of the mighty ocean. I watched several great waves strike the poor little ship and then rush away in foam on the lee side, and it looked for all the world as if this gigantic, imposing wave was giggling. It created in me just the same feeling of scorn and disgust that one would experience at seeing a great beefy giant sniggering hysterically because it had knocked the bottle from a baby's mouth.

To-day is calm and we have spent the morning catching albatross. No less than nine of those gorgeous birds have fallen victims to the wiles of the old Captain. I explained to him that he ought to be ashamed of himself for killing such charming creatures, but he only retorted that the pie that he would make was much more beautiful than the living bird. We shall see. The record bird so far measured fourteen feet from tip to tip, so you can imagine the commotion when they are hauled on board. The captain has promised to make a tobacco pouch out of one of the feet. By the way, talking of tobacco, I started the voyage on plug but soon got tired of the fag of cutting it, and have now adopted French caporal, which I buy from the ship at about $1\frac{1}{2}$d. an ounce. At first I thought it filth, but now I am quite inured to it. It reminds me of your shag, only it's a little worse.

50° something S. 25° E.
April 12*th*.

. . .

I COULDN'T write last Sunday, it was too rough and cold and miserable. To-day writing is uncommonly hard as the old pig is rolling violently, but I simply must talk to you or I shall go mad. . . . I want to see something that isn't dirty. I want to sleep in a bed free from cockroaches. I want to taste some food that is not crammed with garlic to disguise the mouldiness. I want to hear some talk that is neither French pornography nor plantation profits. You will see that I have broken down. The veneer of jolly boon companion has worn through, and the underlying me in all his native cynicism and discontent is nakedly and horribly visible. You may blame me and say that I'm a weakling ; that I ought to stand all this and more for the sake of what I am going to. . . .

You know the style of conversation which begins with a fatuous giggle, and then "You know the story about . . . ? " I can do that as well as another, and have done a great deal of it in the past. I fully appreciate the value of such abominations in their proper place, but I had hoped that I had finished with it. Do you remember that I once told you that if I went to the South Seas with Brookes I should shoot him in his sleep. . . . I have a gleam of hope. He had apparently decided to venture on this expedition because he had made some wonderful calculation as to what one could gain. He dinned the figures into me, but I never listened.

Now it appears that he had made a mistake in the arithmetic (a nought too many or too few or something) and he is horror stricken. He came to me with an absurd face last night and reams of paper, and told me he found that he could make more money in Buenos Ayres. I am afraid I laughed rather rudely and suggested that he went back there. To my huge joy he took me at my word and said that, if he found on arrival that there were only such paltry profits to be made, he would take the next boat back to South America. I am going to play this game for all I am worth. I am not a commercial genius, but my experience as an usher has made my mental arithmetic very sound and I am convinced that the second estimate is the correct one. In this case I shall be left in the lurch in the great Pacific Ocean. What a horrible fate! You can imagine how fearfully upset I shall be at such a desertion. I have not the slightest fear that I can manage to worry along somehow. If I can't get something to do in New Caledonia itself, I shall beg, borrow or steal a passage to some more interesting group of islands and simply plant myself on them.

By the way the albatross pie was absolutely filthy and made me ill for two days. So there was no excuse for killing the thing of beauty.

. . . Curiously enough I came across a product of yours in a little Italian bookshop in Monte Video just before I left. I had been talking to the proprietor (an ex-convict, an anarchist, but quite amusing) and idly turning over a pile of papers on the counter. My eye was caught by my own name on a page. Then I saw that what I was touching was a copy of X Magazine[1] and that it contained a boxing story by you. The man explained that he got the magazine for an English engine driver on the F.F.C. de U. and that he had left the country ; and the magazines which he did not know how to countermand on his (the anarchist's) hands. He tried to persuade me to buy the objects, but I assured him that I could neither read nor write English as I was a Scot.

April 22nd.

I WAS considering things yesterday, and I arrived at the conclusion that I was horribly ungrateful in cursing my trade of ushering. It has really done quite a lot for me. It sent me to Oxford and Egypt, and now it has sent me to the South Seas via South America. Not one of these things would have happened to me probably if I had pursued my original plans and become a doctor. So let us rather bless the profession and merely thank God that I was discontented in it.

45° S. 100° E.
April 28th.

.　　.　　.

WHEN the sky is gloriously blue, and the sun is hot I don't care a bit about England. Then my mind turns tropic-wards, and the palm trees have the upper hand. When there is a huge sea running, and the wind is howling through the

[1] They grossly underpaid me, so I won't advertise them.—ED.

rigging, there is nothing to remind me of England or the tropics, I am full of a sense of health and my mind turns involuntarily to stories of Vikings and Bersekers, and I invent strange sea oaths in various tongues. It is at sunset when the sky is grey, when there is a fog and a greenish sea that I think of home and England. I think of tea time, the most comfortable (? the only one) of English hours, I think of my own home on the Channel, and the lights of the ships on the Downs and the sound of fog horns. Curiously enough I think also of the West end of Piccadilly, the part (say) round about Curzon Street, where one sees the railings of the park standing out black in the evening mist, while the lights of the hansoms are blurred. I pace the deck alone in the gathering gloom and am entirely lost in my surroundings. I love these greys and suggested purples . . . and then Brookes appears and tells me what there is going to be for high tea, and the spell is broken. However, I must not grumble. I contrive to get nearly the whole day to myself. I get up early with the utmost regularity and study the effects of the dawn which are always new and always glorious. The more I see of colour the more I object to the ordinary idea of its gorgeousness. I remember how at one time Turner was the last word to me in colour. Now my tastes have changed utterly. It is the suggestions in a misty sky which give me real joy. In them I can see ideas of colour which exist for me alone, shades that I have never before imagined which speak to me and whisper of mysteries instead of shouting about things popular. Do you know with this taste

developing so strongly I rather dread the tropics.
From all that one has read everything there is
apparent and garish and obvious. I can only hope
that the people who have described tropical land-
scapes and tropical skies have been incapable of
seeing what is really there. . . . The things that
I feel most I cannot express. I think that the mere
giving birth to the expression would kill all that
it contained. I should love to be with someone
who would say what I want to say but dare not.
I do not mean the X.Y.Z. type who treat Nature as
if it was really ' useful to illustrate quotations from
the poets.' What I want is the rare person who
can see in the charming suggestions of Nature the
wherewithal for a perfect piece of art.

150° E. 40° S.
May 9th.

. . .

IF, as I presume you will, you look up our position
on a map, you will see that we are some 250
miles off the East coast of Tasmania. What you
won't see on the map is that we are 57 days out
from Monte Video, that there is a beastly head
wind that prevents us running North into the warm,
that I expect to be out of tobacco this afternoon.
Sunday was a foul day and I could not write. It was
the worst thing we have had, a gale dead ahead.
Fortunately it only lasted a day, but it has thrown
us back a lot. The Captain talks hopefully of arriving on May 29th, which will mean 77 days' voyage
and 81 days on board. . . .

I must tell you two things while they are fresh in my mind. If they don't interest you, at least the telling will pass away some of the morning for me. The first thing is a little scene during Sunday's gale. I rose betimes as usual, washed at the peril of my life, and went on deck where I found an enormous sea running and torrents of rain. I clung hard to some kind of marine contrivance and gasped for breath while I tried to make out what was going on in the pitch darkness. After a bit I discovered that all hands were engaged in pouring buckets of water on the ropes which are in some way connected with the steering apparatus. The idea being, I presume, to tighten the said ropes. The operation sounds simple. It consisted of passing a bucket from hand to hand along a chain of men for about 20 yards which included one flight of six steps. Now that should be easy. Given, however, that every other minute the deck was nearly vertical, item the boards were like ice, item all the crew were in oilskins and wooden-soled sea-boots, I contrived to get a good deal of amusement out of the manœuvre. Every other minute a dark shape would fall with an appalling crash on the deck and go slithering away to bring up with a bump against the lee rails. This was amusing especially as the bucket of water invariably accompanied the faller, and then had to be chased for some minutes. But it was the attitude of the non-fallers which was most pleasing. With most commendable regularity they bellowed with laughter, holding on to each other to laugh, and roaring abominable Breton witticisms at the unfortunate one, only to meet the same fate themselves a few minutes later. The language of the fallen was characteristic of most French swearing ; *i.e.* furious repetition (which seems to give as much force as the multiplicatives of the Arab) and an absurd bathos. Here you have an example, robbed of its real value by the omission of some quite unwritable words (maxima debetur . . .) 'Sacré nom de Dieu de nom de Dieu ! Sacré espèce de— ! Sacré sale bête d'un volier ! Espèce d'oie.' To begin by an enormous invocation of the unnameable, to pass through ghastly obscenity, and then to end up with ' sort of goose ' seems to English ears a little feeble. However, it appears to meet the case, which is all one can reasonably expect of an oath.

The other thing that I want to tell you happened to me last night at sunset. Let me begin by saying that there was no crimson, no gold, no absurd bands of colour to remind one of an Academy picture or Brock's Benefit. There was no colour at all. There was only the suggestion of a thousand shades, all beautifully intermediate between silver, rose-pink and the most delicate purple. It was a foggy evening. We were slipping in a ghost-like fashion through a calm sea, with wet decks and the sails flapping in a way suggestive of infinite weariness. I was leaning over the rail looking aft and wondering what the good fog had in store for me. Nearly all round was dense grey showing no line of demarcation between sky and water ; only in the air there was the far-away rumbling of a great city. Then suddenly I found I was looking straight at the most beautiful thing. The sun was setting somewhere behind all that fog, and the fog was robbing the colours of all their

crudeness. It was all momentary, and formulation
of ideas was almost impossible. I was left merely
with the impression of visible and audible loveliness.
In the centre, where I suppose the actual sun was,
the effect was concentrated. There the suggestion
of lights was very wonderful—rose pink and grey,
but too delicate to be named with the names of any
representative colours. It was all fleeting suggestion—pearls against grey velvet. The smoke of
incense slowly waving from the dark altar to the
dim sanctuary lamps. All the garishness gone and
only the glory and the memory of the music left.
Turning one's eyes slightly from the centre to the
right there was a suggestion of very pale blue. The
sheen on large precious stones on opening the lid
of some old silver casket. Again the incense smoke,
but more visible. Soft, soft footsteps in a dark
wood. And the sea and the sky was infinitely sad,
and there was no light. I was cold, I was wet, I was
miserable. I longed for tea and hot things to eat,
and comfortable people to talk to. I heard the
insistent creaking of basket chairs, and the noise of
the spoons against the cups. I hugged the feeling
to myself, for even when prosaic thoughts follow
fast on a moment of beauty one has exquisite
emotions. I am convinced (and it was not Oscar
Wilde who convinced me) that one's moments of
utter sorrow and loneliness bring more deep artistic
joy than any pleasure can. Then quickly afterwards
I was laughing rather bitterly at my own powerless-
ness to express even my own emotions. Is it always
to be like this? Am I to see things and long to
share them but to be unable through my own

inarticulateness ? I have all the weak human desire
to share my good things with another. So over-
mastering is my desire that I disobey Christ's
mandate and consequently they do ' turn again ' and
I get rent. Last night I was weak enough to throw
tentatively a few of the small seed ones.

"Humph ! bloody cold and wet, and the wind's
going ahead. There's fresh pork for tea—" and
there was. And there is every day. And there
always will be, unless . . .

27° S. 127° E.
May 29th.

.   .   .

WE only sighted Norfolk Island late in the
afternoon about 25 miles off. Before sunset we got close enough to see palm trees through
the glasses. Then the sky clouded over. At night
we came precious near going aground on the said
island, sounding hard all the time, but it was too
dark to see anything. The Captain told me that if
it had been light I could have seen the houses of the
rich Orstrylians, and the hotels where people come
to pass the winter. How manifold are Thy mercies,
oh Lord. Sunsets at present are like an impression-
ist sketch of the last judgment. In order to criticise
them one heaves a sigh, places the head in a becoming
and sentimental position and says " Isn't it wonderful ? " After the proper lapse of time one repeats
the above movements and adds " I wish I were an
*ar*tist. I should *love* to paint that." Then someone
suggests whitewash as an alternative. Then everyone laughs.

June 3rd,
Between Walpole Island and
Ile des Pines.

THE sea is the most vivid blue I have ever seen —so blue that in fact in spite of its wonderful cheering effect some part of me cries against it. I am lying in a deck chair clad in the very thinnest suit of pyjamas, and I feel at peace with all the world. If only I had some tobacco and you beside me (not singing), then my paradise would be complete. It does seem a disgraceful shame that I am going to land on what after all is a Pacific Island in such circumstances. . . . I want to feel that when the silence is broken it will only be by the utterance of some such thought as my own. For example, I should like to talk about colour rather than about my first meal on shore. I should love to hear suggestions as to the music most fitting to be heard on a tropic night; instead of which I hear only the most loathly prognostications as to the physical charms of Kanaka women. Reminiscences of Montevidean orgies are, if possible, more unspeakably beastly than were the orgies themselves. However, I am writing to you, and most of the ceaseless cackle is lost to me. I am beginning to feel quite excited about landing. . . .

June 4th,
In sight of Thio.

I WAS interrupted yesterday by a shout of " Land on the port bow ! " and up I went aloft to have a look. Sure enough there it was, the Promised Land,

or at least it was Jericho. After that I was too
excited to write, so I watched the Captain harpoon
dolphins. Have you ever seen a dolphin ? I don't
mean a porpoise, of which beast I have eaten enough
on this voyage to make me feel sick if ever I see one
again. The fish I mean is called in French ' Dorade,'
and that is all I know of its name. Of its appearance
in the water I could never tire of talking. Its huge
fins are exactly the colour of a mighty electric dis-
charge. Its body is brilliant gold which, seen
through sapphire water, appears the most extraordinary wicked green ; it flashes through the water
in almost a blinding manner. And this old Breton
villain ran a harpoon right through the flesh, and
hauled it struggling on board. There, of course,
it was grotesque. In a few minutes its colour had
been scraped off, and chunks of it were on their
way to the galley. We ate it for tea, and I will say
it was remarkably good, but it was a pitiable thing
to do.

June 6th,
At anchor at Thio.

WE sighted Thio on Tuesday, but it was too
thick to dare to try and get through the
reef, so we sailed away again and beat about all night.
Yesterday was clear and we came in towards land
with a beautiful breeze and signalled for a pilot.
We got no answer from shore for a long time, and
then finally " Pilot away : back to-morrow." That
was too much. Our old man swore mighty oaths, and
then ' Sacré nom de Dieu, je me passerai de pilote,'

and he did. It was the most daring bit of navigation, and for about two hours the chances were even
that we ran on a reef. The place teemed with them.
First of all the big one in which we had to find an
opening, and then patches of reef all over the place.
However, by much skill and not a little luck, we
got in and dropped anchor. The old man was
bathed in sweat and could only totter feebly back
to his cabin, where he called for absinthe, and we
made merry together. I really admired him until
with a leerish grin he turned to me and whispered
that he had gained the 2,000 francs of pilotage for
himself. We were at anchor by twelve o'clock, and
after lunch we went ashore, a pull of about two
miles, and I set foot on an island in the Southern
Pacific.

It was a good job that I prepared myself for a
bitter disappointment. I got it. The coast was
nothing but barren mountains with great ugly
patches scraped in their sides by the nickel mines.
The village of Thio lies in a valley, and is nothing
more than a mining village. True, there are palm
trees and various other tropical plants, but they
could not take away from the general impression.
The foreground was filled with all the usual appur-
tenances of a mining village, trucks, miniature
railway, cable railway, foundry, and so on. In fact,
but for the temperature one might have been in
Cumberland. We paid visits to various French
officials and then *took the train* to the village proper.
True, the train was the merest of toys, but it was
nevertheless mechanical. I won't go on with
description. I simply content myself with saying

that I was very glad that Brookes was with me. I have not yet set foot on a South Sea Island. . . . By the way, besides riding in the train yesterday I telephoned to Nouméa for rooms in an hotel. Need I say more ?

June 7th,
Nouméa.

. . .

NATURALLY the first thing to do was to decide whether we were going to plant coconuts in New Caledonia. We called upon the Governor and presented our letter of introduction from the French Minister in Montevideo. We were most courteously received and then handed over to the Lord High Everything Else to receive full details as to grants of land, etc. To my huge joy things turned out just as I expected. The idea was quite impossible. A large capital was necessary, and the gains were slow and very uncertain. So back to the hotel to reconstruct our plans. Brookes immediately cabled to his brother in Japan, and is off thither via Sydney on the 20th. I found myself left, stranded, a waif in the great Pacific.

A very casual glance at Nouméa (it is nothing but a village) added to information I had picked up at Thio assured me that it wasn't worth while wasting time in looking for jobs in New Caledonia. The place is overstocked with French Govt. officials and there's absolutely nothing else doing. So to the British Consul, whom I found lethargic but friendly. From him I got the names of the only two British copra merchants in Nouméa, and then set out to find them. I struck oil straight away. The said merchant (named Muller) laughed at the idea of coconuts in New Caledonia, said he had been here forty years and would not spend a penny on them in the island, but (and here began the interest) he was largely interested in copra in the New Hebrides, and it is this copra that comes to Nouméa for exportation to Sydney and Marseilles. Hence his prosperity in Nouméa. I found the man a rough diamond, but evidently a man to whom one could say things straight out and get a straight (if somewhat brutal) answer. I told him exactly what I wanted, a job on a copra plantation to enable me to travel about the South Seas getting similar jobs for about three years. I told him also that I wanted to go back to Europe after three years, and that I had no intention of remaining as a copra planter. He tumbled to the idea at once. " If you are willing to work I'll take you on, but you'll never go back to Europe. If you ever write that book you'll do it here." "Who said I wanted to write a book?" " Knew directly I saw you. But that don't matter to me. If you work I'll pay you, if you don't I'll sack you. But you'll never go back to Europe. I am a rich man and I've been going any time this last twenty years, but I can't. I've got my schooners and when I'm tired of Nouméa, I go round the Islands, and then Goodbye to Europe." Well, I liked the man. . . . Took my fancy. He has offered me £6 a month and all found, and I am to give him an answer to-morrow, and, if affirmative, to start for the New Hebrides at daybreak. Needless to say, I have already determined to accept. I have learned much about the New Hebrides. From all accounts they are worthy, very worthy, from the point of view of beauty—typical South Sea Islands, of the stuff of which we have dreamed. There is a draw-back—malaria. Apparently they do not share the general South Sea immunity from malaria, but it appears that it is not of a very virulent type. Muller said that in order to give me the best chance he would give me as much as possible at first the job of going round in a schooner recruiting Kanakas from other groups for work on the plantation. This, of course, fits in most admirably with my plans. I am not afraid of malaria either, because the risks are enormously lessened by proper care and a decent physique. Of course, if I find that it does make life impossible I shall move on. That will be easy once having got a footing into copra planting.

Mosquito Bay,
June 30th, 1912.

. . .

I HAVE just returned from a walk of at least 100 yards along the beach, and I am feeling exhausted. I set out intending to investigate the other side of the headland that shuts in this little bay, but the mid-winter sun was too much for my unhardened body, and, as my pyjamas were speedily losing their Sunday freshness, I returned to my deck-chair on the verandah, where the refreshing trade wind gives one sufficient strength to stretch out an occasional hand for a banana or an orange in the intervals between drowsily ' penning these few lines.'

Really I am very much at peace. Between the verandah and the Pacific there are some palm trees and a stretch of coral beach. I can really hear the incessant booming of the surf on the reef. Away across the calm, blue, sleepy sea I can see other little islands like this. The sky is so cloudless and brazen that the shade of each palm tree looks like a heaven on earth. In the surf, under the shadow of the trees, there are some natives, nothing but their heads showing as they lie in the water and smoke ; and— in the dining-room my fellow-planters are singing ' Our Miss Gibbs ' to the accompaniment of a right bully talking-machine. To think that once a month a boat—an ugly steam boat—reaches us from civilised Sydney, and brings new records for this abomination—' where every prospect pleases and only man is vile '—I thank thee, Dr. Watts (or Mr. Wordsworth ? I forget), for this exceptionally beautiful line. But I must not revile. In spite of ' man ' I am seeing and learning. Remember that in my last letter I told you I expected for two years to be obliged to put up with inconveniences in order to have a year of free wandering. I shall keep this firmly in my mind when I am likely to curse the fate that sent Orstrylyuns to these beautiful lands. For these New Hebrides are beautiful. I have seen all the islands and landed on most. They have not the lotos charm that I expected. I am told that that is only found in the groups further east. But they have an indescribable charm, a remoteness which is beginning (in spite of ' phonos ') to eat into my heart. They are covered with a mass of green ; small hills dense with ' bush,' and here and there a plantation with its not ugly bungalow and store. There is no gorgeous foliage ; and tropical fruits are not as common as I had supposed ; but, really the bush is wonderful. It is dark and silent and a fit home for dreadful mysteries. (As a matter of fact it is still the scene of cannibalistic orgies—in spite of missionaries or perhaps because of them.)

I will stop description for a bit. I don't feel quite in the mood—thanks to ' Yip-i-addy,' etc.—so will content myself with a hard statement of facts such as they have occurred to me since posting my last letter to you. My last news to you was that I was just about to set off for Muller's plantation where I now am. In order to reach this island I had to journey from Nouméa to Vila. The voyage took three days on an evil-smelling 80-ton auxiliary steam cutter. The weather was horrid ; the engines broke down ; my bunk (in the dirty and only cabin) was situated just over the ship's store of garlic ; the rest of the ship was full of mixed cargo and Kanakas returning home from their three years' work in New Caledonia. It was not a pleasant trip, but it took me on my way.

Vila is a typical South Sea town—beach, stores, and bungalows. I had to put in four days there while waiting for a boat to take me to Mosquito Bay, and I made the most of my time. I had heard news in Nouméa that made me take special interest in Vila—the possibility of a well-paid job. These islands are ruled over by a French and English Condominium. This régime is of fairly recent installation, and more recently still there has been started a High Court (3 judges—one Spanish, one

French and one English) to ratify titles to land in the group. Aforetime planters bought or stole land from the natives, and now all these plantations are to be surveyed and title-deeds to be granted by the High Court. These cases will begin about September and will last for years. Well, I smelt jobs here as sworn translator or as surveyor, and I was not disappointed. I got letters of introduction from the Governor of New Caledonia to the British and French Resident Commissioners, and called on them as soon as I arrived. I likewise called on the Spanish President of the High Court, and jawed with him for some hours in his native tongue, which pleased the old man hugely. I got considerable satisfaction out of my visits. The B.R.C. was most friendly and most encouraging. He said that there was work for me in plenty as sworn translator at 35s. a day as soon as the High Court began its sittings ; and also there were other jobs which I could hold in conjunction. While waiting he advised me to go and learn all I could about planters and their ways, as the information would be useful. I thanked him heartily and said that I would take his advice. I didn't tell him that I had broken into my last sovereign to pay my hotel bill at Vila, and that consequently I could have no choice. He likewise offered to take me for a trip round the islands on the Government steam yacht the 'Medea,' and drop me afterwards at Mosquito Bay. This also I thankfully accepted as I didn't know how I was going to make the trip without any money. I had two nights in the hotel at Vila, and it was enough. My room was an outhouse, and I shared it with the most awful collection of creeping things. The hotel was full of the most fearsome collection of beach-combers, ex-convicts, etc., who drank and fought all day and all night. I slept with my Colt's Police Special in my hand, and was jolly thankful I had nothing worth stealing.

So I am only waiting here for a few months, and then I shall be back in Vila earning a good screw, and being more or less respectable. I debated long with myself before deciding on this, but I concluded eventually that it was the most sensible thing I could do. That was before I had seen the planters. Now I am doubly glad, as I couldn't stand these folk for long. In Vila I shall have to be more or less correct and official, but I shall be piling up money, and I shall have leisure to read and write. Also I shall be daily improving my French and Spanish with a view to the future.

... It is only necessary to mention the name of X.Y.Z. to raise a shriek of laughter in any part of the South Sea Islands. Its fame preceded it, and everywhere it was met with the most hopeless yarns in lieu of information, and with carefully prepared fakes. It never stopped more than a few hours anywhere, and then wrote as if it had a life-long acquaintance with the islands. It even (in some books) goes to the length of describing conversations between natives, when there is not a white man in the islands who knows so much as one word of any of the languages. In Epi alone there are more than 20 tribes each speaking a totally distinct language. Natives from one village cannot understand natives from another village. Everybody talks to the natives in Biche-la-mar, which is a kind of pidgin-English. It is used by French and English; and by natives themselves when talking to men of a different tribe. Even French and English people talk it to one another. It is a weird kind of Esperanto. I haven't got the hang of it yet, but will give you examples later on. So much for X.Y.Z.—the shallow journalist. I was glad to hear my opinion confirmed. But I bear it no grudge. Certainly it, in conjunction with B.L., revived the fire in me that had been lighted years ago by Stevenson. By the way, there is an old man in Vila who was for years with Stevenson in Samoa. . . .

(The Plantation),
July 12*th*, 1912.

AS you see, I have once more changed my address. This is another plantation owned by the same man. It is about 12 miles by sea from Mosquito Bay, and as the plantation is just being begun, the boss-man thought I should learn more here than on a finished plantation. I willingly agreed in order to get free from the ' cornstalks.' I had got a little tired of being addressed alternately as ' Mister ' and ' New Chum '—(imagine how you would like to be called Neeew Chem). One youth riled me so much that I thankfully accepted his offer to teach me how to box. I said I had always wanted to learn, but there were no boxers in England. It was only in the Commonwealth that men were found now. The youth was entirely self-taught, or else had imbibed his notions from a pugnacious maiden aunt. His one and only wile was to go down on one knee and then jump up like an intoxicated kangaroo with an attempt at a swing under the chin. I managed to get him twice as he jumped, and then he said he was weak from recent fever and would give me a few more lessons later on. I felt so pleased at dinner that night when I saw the curry get into his split lip.

Here on the plantation I have only got one companion, and I like him. He's a New Zealander, and about as rough as they're made, but he's a thorough good sort. He has been ten years in the islands knocking about and making enough money to supply funds for his own plantation, which is being looked after by his partner (oddly enough a Cumberland man and an ex-member of the Climbers' Club). This man (my companion—'mate' is the proper word) pleases me very much. He has very sound ideas on half-castes (who swarm in these islands), and on niggers generally. He is a tremendous big chap, and to see him handle a refractory mob of Kanakas cheers me wonderfully. There is a nice little bungalow here; we do our own cooking and are very comfortable. Also there are practically no mosquitoes at present, and the trade wind blows right through the house. Also Cameron (my 'mate') goes to his own place from Saturday till Monday, so I shall get blessed weekends free from all thoughts of Sydney and the sale of copra. . . . About the old missionary. I think he was a pretty fair specimen of the New Hebrides missionary. They are all Presbyterians here and bad at that. We landed at his place so that the Commissioner might hold an enquiry into a case of murder. A French planter and his wife had been shot by natives and the mission natives were strongly suspected. The missionary insisted that the murder was done by the ' heathen ' (he used the word repeatedly, to my intense joy), and nothing would shake him till the Commissioner threatened to send a man-of-war to shell the whole place. All the natives had retired to the bush, which is their usual custom after a murder, and no one could touch them there. We could see from their fires where they were, and shells would soon have driven them out. The old pig couldn't stand the idea of his pet Christians being shelled, so he owned up and within ten minutes we had six of the ringleaders on board and in irons in the hold.

These missionaries are just like kings to the natives. They pinch all their copra and all their land, and forbid them to trade with anyone else. There is perpetual war between the Presbyterians and the Catholics. The Presbyterians spread the most abominable lies about the Priests, who are really good chaps. They even tell the natives that French money is ' no good,' so that now it is impossible to pay a native in French money. They hate the planters like poison, and the traders even worse, and do all they can to hinder the planters from recruiting labour. They bombard the Commissioners (both French and English) with complaints about illegal recruiting. The French Commissioner answers politely in a long and charming letter. The English Commissioner tells them to go to the Devil, and fines the miserable planter. Concerning this recruiting, the place teems with yarns. It is only in certain islands that the natives will work, and from these they are recruited. Every planter keeps a schooner and goes round to try and get niggers to work for him. They are signed on for three years, and then shipped back again. Needless to say there are very strict laws and regulations. The dear things are not slaves, they are free and enlightened fellow-men. Needless to say these laws are set at defiance, openly by the French, secretly by most Britons.

There are two principal offences which are punished severely by the British authorities. One is giving drink to natives, the other is any suspicion of compulsion in recruiting.

I heard of a good trick played by a French captain the other day. He arrived at an island where the natives are good strong men (the average Kanaka of these parts is a phthisic wreck), but absolutely refused to go away and work. The captain told the chief that he did not want recruits, but only about thirty strong men to help him shift a large tank in his hold. The job would take about an hour and he would give them 2s. each for it. Thirty of the best braves in the village came and toiled away trying to shift the tank. Their efforts were not very successful owing to the fact that the tank had been carefully bolted to the ship's keel, and when, weary of the work, they came on deck, they found the anchor up and the ship well out at sea. The Captain grogged them all, and as they could do nothing else they all signed on for three years.

The same man has a plantation on Ambrym. There there is an active volcano, the demon of which the natives were in the habit of pacifying with loads of coconuts. The captain saw the idiocy of this from a trade point of view, and posing as an authority on volcano-demons, assured the natives that the only successful offering for the malignant spirit was tinned meat. The guileless Kanaka believed him, and now the good man does a roaring trade in tinned meat, and the natives bring him the coconuts which before had been wasted on the volcano.

I tell you these stories to show you the class of unhung villains that I meet. There is nothing to choose really between English and French. The choicest rogue I have met so far is the carpenter and boat-builder at ———. He is a drink-sodden old ruffian, who has been over 60 years in the islands. When he is really full he starts telling his yarns, which are of the most abominable variety. He boasts openly of things such that it would kill an ordinary man with shame even to think of having done the tenth part. He was ship's carpenter with ———. He talks with great admiration of ———, and sighs for the good old days of piracy and black-birding. This recruiting is only black-birding under a new name. The niggers are supposed to be paid 10s. a month, but at the end of their three years they find that all their pay has been swallowed up in gaudy calico and tobacco, or else it has been stopped for refractory conduct. Then the poor nigger is so disgusted at having to go back to his home empty-handed, which would cause him to lose caste for meanness, that he signs on for another three years, and so on ad infinitum.

Many more things I could tell you, but I have said enough to show you that I have not yet struck the idyllic life in the South Seas. Of course, the New Hebrides are wild and savage compared to the groups further east. The natives on many of the islands are dangerous cannibals, and they are all as ugly as sin. In spite of this, as I said before, there is a strange charm about the islands. The scenery, especially on the shore, is gorgeous. The bush, too, is full of fascination to me. It is the most impenetrable jungle, and even on the brightest days is dark as night. Huge banyan trees mixed with every other variety of tropical tree, and the whole knitted together with enormous vines as thick as a man's leg which hang in the strangest shapes. A sharp axe is absolutely necessary for even the shortest stroll, and as the temperature is a bit high for Gladstonian exercise one does not do much of it. There are a few tracks cut by the natives, but they are only one-man wide.

Last Sunday I saddled me the plantation horse and rode across the island by various of these tracks. I was warned of the danger, but helped by curiosity, and fortified by a revolver, I scorned the advice. The ride was mostly performed on foot dragging the unwilling horse after me, but in the clearer parts I made the brute carry me while I hung round his neck to avoid smashing my head against branches and vines. Not a human being did I see all day though I passed close to several villages and the bush was probably full of niggers. The only beasts that one sees are flying-foxes, crabs (enormous brutes), and wild pigs. There are no flowers, no gorgeous spicy smells, only everywhere a dank, weird darkness and a feeling of solitude that makes one want to scream for the sake of company. I got back soaked with sweat, and in the evening had my first touch of fever. It was very nasty, but I soon scotched it with quinine, and I had experienced some emotions in that jungle that were worth much malaria.

July 13th.

MY lonely week-end has begun. Cameron has just ridden away on my friend the horse, and I shall be gloriously alone till Monday morning. I am hoping that in these oases of solitude I shall be able to formulate some of the indefinite impressions caught during the week of work. It is particularly at night that I have been impressed so far. After dinner, bathed and dressed in clean pyjamas, I seem to shake off the incompetent agriculturist of the day-time, and become once more the savourer of pleasurable emotions. I leave Cameron reading in the house. I have introduced him to R. L. S., and in spite of Colonial birth (I urge extenuating circumstances), he is still sufficiently a Scot to appreciate. After the first night I could see his eyes sparkle, and his " Aye, man, it's grand " was really sincere, so sincere in fact that in spite of the thought of getting up at 4 a.m. he read on till past midnight. This should be accounted to me for righteousness.

Well, I leave him at it and stroll slowly along the coral beach. The bay is so sheltered that there is no ripple on the water inside the reef. Last night I could see the whole of the Southern Cross reflected on the surface of the water, water so clear that the image of the stars was confused with the sparkle of many coloured shells, and crossed with shoals of little phosphorescent fish. Everywhere the trees dip into the water like tired animals resting and drinking after the burning day. Just beyond the headland at the entrance to the pear-shaped bay the surf rumbles and roars on the reef, far enough away to make a low, continuous music of the sound, a running bass accompaniment to the sonata of the night. Ceaseless and higher pitched is the busy whispering of the trade wind to the palm trees, and joining the two sounds is the monotonous singing and foot stamping of the Kanakas, glad with me that a day is just dead, and a new glorious night is born. Away across the calm sea the great golden stars light up the islands of Malekula and Ambrym, while the passage between the two remains dark and mysterious, the high road calling to further beauty and fuller peace. On Ambrym the great volcano glows fitfully, a giant grumbling at the desecration of his own work, but too much imbued with South Pacific peace to be really angry. Can you wonder that I am glad when day is done ? Can you wonder that these Kanakas are not eager to work ? Can one expect them to love leaving their days of idleness and nights of languorous pleasure in order to toil for another man's enrichment, to be driven and cursed and struck, and finally swindled by a civilised

up-to-date Christian from New South Wales ?
I am firmly resolved that I shall never settle in these
islands as a planter. The thing is sacrilege and
desecration. It may sound romantic in the pages
of X.Y.Z., but the reality is sordid. The mere
cutting down of gorgeous trees is bad, the treating
of the coco palm as an article of commerce is worse.
Would you believe that they plant this lovely
creature in geometrically straight lines a few feet
apart ?

Then again the working and driving of Kanakas
is full of beastliness. One must drive them like
beasts and one must also care for them like beasts.
Imagine that every morning just as the colours of
the coming day are most glorious, I have to inspect
sores and scrub-itch on natives' legs and imbibe the
unspeakable stink of these and other maladies to
which the unwashed Kanaka labourer is prone.
To the mere idle spectator the planter's life is heaven.
To the initiated it is very nearly hell. It is full of
punishments to those who try to make accursed
gold out of the few remaining spots on this earth
where beauty unspoiled by man may be worshipped.
The money is to be made in plenty, but why should
not such money-making be confined to Walsall, and
Huddersfield, and Montevideo and Sydney ? No,
the islands are no fit place for workers. By working
one loses all the spirit of the place. Can one imagine
' a mild-eyed, melancholy ' worker ? A worker, a
life-force man must be brainy and pushful. He
must know how to get right there, and do it just one
second before the other swine of his own species.
I quote either from an ad. for somebody's electric

belt or an unsolicited testimonial for a bean-food diet. Britain wants such men ; the U.S.A. wants them ; Sydney wants them. Well, let these hives of industry have their fill, but God keep them from the islands. I wish you knew Italian. I quote you a few lines of a sonnet of Dante. Even without translating the sound will tell you what I mean.

> " Tanto gentile e tanto onesta pare
> La donna mia, quand'ella altrui saluta,
> Ch'ogni lingua divien tremando muta,
> E gli occhi non ardiscon di guardare."

Contrast this spirit of speechless admiration at the mere idea of his lady's salutation of another with the modern vulgar hustling to get rich, and you have an idea of what I want in the islands, and what the Colonial would give me. I want to be alone with all that is left unspoiled, so that in such surroundings I may say over and over again such glorious words as I have written above. How could I explain such a longing to a man who estimates the islands in tons of copra ? And, I fear, the so-called educated classes are just as Philistinic. Q. was full of snorts and grunts about ' the sentimental fools who write sentimental rubbish about these islands.' ' My year's leave is the only one in five that I care about.' ' Low Islands ? Yes—simply hideous. Rings of coral and a few old palm-trees and stinking natives. Give me a comfortable hotel in London and my club for the afternoons, and a rubber of bridge, and you can keep all the South Sea Islands.' Thank you, Mr. Q., I intend to keep them. They are not meant for you. You naturally, through no fault of your own, turn again and rend. You infinitely prefer banana-skins to pearls. They will fatten you against the days when I want to kill and eat you for my bodily needs.

Did I say any such things ? Not I. I know how to talk to the Mammon of unrighteousness. He shall think that I am a convert to his Philistinism. He shall help me on my way, and by and by I shall gather up the pearls he has rejected. I have learned enough here to keep all my hopes and longings hidden. I shall save during the years of my slavery and then close to my hand lie the things I have promised myself for many years. Don't think that even now my time is wasted or abhorrent to me—it will not be so in Vila. Compared to English ushering, compared to Montevideo, my life is wonderful. And then I am so near. There is no longer the thought of a long expensive journey to confront me. For a few pounds or even for nothing as supercargo on a schooner, I can reach in a few days realms of bliss. And, with the saved money, I can live as I want to live, and know for myself what I am convinced is there awaiting me.

Later.

I have just had dinner and feel inclined to write a little more before taking my nightly stroll.

During dinner I amused myself by talking to my Kanaka maid-of-all-work who helps me in the kitchen. I selected him for the job partly because he is a cheery ruffian and partly because I can understand his lingo, which is more than I can do with most of them. The only point I have against him is that he is a Christian. The outward and visible

sign of this is that he wears a hideous suit of dungarees instead of the delightfully becoming lava-lava
of ' the heathen.' I thought I would put his inward
and spiritual grace to the test, so I catechised him
thus :

" Time you altogether dead-finish, Nirawa, where
you stop ? "

" Me no savvy, master. Missie (missionary) he
speak body belong me go in ground, wind belong
me go up-tree (on high, aloft, etc.). Me think he
speak altogether gammon too much. Me think
time me fellow dead-finish me stop altogether same
pig."

Thus Polynesian belief in metempsychosis
triumphs over the Calvinistic adaptation of Greco-
Hebraism. As this man was a missionary teacher
in his own village, it is obvious how ' the Lord
prospers the handiwork of his faithful servants
among the heathen.' I tried to persuade the ex-
teacher that his native costume was infinitely
superior to ours, but he would have none of it.

" Oh, no, master, me fellow altogether flash more
when me have calico (clothes) belong white man."

Poor deluded creature. Curiously enough, these
lava-lavas come very largely from Japan, and are
beautifully embroidered, and the colours are exquisite. An intermediate stage between them and
dungarees (when the spirit of John Knox is faintly
felt at work) is seen in the substitution of store
calico (Horrocks' best Manchester variegated) for
the Japanese article. Then comes the full measure
of saving grace and trousers. In the wilder islands
of the group—Espiritu Santo, for example—not

even a lava-lava is worn. A man's costume consists in a narrow band of banana fibre . . . the females wear absolutely literally not a stitch. In consequence, consumption is unknown equally with the metrical version of the psalms of David.

Now the stars are getting bright and the beach calls me. . . .

July 21st.

TO my intense annoyance, last Sunday was absolutely ruined for me. I had had my petit déjeuner at 6 o'clock and was looking forward to a long day's talk with you when, just as I was about to begin, there arrived a boat from Mosquito Bay bearing my two pet Sydneyites and their ' phono.' They had come to pay the ' Neeew Chem ' a visit lest he should be lonely. They stayed the whole miserable day and nearly killed me. Why are such people allowed to live ? I had flattered myself that I was unassailable here, but these people wished to show me that Colonial hospitality laughed at roads and distances. . . .

Later.

I am a little recovered from my malarial peevishness and just want to broach the subject I should have talked about, fever permitting. Perhaps the least mental effort will be involved by my copying out the lines which started in me the desire to talk to you. I need not tell you who wrote them. With a large amount of the doctrine preached by this man, a weird mixture of nonconformist parson and profound critic, prosy moralist and intense lover of beauty, I am absolutely at variance. I forgive him his heresy on account of his splendid prose.

" Ask yourselves what is the leading motive which actuates you while you are at work. I do not ask you what your leading motive is for working —that is a different thing ; you may have families to support—parents to help—brides to win ; you may have all these, or other such sacred and pre-eminent motives to press the morning's labour and prompt the twilight thought. But when you are firmly *at* the work, what is the motive then that tells upon every touch of it ? If it is the love of that which your work represents—if, being a landscape painter, it is love of hills and trees that moves you—if, being a figure painter, it is love of human beauty and human soul that moves you— ... then the Spirit is upon you, and the earth is yours, and the fulness thereof.

" But if, on the other hand, it is petty self-com-placency in your own skill, trust in precept and laws, hope for academical or popular approbation, or avarice of wealth—it is quite possible that by steady industry, or even by fortunate chance, you may win the applause, the position, the fortune that you desire—but one touch of true art you will never lay on canvas or on stone or on paper as long as you live."

I don't know, I don't know. I wish I did. This ' motive for ' and ' motive when at ' smacks to me something of the public school Latin Primer, also somewhat of legal quibbling. What about the beautiful grotesques such as Beardsley made ? Were they prompted by ' love of hills ' or ' love of

human beauty ' ? Is not the mere production of
a beautiful thing, whatever prompted the production, a ' touch of true art ' ? Need one necessarily
have a touching, seventh-day Baptist belief in the
literal truths of the Hebrew scriptures in order to
be an artist ? Tell me all these things when you
write, and I shall be grateful to you. Tell me what
is your ' motive for,' also what is your motive
' when at.'

August 11*th*, 1912.

A WEEK ago I firmly made up my mind to
leave the islands by the first boat and never,
never to come back to them. That was because I
had fever and had it badly. I had several goes of
ordinary malaria, but that only lasts a few hours
and is nothing. This was a sweet variety known às
' bilious intermittent fever.' It wasn't intermittent
but it was very bilious. My temperature was over
106 at intervals for five days and all the time I could
feed on nothing but water. For two days I was
alone, as it came on at the week-end. I can tell you
it was lovely. I was alternately shivering with cold,
burning hot and then soaked in sweat. I daren't
get out of bed to get dry clothes for fear I should
never get back again. I really thought I was going
to peg out at one time. I kept wandering away into
unconsciousness and then back again to the wet bed.
I am just getting over it now, and with the departure
of the fever more reasonable counsels have prevailed.

This bilious fever is never so bad as at the first
attack. There is nothing worse except blackwater,

and that is not very common. Dysentery one can
guard against. Ergo, being in the group and
having the chance of making some money here, here
I shall stop in spite of fevers. . . . I am feeling so
disappointed. I had looked forward to such a lot.
I cannot quite explain to you what I expected to
find in the South Seas—you know how indefinite
such feelings are—but I am sure I have not found it.
I tell myself over and over again that these are not
the South Sea Islands at all, that I must wait until
I have seen Tahiti and Aitutaki and the Marquesas.
I repeat to myself ad nauseam that when I see those
islands I must be free from sordid cares, free to do
nothing or anything that pleases my fancy. I say
that the near presence of even one Cornstalk is
enough to spoil anything, however intrinsically
beautiful it is. For these people are vulgar and
horrid and petty-minded and ignorant. They
would be abominable anywhere. And then the
natives here are loathsome. They are simply
hideous, mis-shapen, lice-stricken savages. And
the scenery is only very mediocre. There are times
when I wax enthusiastic, but to be absolutely honest
I have seen infinitely more lovely scenery in England
and without the unpleasant accompaniments of
fevers and mosquitoes and cockroaches and rats.
No, I am not there yet. I must be thankful that
I am on the way, and that I am within reasonable
distance of realising my dreams. Remember that
I am passing no judgment on the South Seas. I
merely suspend it, which is, after all, a fairly reasonable thing to do.

August 31st.

M Y yarns are collected from all the hardest old cases that I come across. Lots of these beauties congregate once a month at ——, as this is the only station at which the mail-boat calls. They come in every imaginable species of craft from the surrounding islands and camp out round the plantations. Their talk round the dinner or high tea table is an eye-opener. It is mostly French. Nearly all these old stagers are quite bi-lingual, and they always talk of their villainies in French.

Here is one yarn. The man was a Melanesian missioner, Eton and Cambridge. He had the ' artistic temperament ' (blessed word !), and fell as greater men have fallen before him. The Melanesian mission chucked him out. Of course they were bound to, as the affair was a scandal, but as the M.M. is at least organised by gentlefolk, they let the matter stop there. But now stepped in the ' unco guid,' the righteous overmuch. Delighted at having caught one of their hated Episcopalian rivals tripping, they persecuted the wretched man for thirty years. Wherever he tried to settle they found him out through their native spies and hounded him out. Traders refused to sell him the necessities of life. Niggers were set to rob him, to mock him and to burn his house until he was forced to fly to other islands. He went on from island to island, always a charming gentleman, always a cultured scholar. He went from island to island in Santa Cruz, learned the language and translated the Bible into the Santa Crucian tongue. He was credited with being able to speak fluently twenty of the Papuan languages. Then the godly Presbyterians threw him out and he had to fly again. This time he came south to the Torres Islands and found there the man he afterwards described as the only Christian in the Western Pacific. This was a French priest who took the man in and hid him for fifteen years. During this time he became a Catholic and translated missals into many languages. The poor chap was desperately ill, suffering from one of the worst forms of elephantiasis, a poetic justice having decreed this punishment for his youthful sin. Then here again the predestined and elect found him and started their old games. But he was too old and tired to afford more sport. He wrote a pathetic letter to my boss Muller, who, owing to French training, had always done his best to be kind, in which he complained that the Christians would not let him live, and then shot himself. He sent his diary in Santa Cruz also to Muller, who has given it to me. With the aid of one of the Santa Crucian Bibles and a small dictionary I am trying to translate it. It is too awfully pathetic. There is none of the unctuous soul-baring of *De Profundis*, but the man had been through depths that Wilde never knew. Can you imagine the poor wretch trekking from island to island, often in native canoes (the heathen natives always recognised the sahib in him ; it was only the cheeky missionary-fed beasts who dared to taunt him)—clinging pathetically to his ruins of gentility, his books, his whisky decanter and an old school rowing blazer. It may be bad to be scorned by white men and by gentlefolk, but to be howled at by niggers and by Presbyterian missionaries must be a bitter pill. Several times his house was burned over his head in the night, the grass hut which he had built with his own hands and into which he crawled and lived like a wounded beast. He spoke Arabic and has written verses in Santa Crucian which he tabulates side by side with comparable verses from the Koran to show the great probability of an African origin of these Papuan (as distinguished from the Malayan) South Sea races. The whole story as told me by Muller and what I have learned since has made me horribly sad.

September 1st.

I INTENDED to write for a long time last night, but I was interrupted. I had to get up to eject two rats and one large crab, and the rats offered such exciting sport that my train of thought was broken, so I went to bed and chased smaller game. You have no idea how horrid flying-foxes are. I am quite sure that they are the souls of journalists. . . . However, this is a digression. To-day it is pouring and the wind is howling from the sea. In spite of the wind the heat is stifling, and everything is teeming with warm, sticky water. I don't know how I am going to stand this climate in the hot, wet season. It is bad enough now. One can smell the malaria hanging about, and to walk anywhere except the beach after nightfall is asking for trouble.

I have kept fever at bay this month by living on quinine, but it is a wretched form of life and too much quinine spells ' blackwater.'

... Now that the fever is over, I look at this life here with more interested eyes. It is not bad; certainly it is ten thousand times better than ushering. I wish, however, I had gone to healthy and more beautiful islands. Also, I wish Australia had never been discovered. Muller, who knows the Pacific like a book, says that a strict line divides the South Sea Islands of Stevenson flavour from the merely interesting islands inhabited by ugly semi-cannibalistic savages. This line is drawn from the south-west corner of New Zealand to Honolulu, and passes between Fiji and the Tongan Islands. To the west are the Papuan races of ugly savages; to the east all are Malayan stock. The eastern islands, too, are absolutely different, being the real lotos lands.

September 7th.

I WAS thinking the other day of my curiously futile life, and the phrase flashed across my malaria-befuddled mind, ' The aspirations of the irresolute in common with the aspirates of the illiterate are often dropped, often misplaced, always misunderstood.' This is a fair example of my mental condition. I am forgetting how to talk, how to think, how even to eat. I feel almost at the end of my tether and cannot tolerate this crowd of Commonwealth yobs any longer. Their conceit is insufferable, and their ignorance is unplummable.

I cannot even understand their language. Could you feel interested in a ' bosker come-back ' ? Would you at my age like to be called a ' Jackeroo ' ? And they are so omniscient. Query—what do they know of England who only Sydney know ? Answer —everything. . . . Frankly they are insufferable. Their newspapers are mutual admiration societies. They speak openly of ' our magnificent race,' ' how we saved the Empire,' ' decadent Britishers,' ' the one bright spot in England's gloomy future,' ' the nursery of artists and poets such as England has never known,' etc., etc. ad nauseam. I saw a photograph the other day of a banquet given in Sydney to the Prime Minister of the Common-wealth. The costumes and the faces told a tale. It was just what you could imagine if you took a crowd of Scottish wee-free crofters in their Sunday ' blacks,' clean-shaven upper lip, blacking-brush fringe of beard, and mixed them with another crowd of the brainy, hustling, mind-power, vegetarian cultured ' college graduate,' the latter part of the crowd having their hair too long, and their evening costume like a mixture of a Soho restaurant waiter's and the star lion-comique's representation of Lord Halgernon. In fact it is just what one would expect the English House of Commons to look like in twenty years.

. . . I had to take a gang of niggers round to Mosquito Bay on Tuesday to make copra to ship on the Burns Philp steamer. When the steamer came, I went on board out of curiosity, and was well rewarded. There was a deputation of mission-aries from Malekula journeying to Vila to complain to the Resident that their lives were in jeopardy and to demand a man-of-war. They had a shocking story to tell, and were so frightened that they had left their wives and children behind in the danger while they went for the jaunt to Vila. It appears that the natives had been getting truculent for some time. Last Sunday week they made a descent upon a quite inoffensive English planter, killed him, ate him, and then retired to the bush with six of his labourers, and ate them alive there. All this I could have seen with a telescope, as Malekula is only about five miles from here. There is no doubt that the Government will do something serious now. This same tribe has murdered several whites with impunity, and each murder has made them cheekier when they have seen it go unpunished. This is the first open outbreak of cannibalism for years, although plenty goes on in secret. Now the Presbyterians are frightened. . . .

I was savage about my Sunday being spoilt. You have no idea how necessary these oases are to me in this hard, rough life. Another thing enraged me. I had been nursing carefully one of the wretched Kanakas here during the week. The poor beggar was frightfully ill, a mere bag of bones through tuberculosis ; willing enough, but absolutely past all effort to work. I felt horribly sorry for him, spite of his lice and dirt. He couldn't speak a word of even Biche-la-mar, and as I don't know a word of his lingo, he could only look at me with appealing eyes. I knew he was dying, and tried to compensate to the poor wretch for the brutality of the treatment they get at the hands of these planting beasts. I

had to report him as sick and said that I didn't think
he would last long. " Pooh, he's only shamming.
That's the way you jackaroos are always taken in by
niggers. You're too soft for this life. Let me look
at the rotten swine. I'll soon turn him out." So
off we went to the man's hut. He was obviously
at his last gasp, his face turned to the wall, trying
to think of his own island that he had been kidnapped from to make gold for Sydney's civilised
sons. " Come on out of that, you rotten swine, you
lazy, shamming—" this, accompanied by a kick
which made the poor wretch fall on the floor. " You
see that's the way to treat 'em. You new chums
have got to learn. Now, then, on your legs, you
swine." The fall had finished things. The poor
creature was dead, and the Orstryliun hadn't the
grace to be ashamed. He simply swore and called
some of the man's fellow-islanders to bury him
quick ' before he begin to stink,' and then growled
about the loss of £20, the market-price of a Kanaka
labourer. Yes, I am too soft for this job.

I know this sounds like ' Uncle Tom's Cabin,'
but the treatment of these poor wretches makes me
writhe. People howl about Chinese slavery. I
could tell them things about the recruiting and
treatment of Kanakas that would open their eyes a
bit. Imagine a poor wretch tied up to a post to be
flogged by his own wife and friends because half-
fed he had dared to eat one coconut found by him
in the bush, his own land stolen from him by these
cursed money-grubbers. That I heard yesterday,
and it was told as a huge jest. I am no ' black man's
friend,' and the Christianised, civilised nigger I

detest. But these poor beggars have more manners
and more virtues than their masters. They are
simple, courteous and generous to a fault. They
have unbounded trust in the white man. When this
trust has been betrayed, can you wonder that hatred
is born and they revenge themselves on their
persecutors. The planters complain bitterly that
the niggers won't come and work for them. Why
should they ? They have all they want, and, like me,
they hate unnecessary work. They are enticed away
by every species of trickery, often by actual violence,
and then the gold-greedy white man wonders that
they don't toil for twelve hours in the broiling sun
with one meal of rice willingly and heartily in order
that ' master ' may become rich.

   . . . You must remember that the Presbyterian
missionaries are medically trained. They are the
only doctors in a group of islands teeming with
diseases deadly to white people. They are paid
£300 a year and get a house, a large launch and all
their provisions free. They get all goods free of
freight and use this privilege to undersell the
wretched men who are trying to earn a hard living
by ' trading ' in this pestilential climate. They
use their spiritual influence over the superstitious
natives to make them bring all the copra to the
mission instead of to the store, frankly telling the
wretched Kanaka that ' great big devil he get you
belong night if you no bring plenty copra.' They
swindle all the natives out of their land, and set
them on to attack and rob the planters. Can you
wonder that the missionary is adored both by the
black and white ? After a few years they have

accumulated enough money to go and live in England, where they talk of the martyrs of the mission-field. The other variety that prevails here, the Melanesian mission, I have not struck yet. The 'Southern Cross' is due here soon, but they have little dealings with this group, confining their attentions to the Solomons and the groups round them. I believe they are better, but very wrong-headed, insisting on the horrible doctrine of equality of races and putting their doctrine into practice. I heard of one of them who went to stay in Auckland with a parson there, quite a decent man, and his wife. The missionary brought with him a pet native teacher. The Auckland parson's wife natur-ally arranged that the teacher should feed in the kitchen with the other black servants. But no. The missionary insisted on his brother sitting down at dinner with the whites. The parson's wife, however, was even with him. When they were about to retire, she remarked sweetly to the missionary, "We're so very pressed for room, Mr. X., I'm sure you won't mind my putting dear Mr. Mapuna in with you. It's a large bed." The man who told me this said the missionary's mug was worth a long drink to see. Next morning Mr. Mapuna was dispatched on urgent business up country.

October 6th, 1912.

.   .   .

THEY only keep me because I do a man's work for nothing. What they want is a hard, callous, slave-driving nigger cheater. Such men abound in the group and can generally be trusted to keep sober enough to make the niggers work. They only stop at one job long enough to get money for a fortnight's ' drunk,' but there are plenty of them. Where they come from, where they go to I don't know. Anyhow it's beside the mark just at present.

I am afraid I have bored you with this pro-nigger tirade. It was largely induced by my rage at the intrusion of these bounders. Tell me when you answer this whether the general tone of my letters is boresome or not. If it is, I will try and cut down the quantity of *ego* in them. I feel so much in need of someone to listen to my outbursts. It is just possible that this mail may bring something. Then, for the Lord's sake, don't miss a single month, and don't stint me. Remember I am in the veriest wilderness. Anything will be acceptable; news-paper cuttings, reviews of books, anything, every-thing, provided that it makes no mention of cattle or Orstrylia.

. . . I feel strongly disposed to come back to London for a spell. It seems rather absurd to turn one's back on Aitutaki before even seeing it. But I have talked a great deal with various old villains who have wandered the Pacific from 'Frisco to Sydney, and from all that I can gather the conditions are very similar everywhere, bar the fact that there is no fever further east. Otherwise it appears that Orstrylians, traders and planters flourish every-where. I don't think the South Seas is a good place to earn a living in—especially for a fool who is cursed with the smallest grain of sensitiveness.

The dolce far niente may or may not be good.
Personally I am inclined to think it would pall
quickly except in very congenial company. You
see, sweltering heat, mosquitoes, flies, fleas and
other pests are all against quiet enjoyment. Certainly I should like to travel further afield in the
Pacific and see things for myself, but I should like
to have just enough money to move on if a place did
not please me. For example, I should not stop in
the New Hebrides another day if I could get away.
I don't want money in order to travel about like a
tripper ; I am quite content to journey on any old
craft that turns up. But I do want enough, when on
my journeys, to be independent of applying for jobs
to these damnable bounders, and being obliged to
associate with them.

I don't think that even for a good screw I could
stand this plantation life much longer. It's the
nigger-driving that beats me. The mere fag of
tramping about from dawn till dark I don't really
mind. One has a bath and feels rather fit than
otherwise. If it weren't for fever I could stand that
part of the life and rather enjoy it as long as I had
no beastly cornstalks within ten miles of me. No,
it's the slavery business that I cannot stand. I
absolutely refuse either to thrash the niggers or to
trade. Trading simply means wholesale thieving,
and I haven't sunk to thieving from a black man yet.
The thrashing is probably necessary, for the Kanaka
is born lazy. But I do sympathise with him
thoroughly. As I have said before, why should he
work to make money for people if he doesn't want
to ? The wretched Kanaka gets no money for

himself. His legal wage of 10s. a month is paid
him in 'trade' which he doesn't want. More often
than not his wages are stopped for sickness, mis-
demeanours, etc., although this is absolutely illegal.
Why then should he slave cheerfully for a white
man ? I manage to get the beggars to work fairly
well. They love a joke, and one good laugh (which
is easily raised, I have about four stock jokes, all
quite indelicate) will make them work better than
torrents of abuse. The way they laugh is quite
refreshing. It is so different from a civilised laugh.
The laugh begins absolutely suddenly, and then
goes rumbling on like summer thunder to burst
out again just when you think it's finished. There
is no hypocrisy or sycophancy in the laugh. They
laugh because they enjoy the process. They know
all my jokes, but familiarity breeds content. I even
use laughter as a splendid medicine. It is perfectly
extraordinary the enormous power that imagination
has over these people. If a Kanaka imagines he is
ill (he may have just a little fever to begin with) and
is allowed to stay and mope in his house, he will die
of absolutely nothing at all. That is a well proven
fact. Turn him out to work brutally and he will get
better, but he will hate you ever after. Make him
laugh ; pretend you think he is a heavy woman ;
tell him 'me think picanniny belong you he close
up time he come down,' he'll howl with laughter and
be out to work forgetting that he quite meant to die.
It sounds very childish, but in his unspoiled condition the Kanaka is nothing but a small boy. It is
contact with missionaries and white people that
makes a cheeky nigger. Fortunately, I have got

very few Christians amongst this gang ; and I sit
on those pretty hard. One chap, who had been
some years in Queensland, had the cheek to lift his
hands to me the other day. I very rarely lay hands
on any of them, but I caught this chap thumping
his woman with the butt end of a musket so I
handed him one. Instead of caving in at once, he
stuck his fists up and howled out, " You no fight
me, master. Me savvy fight all same white man."
Then he got it. I really hurt him and meant to.
After about half a minute I dropped him and
immediately he started howling like a dog. He had
evidently been used to Queenslander's ways, and
seemed quite surprised when I didn't kick him in
the face merely because he was on the ground. I
couldn't make him get up so I left him howling, and
he has been mighty respectful ever since. He may
try and pot me some day, but I'll take my chance.
For the benefit of possible shooters I sit in front of
my house on Sundays and clean my Winchester and
a Colt's revolver. I rattle the cartridges in and out
of the Winchester, and look cunningly along the
barrel. They don't know that I probably couldn't
hit the house itself with either of the weapons. They
think all white men are crack shots, and, to do them
justice, most of these Australians are extraordinarily
good rifle shots. In a recent punitive expedition to
Malekula, an officer of H.M.S. —— bowled over
the chief of the revolting tribe at about 600 yards,
and the wonder of it caused the whole tribe to give
in on the spot. A Kanaka's shooting distance is
about five yards with a shot gun and about two
with a rifle. Of course rifles and rifle-cartridges are

absolutely contraband, but all the traders sell them.

You see, in spite of talking of London I get back unconsciously to Kanakaland. So I suppose the place interests me. It is bound to interest, but that is not everything. I could fill you pages with yarns about these people, but you can find such yarns better told elsewhere. I don't know, though, that anybody has written about the Kanaka labourer and coconut planting. Most of the written yarns are about traders. I chanced to look through *Island Nights Entertainments* the other day, and I was absolutely staggered by the vivid truth of it. The story ' The Beach of Falesá ' might have been written yesterday about the New Hebrides. Everyone of the types from the schooner captain to Papa Randall is here. The same drinking, the same roguery, the same war with the missionaries and the same tub-thumping natives exist to-day. There are men that one sits at table with who are known murderers, whose murders have been committed too far from justice ever to be punished. You remember I told you of the carpenter who had been with —— ? I heard the other day that he had been sacked for pulling out a revolver at dinner and letting fly at the Kanaka boy for not bringing him the mustard quickly enough. This man is known to have shot a partner when he was trading on Pentecost. It was put down as an accident, but the old ruffian boasts of it when in drink. " I say, old Jack was a mean feller, that's what 'e was. 'E stole my money ; 'e stole my booze ; and 'e didn't act fair with me over the trading. Then 'e stole my woman when I was drunk. Damn 'im. Shot 'im, of course I shot 'im, and I'd shoot 'im again to-morrow. Such a mean feller has no right to live." These words I heard him say myself, and everyone assured me it was the truth. When with —— he used to kidnap niggers for work in Queensland. He used to entice them on to the ship, and then lock them down in the hold. If a nigger got the chance he jumped overboard and swam for the shore. Then this beauty used to shoot, not to kill, but to maim " so that the sharks'd get 'im. Oh, it was rare fun in those days." The kidnapping and the shooting go on as merrily now as ever. Certainly it is chiefly done by the French, because the British Government go jolly hard for anything of the sort. This firm, by the way, trades under the French flag, as do many other Australian Britishers, so as to profit by the criminal idiocy of the French officials.

. . . Gracias à Dios, it is a pouring wet day, so I get an extra holiday. I seem to have meandered on with this letter yesterday, without saying very much. I only hope you'll find my letters give you as much pleasure as they give me to write. You can't think what a joy it is to me to be alone here. Spite of heat and fever, I not only tolerate, but actually like this life as long as I am alone. The work isn't really irksome. A large proportion of it consists in sitting on a log smoking a pipe while my niggers pretend to perform their allotted tasks. Every now and then I sing out " Go ahead there," just to show the slaves that master isn't asleep. Occasionally I stroll round and pretend to be in a

terrible rage just to maintain the proper respect
due to the presence of a white man. These Kanakas
don't pretend to try and understand a white man
or his ways. They are quite convinced that white
men are all mad. " Suppose white man he got
plenty kai-kai (food) in place belong him, which
way he want to work belong sun ? Black fellow
time he got kai-kai he no work. Me think white
man he all same devil-devil." This is their philosophy, and it's quite workable. They have an
extraordinary pride about work. No man would
dream of hiring himself out to work in his own
island, but will go and be a labourer on an island
five miles away. The only willing recruits are those
who have got into trouble on their own island and
are ' wanted ' either by their chief or by the authorities in Vila. The rest are, practically speaking,
kidnapped. Some few ' recruit ' because of their
love troubles. The marriage arrangements of the
labourers here are a great source of joy to me. We
have a fairly large number of women labourers,
and from these the boys are allowed to select a wife
to have and to hold during their three years' service.
All marriages have to be first sanctioned by the
white man in charge, and it is here that the fun
comes in. The man is too shy or too proud to come
and say he wants such and such a woman. Generally one of the women (not the selected one) is
deputed to come to me. Usually she arrives when
I am at dinner. I hear a sort of cough-giggle, and
then out on the verandah I see a woman, dressed up
in her best, hugging one of the verandah posts and
keeping well in the dark. I take no notice, or she

would run away. After about ten minutes she will
come sidling in leaning up against the door and
simpering like a school-girl. Then I ask her what
she wants, and she pitches me a long-winded yarn
full of giggles and smiles. I don't catch more than
one word in ten, but just listen for names. Then I
tell her to send the boy to me. He, I know, is
waiting at the gate, but he takes quite ten minutes
to get into the house. After a little general conversation about pigs and pigeons I come to the
point.

"Well, Taoniape, we hear you want marry
belong Poussiba." (Loud giggles from outside.
All the women are hiding there in the dark.)

"No, master, me no want marry belong him (her)
but woman she want me fellow too much."

"All right, Taoniape, take him he come (bring
her here)." Then the blushing bride is pushed in
by all the other women and I perform the ceremony.
This consists of writing on a piece of paper ' I,
Taoniape, do take Poussiba for three years.' The
couple affix their mark and off they go. The
shameful part is that from the day of the marriage
the wretched couple are bound to serve for another
three years, quite irrespective of whether their
real time is nearly finished or not. This is quite an
arbitrary arrangement, and is against the law, but
it's no concern of mine. I have performed seven
marriage ceremonies already and am very sorry
that only two single ladies remain. Of course they
have husbands (probably three or four, as women
are scarce) on their own islands, but that doesn't
count. The missionaries are frightfully against

this ' labourer marriage ' business. That also is no concern of mine. They try and enforce mono-gamy, and the natural result. . . . This practice, which a few years ago was punishable by death amongst the natives, has spread amazingly, thanks to the Calvinistic saints. Also the islanders are now decimated by pulmonary phthisis owing to the fact that the missionaries insist upon the Christians dressing decently. Of course they love wearing clothes, but they naturally don't know how and when to wear them. On a fine hot day a man will wear trousers, a thick woollen jersey and a double-breasted pea-jacket. If it comes on to rain, off come his clothes one time, and his sweating chest is exposed to wind and rain. The missionaries deny this, but facts speak for themselves.

September 10*th,* 1912.

A CURIOUS thing happened last night. I had just fallen asleep about 10 o'clock, and was awakened by a most fearsome din. Someone or something was uttering the most awful screams that I have ever heard. Every scream was worse than the last, and each one spoke mortal terror. Mixed with the screams were reports of guns and a general shouting and hulabaloo, but the screams dominated everything. My first thought was an attack on the plantation by bush tribes. I hopped out of bed, put on a pair of top-boots and my revolver belt and collaring a Winchester nipped out at the front door. The row was all coming from the back, so I thought

' to fetch a compass ' about the attackers and at any
rate have a bit of a run for my money. However,
to my surprise at the gate of the house I found all
the ' labour ' assembled and clamouring for ' master.'
I could see at once that they were in an awful state
of funk, for they were all stark naked. (As soon as
these Kanakas are either frightened or ill, off come
their clothes.) I called for the head-man, and he
came up shaking with fright and pitched me the
rummiest yarn I ever heard. (I will omit the
Biche-la-mar and give you the gist of his story.) A
certain labourer named Siva had seen a devil at
sunset when he went to draw water at the well.
The devil had said that he would come and take
him off to the bush during the night. Siva had told
all his pals and they had sat up with lights and
singing all the proper songs, but apparently to no
purpose. The devil had come and dragged Siva
from his hut and was now trying to catch him
behind my house. His pals had rushed after him
with their guns and were firing at the devil. As
long as they fired the devil couldn't catch Siva, but
their weekly allowance of four cartridges apiece
was giving out. Would I come and fire some
dynamite to frighten the devil right away ? I
persuaded the head-man (who is a dungaree-clad
Christian on ordinary occasions) to come round to
the back of the house, and there in the moonlight
I saw the strangest sight. I could never have
believed it, but for the unmistakable evidence of
my own eyes. In the clearing behind the house the
wretched Siva was running for his life, doubling and
dodging backwards and forwards, his eyes starting

out of his head, and uttering the awful screams that had awakened me. Three or four pals shouting at the top of their voices were loading and firing as quick as they could. They were firing apparently at Siva, but really just behind him. I made sure he would get a charge of shot in him, so I ran towards him and roared at him in my most mighty tone of command. Ordinarily he is a most tractable youth, and obeys me like a dog, but he took not the slightest notice of me. When I was about thirty yards from him and was beginning to be afraid of getting shot myself, the firing ceased. Immediately after the last shot he set off hell for leather towards the bush and—here is the odd part—his right hand was stretched out to the right front of his body as if clasped by somebody running beside him, and fast as he went he seemed to be leaning back and pulling against a resistless force. I was too blown to follow, and top-boots are bad for running through thick scrub, so I turned back expecting to find all the other niggers where I had left them. There was not one to be seen. Every mother's son had bolted for his hut, and was safely inside with lights burning howling songs for all he was worth. I went from hut to hut trying to cajole and threaten them to make up a party to go and catch the poor beast. I could do absolutely nothing. Ordinarily servilely obedient, now they were as stubborn as mules. I offered lanterns, dynamite, cartridges, even ' trade ' mouth-organs, but nothing would give them confidence. I could do nothing by myself, and feeling fever coming on I turned in to see what morning brought.

In the morning I sent for the head-man and gave him a long jaw. He seemed partly ashamed and partly sulky at my interference with what didn't concern me. He would only tell me his old story over and over again, so I sent them all to work. About an hour afterwards in walked Mr. Siva not a penny the worse for his adventure. He wouldn't tell me a word about it, but went and got his tools and went off to work. I noticed that none of the other men would work near him all day, and if he tried to speak to a man, that man immediately put his fingers in his ears. Whether the fact that Siva had returned whole meant that he had made some fearful pact with the devils or not I can't say. Anyhow the whole thing was odd.

September 11*th.*

THE wretched Siva is dead. When I called the roll this morning he didn't answer, and no one would tell me anything, so I went straight off to his hut and found him stiff. I am convinced he has been poisoned, but what can I do? I couldn't perform a post-mortem even if I wanted to; and these beggars use vegetable poisons that are instantaneous in action and quite undiscoverable. I don't know what to do. I suppose I must let the matter drop. If I pressed things much further I should have an open revolt, and I can't fight a hundred niggers with guns single handed. I have the moral support of the man-of-war at Vila, which might arrive six months after I was dead and buried (or eaten), so I shall wait on events.

Sunday, *October* 13*th.*

ONCE again peace and rest. I completed yesterday something that pleases me, and which I
think would please you also. This bungalow has
always been a distress to me. It is built of wood
and galvanised iron, and its squareness and bareness
is simply horrible, also the heat at midday is quite
unbearable. Unfortunately, the galvanised iron
roof is a necessity, as owing to the entire absence of
rivers and the poisonous nature of the few springs,
rain water is the only kind that one has to drink.
The matter was one that gave me much thought,
and I have solved the problem rather nicely. I
have thrown out two verandah wings, one for
morning use, one for afternoon use. The roof is
thatch, the walls made of plaited coconut leaves.
A big leaf is about 10 feet long. One splits the
mid-rib longitudinally and then plaits the what-
d'you-call-'ems. The result is delightful ; shade,
coolness, and a beautifully diffused light. The
whole thing cost 2s., the labour of two Kanakas
for two days. I have divided one verandah into
two parts, thus giving myself a bathroom. Can you
believe that even in this climate the white men don't
bathe ? Sea bathing is, unfortunately, impossible
owing to sharks and other worse beasts. They also
say that cold baths induce malaria. I say ' rot ' ;
they've never tried ; and the water never is cold.
My mate, Cameron, used to wash his feet on
Saturdays !
    To return to the house-building. I don't know
why all the houses are not built in native fashion.

They are cool, absolutely rainproof, and beautiful. (I suspect that is why they are not used.) Also they cost nothing. All the materials grow in the bush. One uses tree ropes instead of nails. For doors the natives use plaited coconut leaves, but to my mind that is rather clumsy, so I fashioned another kind of door which is a great success. It is made of cane grass (a kind of small bamboo) fastened together with string made of coconut tree fibre. It rolls up like a blind, and is in admirable keeping with the walls. Altogether I am pleased.

November 10*th*, 1912.

I AWOKE to the fact that all the letters I had written from the New Hebrides had been rather dreadful. I seem to have got into a horribly materialistic Philistine train of thought and my letters must have shown you my frame of mind. At any rate they were a faithful reflection of my actual mental state, and as such you must take them for better or worse. It is very hard in the life I live to be impressed with anything but the purely material. Remember that my day is full of little agricultural worries. My mind is rarely, if ever, used. I am tormented by ill health, and the awful, stifling, damp heat. Altogether it is a wonder that I can write anything at all. I am firmly resolved that I must speedily go back to London. I want health, I want books. I want music. I think the ideal South Sea Island must be left as a beautiful dream. As such it is far, far more beautiful than the reality. Why then disturb a beautiful picture ? I feel sad about it, but an unsatisfied longing is better than a shattered dream. And I am craving for London. Even if it necessitates a return to usherdom, it must be done. I can always get a non-resident job in London and spend the holidays wandering abroad. At least one gets thirteen weeks of freedom, and that is no mean thing.

I have definitely got that surveying job, and as soon as Cameron gets back from recruiting I shall start work. A very few months of that should give me enough money for a tramp steamer home and enough money to live on while I am looking for a job.

December 15th, 1912.

.   .   .

I GOT thus far three weeks ago and then a variety of things have happened. First Cameron returned from his recruiting trip and I went out surveying at once. I had been out a fortnight when the quite unexpected happened. The Government yacht came chasing round the group for me with orders to take me back to Vila immediately. The interpreter-translator to the Court of the Condominium had suddenly resigned, and his place was handed over to me. The appointment was dated December 1st, but the yacht did not catch me till the 10th owing to my erratic wanderings in a cutter. Needless to say I jumped at the job and embarked one time, calling in at the plantation for my baggage on the way. I hailed with joy the return to even the civilised officials of Vila.

The job is a very fair one from the filthy lucre point of view.

I made my first appearance in Court on Friday last. It was a bit of an ordeal. Every word spoken by Judges, Counsel, witness or prosecutors has to be interpreted in a loud voice by me. The Court consists of a French judge, an English judge, and a president, who is a Spaniard. The Public Prosecutor is a Spaniard. The Native Advocate is a Dutchman. The witnesses are chiefly natives who speak Biche-la-mar. The accused are mostly French traders. Can you imagine the babel? On Friday the Court sat from 9 a.m. till 6 p.m. in stifling heat, and at the end of the day I was nearly dead. This was the last sitting until February 14th, so I shall have two months' peace with nothing to do but sit in my palatial office and translate documents at about 7s. 6d. an hour extra pay. Ordinarily the Court only sits for two hours a day twice a week, so I shall not be overworked. All this week I have spent paying official calls ' upon appointment '— a small price to pay for a job that suits me down to the ground.

1913

January 8th, 1913.

$\cdot$ $\cdot$ $\cdot$

BY the way, Vila is beautiful—really beautiful. It is almost impossible to imagine that one is in the New Hebrides. You see, the bush has been largely cleared all round the town—which makes an enormous difference. Nothing is left standing except coconut trees and banyans. Then it is all grass covered. Again, there is a bay which is a very pearl. Also it is healthy—fever being practically wiped out owing to the bush-clearing. Also there are two doctors and a hospital and fresh milk and fresh meat and ice ; so altogether I am feeling happy.

There is a man here who rather interests me. His name is Mowbray. After Oxford he went to Paris and qualified in law there, and is also a member of the English Bar. He used to be Assistant-Commissioner here, but chucked it up. He works for natives, and is instrumental in worrying the Government folk into a fit. To his intimates he professes no love for the nigger. . . . He tours the islands, and at every landing-place the tribes are waiting for him with (literally) huge bags of gold. The niggers look upon him as their saviour. The French would shoot him if they dared, but instead they

71

invent the most dreadful stories about him in the local French rag. Really he is most amusing, and a rare find in a place like this. I went to his house last night and found Aubrey Beardsley on the walls. Ye Gods ! in Vila !

February 2nd, 1913.

. . .

MOST of the work that I have done so far has been for the man Mowbray. He lives in the next house to my present abode and I have seen quite a lot of him lately. To say the least of it he is an oddity. He plays the piano quite well and plays the most extraordinary things. There is quite a nice piano in this house and he rushes in at all hours of the day and night to play on it. He always comes accompanied by half a bottle of champagne, which he makes me drink before he will begin to play. Then he plays for about half-an-hour and rushes off again to get up cases on behalf of his nigger clients. I am sure the man is mad ; but after my Orstrylyun experiences his madness is very, very soothing. The type produced by a grafting of Paris University on Oxford is one quite new to me. He writes verse too in the Verlaine manner. It doesn't appeal much to me. Too many ' oh's ' about it.

By the way, here is another true missionary story. Don't let your ancient Anglican prejudices put you off. The story was told me by a Presbyterian, and, as you know, there are no sacred mysteries to them. It was at the Première Communion (called by the

U.P. ' the Lord's Supper,' and partaken of while sitting round a table) of a new batch of nigger converts. One brand from the burning named (say) Woivira Kilu-Kilu had been passed the cup of wine rather late when not much of the sacred liquid remained. He drained it with great gusto, and then, smacking his lips with the air of a connoisseur called out to the shepherd, " Here, missy, what name here (=quoi donc) ! No plenty he stop. You fill him up back again. Me fellow love big-fellow-master-on-top (=le bon Dieu) altogether too much." I suggested to Mowbray that he should take out summonses against all the missionaries for a breach of Article 59 of the Convention (' selling or giving or in any way whatsoever delivering alcoholic drink to natives '). He has promised to ponder the matter. . . .

February 7th.

I CAN'T go on with this now. It is very early morning and so I thought I would write before the great heat came. But I was working till late last night and I feel slack and languid. I think there is a hurricane coming, there has not been a breath of wind for days. The sky is covered with clouds, but by 8 o'clock the heat will be gruelling. The palm trees are extraordinarily quiet—frightened, I suppose, because they always suffer in the hurricanes. I have a three-fold longing : to scream, to drink much whisky, to sleep very peacefully. I shall do the last.

THE greed for gold has eaten me up. I don't like to tear myself away from the stacks of work that await me. I drive my pen to the tune of ' Gold, gold, gold.' Curiously enough it works out at 1d. a line, but I don't have to write journalese— it is all done in pseudo-legal French. I am also busy with the house. I have selected a new site and about one acre of ground. I won't describe it to you now. It is two miles from Vila on the shores of an incredibly blue lagoon. The trade winds ripple it now and then, but usually there is nothing to break the reflection of the palm trees. Think of me on Sundays, on the verandah, looking into the water. I never dreamt that such a spot existed in the New Hebrides. . . . I shall go into the house on the night of the next full moon. There will be fire flies also. Vila and its cornicopradom will cease to exist for me at 4 p.m. every day. I have got a horse, because one can't walk two miles. My first care will be to build a spare room. There are no sharks in the lagoon. The temperature of the water would average about 80° F. Full in front of me is the bay with its little islands, with its reef and its tear-compelling myriads of colours. There are no names for colours. One cannot say blue or green ; the words are banal. More specific terms are merely reminiscent of drapers' shops. Fancy saying that the colour produced by the filtering of tropical sunlight through palm trees, and its subsequent incidence upon coral-reef water was shot-green or ' Liberty Blue.' The other names belonging to nasty messes of stuff in squeegy tubes are equally unconvincing. I can only make comparisons with precious stones possessed of pleasant names ; and I don't know enough of these names and colours.

Port Vila,
February 16*th*, 1913.

I AM angry. The man who sold me my acre of land has swindled me. The said acre didn't belong to him. I ordered my gang of niggers down to start clearing the bush and the very next day I received indignant letters from two Frenchmen, who both claimed the land. I was threatened with actions in the Joint Court so had perforce to retire. I found later that all three of the people have an equally bad claim to the land, which really belongs to some nigger tribe. I shall have to wait until the matter has been decided by this precious Land Court, which may be one year or ten—gornose. In the meantime I am having the house built on the site which the Condominium Government gave me. It is not bad really, but cannot be compared to the lagoon. The failure annoys me, as I had made so many plans round that particular spot. I shall rummage round in my spare time and look for bits that I can buy.

Of course at present I am spending money wholesale in ordering from Sydney those little necessities of life which I have denied myself for so long. Silk pyjamas are expensive, so are good whisky and tobacco and cameras and a host of other things.

April 6th, 1913.

.   .   .

UNLESS I am very careful I shall start ' to sleep upon the shore,' and from that sleep there is no awakening. I notice one thing strongly marked. All enthusiasm for man-made art is leaving me. Instead of Europe and its wonders my mind is turning slowly but surely to Cathay. God alone knows if I shall ever see Europe again. I think and think with growing longing of everlasting warmth, of natural loveliness flavoured and made more lovely with Oriental mystery. I shudder at the thought of an auto-bus. . . . In the week I have little time for any thought. I eat and sleep and translate or interpret. It is not an exciting life. The translation is deadly dull, the interpretation is damnably fagging. Imagine standing for three hours and shouting in three or four languages. It would be hard work anywhere ; in this climate it is killing. After a morning in Court I can do nothing but sleep for the rest of the day. The Court is nominally only held on two mornings a week, but lately there have been some bad kidnapping cases, and two weeks ago we had a whole week's Court morning and afternoon. Oh, those afternoons ! That culminated in an attack of fever for me from which I am not free yet.

The people here are nearly all impossible. The place is merely a seething pit of racial hatred, and every man, English and French alike, has his own pet grievance against some other fool. "The French flag on the Post Office is an inch higher than

the English ditto." " Chose a fait une visite de
10 minutes a Un Tel, chef d'un magasin, mais à
moi, fonctionnaire de la Résidence de France
(Marseillaise : Musique de la Garde Républicaine)
il n'en a fait qu'une de 9 minutes. Ah ! mais ! "
etc. So you can imagine that I don't frequent the
society of the place. There is a certain ———, aforetime trader, recruiter and planter, who interests me
not a little. He was in Samoa with R. L. S., and knew
him well. Some of his yarns are almost unbelievable,
but they are all worthy. At present he is trying to
to be respectable as befits his age and position.
' 'Tis but a mere veneer.' After three goes of rum
he takes his coat off and begins to regret what he
calls ' the wild and woolly days.' And then he
begins to talk : what villains, what pirates they
were then ! The pirates and the kidnappers still
exist, but they dare not talk, and their crimes lack
the sanction of antiquity.

April 10*th.*

AS far as any place can be cool this weather this
house is. I am charmed with it ; though the
Philistines scoff at me. At least I am removed from
officialdom and once inside can do what I damn well
please. Also it is mosquito-proof—which no other
house in Vila is—and this is a boon which can only
be appreciated by one who has scratched every
square inch of skin off his body for a few months.
It is quite a fable that one becomes acclimatised to
mosquitoes. It is true that the bites don't affect one
after a time, but the vile insect never ceases to sing.

The mere sight of a mosquito rouses me to fury and the singing makes me dangerous. . . . I want to see you in my little grass house in the Western Pacific, but I don't think my dreams must ever be realised. I should hate you to get fever, which you would do sure as fate. I have got it now and it is beastly. I drank too much absinthe last night because the sunset was so lovely, and the fever is the result. It is such a pity, because I love absinthe and I love the additional powers of appreciation of colour that it gives.

May 25th, 1913.

I DON'T want to live in England again. I could not live anywhere near a British colony; the accent carries so far. I doubt whether the dreamed-of Pacific Isle exists now. The horrible octopus of missionary-cum-trader-cum-official has spread his tentacles everywhere. Also I shall always be a Wandering Jew, and it is so damned hard to wander from a Pacific Island. Here, of course, one is comparatively close to means of communication, but I couldn't settle in the New Hebrides for many reasons. I feel irresistibly drawn Eastward sometimes, and I shall probably sample it with its joys and mysteries, unhallowed as they may be, but I shall go with my eyes open and my mind made up. I shall learn a little and taste a little, and it will be so much added to the stock, the cud, the store for subsequent rumination. I am sure that it is only amongst the very old things of the world that one

can find that really blessed state where things are
not classified as good or evil, ' done ' or ' not done.'
Why should I be the slave of other people's convention, their paltry laws and accursed consciences ?
My life is all my own to play with and experiment
upon just as seems good to me.   I know that this
is foolish, and very largely impossible, but I intend
to have my times of freedom, if only to chortle about
them when I return to live amongst folk who dare
not form an opinion for themselves, let alone perform an independent act.   Ouf—I nearly got started
on a tirade. . . .   But really, what a rotten, petty
place England is.   What miserable slaves folk are
there.   Your country squire who bawls that he
' never shall be a slave,' and daren't even wear a
green tie if it tickles his fancy to do so.   Your
pedant who spends his life snouting up the crumbs
of knowledge of baked and stale and forgotten
loaves.   What will anybody ever know or do compared with what has been known and done ? Think
of all the sloppy-bloused, dishevelled young women
hacking monstrosities out of stone that was once
noble in form, the self-same stone that served for
Phidias.   Think of—— no don't, it might dis-
courage you.   Don't think of any of the things
that I have or might have said.   It is really only
the result of so much fever and quinine that
makes me like this.   Really I am the gentlest
of things, the mildest and most law-abiding of
bourgeois. . . .

June 29th, 1913.

Sir,
        Yours of April 17th safely to hand and
note contents, also under same cover drawings,
art goods, etc., for which our respectful thanks.
Think how nicely I could do that sort of thing if I
were only a senior student at Mr. ———'s academy.
Lord, what funny ideas seize me sometimes. Fancy
me a-wearin' bowler hats and reading ' all about
the Spurs front line ' during my daily journey in the
' toob.'

I am literally killed with work here, and after
hours of furious writing for money my hand and
my brain are too tired for further effort. That is
going to stop and soon. This job here is no good to
me. I am making money, but it is at the expense of
my bodily and mental health. I have just had a bad
breakdown through overwork, fever and insomnia
combined, and I nearly had to clear out and go to
hospital at Sydney. It's not good enough. Also
one has to be too respectable and respectful. I have
to bow and smirk and say " Parfaitement, Monsieur
le Président." " Je vous serai infiniment obligé,
Monsieur le Procureur," etc., when what I should
like to say would not bear writing. All the folk
are such fools and so dull. Igitur, I move on. It
is the first time in my life that I have not been able
to call one single moment of the day my own. At
first I liked it and hailed with joy the enormous
amount of work, because it all meant more money
which I was badly in need of just then. But it is the
kind of work that eats into the soul and destroys
all that I have been trying to nourish for years.

You have probably noticed the absolute dullness and lack of spontaneity in my letters since I came here. The cause is absolute brain weariness. As long as I was living near Mowbray I was stimulated by his madness and by much champagne : but they are stimulants which have no lasting effect ; and the reaction is terrible. And I am longing to be free, to do, say, wear and think what I damn well please. I didn't leave usherdom to become a ' rond de cuir,' and that is what I should speedily become here, if I didn't die or go mad first. Also, being in with Muller I shall get a chance of some fun. He told me in confidence that he had just returned from a voyage to the outer islands of the Gilberts in his steamer, and had netted over £6,000 in shell and pearls—absolute piracy, of course. He is a great, big devil, and howls with laughter at the Joint Court. The bailiff of the said Court boarded his steamer to serve a summons on him for a breach of the Customs Regulations (in the New Hebrides !). Muller, after urging the good man to depart quietly, took him by the seat of the breeches and threw him overboard. Then when he saw the ' fonction-naire ' couldn't swim he jumped in after him, pulled him on board and made him as drunk as an owl on champagne, and sent him back to the Court. For this little jest he was fined £50 by the Court. But, good God, give me a man like that ten thousand times rather than these ruddy idiots of officials. And this group is really a good place to live in. I damned the place when I was at the plantation because the Orstrylyuns bored me and because I was anxious about money. But, really, it is very beautiful. At —— I shall be free from Orstrylyuns, and the scenery is lovely. I shall be my own master and need not care a damn for anybody. Malaria I have got used to. I have had it badly in Vila (more by token I have got it now, the ague stage, hence the writing), because I have kept rotten hours and drunk too much absinthe. In fact I have worked and lived as if I were in London instead of in a tropical climate, and one can't play games like that with impunity. However, once clear of Vila I shall be very ' sage.'

Later.

It's all over. Cold, shaking, hot, sweating—finish. I left off writing at 9 o'clock this morning and it's 4 o'clock now, so you can see that an attack eats into a day pretty considerably. I deserved that dose, though. I spent the evening at the Club with Muller and some ' types ' from Nouméa. Hinc illæ lacrymae. I am told that —— is free from fever—it all depends on the mosquitoes—but I don't much care. One gets used to it, and it doesn't leave bad effects as long as one is careful and leads a decent out-of-door life. It is this wretched work here and no exercise and hourly apéritifs that do the mischief. You should just see some of the things that haunt the ' beach ' in Vila. Their only sustenance is absinthe and cigarettes, so fever takes them properly. They earn a precarious living by selling grog to Kanakas and gambling in the Chinese opium hovels. It is rarely that they venture out in the daylight, but if one does chance to see them the object lesson is salutary. I am sorry for some of the poor devils. They are all ' libérés ' from Nouméa, not allowed to go back to France, unfitted for work, and with every man's hand against them. There is one poor old chap who has my especial pity. He is ordered about and cursed and bullied by these greasy bourgeois fonctionnaires and négociants. They even ' tutoyer ' him. I have seen the old thing sneak out on to the verandah while we were at dinner and drain the dregs from the apéritif glasses, and then come back and stand in the dining-room as impassive as a judge. He has got a really aristo-cratic face—a damn rare thing for a Frenchman—and I sniffed mystery in him from the first. I had several jaws with the old man when I found him alone in the Club, and I gathered from his talk that he had travelled a devil of a lot ; but never a word of any previous superior position. I didn't like doing it, but curiosity got the better of me one day, and I asked one of the aforesaid greasy bourgeois the old man's history. It appears that his father was Governor General of ——, and he a high official at ——. Wine, women, etc., brought the usual story—defalcations, father's suicide and a life sentence for this old man. That was forty years or so ago, and now he is called for to wipe a table-top before a greasy store-keeper can put his greasier helmet on it. I am quite sure that this old man is the only Frenchman in Vila with any pretensions to gentle birth. Why the hell hasn't he shot himself years ago ? I suppose French convict-prisons break one's spirit a little, there's too much fraternity and equality about them. Talking of Chinese, there are about 150 Orientals even in this little town—Javanese, Tonkinese, Japs, etc. They're a foul mob—the Tonkinese at any rate—but they can cook. They rob the wretched Kanakas right and left and teach them to smoke opium, which kills them off like flies. The wise Condominium Government places no restrictions on their coming, and they are arriving by every steamer. The Tonkinese, of course, are French subjects, so they do get looked after a bit, but the rest can do what they like. I hear, for instance, there are thousands of Japs in Queensland alone, and Fiji is fast filling up with 'em. Really some people are fools. The Australian Government has shut out Kanakas from the country, and thereby ruined all the plantations in Queensland, and yet they allow these yellow swine to come in who simply batten on the country and are no good as agricultural labourers. Some of the fools who are wasting their time in dividing Europe into lots ought to come out to the Pacific and see the way these yellow races, by sheer force of numbers, are running over and trickling in everywhere. Howsomever, it doesn't really interest me ; and as I don't suppose it interests you, we will leave the question.

July 6th, 1913.

TALKING of the conventions of life here, an amusing thing happened yesterday. My ' humpy ' is situated close to and overlooked by the pretentious mansion of his Honour Judge ——. The creature had had the effrontery during the last

month to have a lot of female relations from Seednee
staying with him. Naturally I took no notice of
them and expected the same politeness on their part.
Imagine my feelings when he called on me yesterday and told me that the ladies objected to my
walking about in a sun helmet and pyjamas in the
afternoon. They are very nice pyjamas and the
helmet is of a most becoming shade of grey. Naturally I refused to change my habits. Then the good
fellow became petulant and said that the " Court
would consider the matter." I being weary of the
discussion said the Court could ———. It was
rude of me to say what I did, but the man was boring
me. I await the result of the Court's deliberation
with much joyful curiosity. They daren't offend
me because they would be absolutely in the soup
without me now, and it would take three months
to get a ' remplaçant ' from Sydney. If the judge
had admitted that my pyjamas quâ pyjamas were
of tasteful shade I would perhaps have given way ;
but he is no judge of colour, and would, I am sure,
write the word without a ' u.' So what could I do ?
. . . Yes, of course H. shall be a mighty man with
his hands. It will harden him and teach him proper
contempt for foreigners. (*N.B.*—I am fast becoming
a blatant Briton in some respects. The Latin races
nauseate me with their excitability and lack of self-
control.) But also he must learn to fence. You have
no idea how I have longed to fight some of these
Dagoes and Frenchmen and hurt them really badly.
They despise us because there is no manner of
settling disputes among men in England except by
fisticuffs or the police court. H. will, of course,

travel, and he will (equally of course) inherit the quarrelsome tendencies of his father and the said father's very reasonable objection to sitting down under an insult. Therefore, he must be prepared to make his quarrels good. Don't talk to me about Christianity and the 20th century. Man, if he is really a man, will always want to fight. Well, then, let him be in the position to do so properly. I should love to be able to spit my enemy through some part that would hurt him and ' make him sabby ' (as the Kanakas say). Of course, I don't refer to the journalistic, theatrical idiocies of the French duel, but a man really cunning with the sword (do you remember Esterhazy ?) can hurt his opponent very badly and yet do it in a courtly and dignified manner.

Just to touch on the boxing question for a minute. I have seen a good few scraps down here and in most of them a knowledge of boxing was far more hindrance than help. The fights were chiefly of the ' all in ' variety in which the weapons included teeth, chairs, bottles and feet with a revolver as the trump card. You see, a boxer makes the foolish mistake of imagining that his opponent is going to fight fair and consequently he neglects to take advantage of the furniture. Of course between two average Englishmen the best boxer will generally win if he can hit, but in a mixed fight among Australians, Frenchmen and half-castes boxing is a very ineffectual asset. I saw one instance in Vila in connection with a baccarat row. A Frenchman challenged an Englishman to come outside and fight. The Englishman naturally accepted and led the way, taking off his coat as he went. The Frenchman

began the fight from behind with a bottle while the
Englishman was foolish enough to be entangled
with his coat-sleeves. Naturally the fight ended
there, and the Englishman recovered consciousness
two days afterwards to find that owing to the unfortunate absence of set rules he had sustained three
broken ribs as a result of the Frenchman's entire
ignorance of the heinousness of hitting (or kicking)
an unconscious man. The row ended up quite
merrily with revolvers and lasted as a faction fight
for some days. And then the original Frenchman
sued the original Englishman for damages for
abusive language—and got 'em. My motto for
these mixed melées is ' If you haven't got a revolver
or are not prepared to take the consequence of using
it, clear out quick and lively.' Neither honour nor
cowardice can possibly be appreciated in such company, and after all, I should hate to think of dying
in such a vulgar way.

. . . I am beginning to see many virtues in the
public school type. Whether the virtues (you know
enough about ' foreigners ' to know what I mean)
really arise from the public school training or
whether they are inherent I have not yet decided.
I think that very probably a good school counter-
balanced by a judicious admixture of travel and anti-
philistine instruction in the holidays might be
effective. It is a very difficult thing to decide. The
stereotyped public school athletic Philistine is
obnoxious in many ways, but the pampered, home-
trained neurotic is infinitely more so. The great
objection to my mind about English public schools
is the absurd importance attached to skill in games.

General athletic excellence is admirable, but English games are not. They do not tend to a reasonable and artistic development of the body, but rather the reverse. The best that can be said of them is that they teach courage and self-restraint—excellent qualities which could, however, be instilled in a much more sensible way. Then again the pleasant things of life are so utterly neglected in English schools. How many thousands of public school boys are there who curse as men the fact that as boys they were not taught music, drawing, and a proper use of European languages. These three things are of such great importance in life ; and they cannot be properly acquired except in early youth. Some people think that by sending a boy abroad for six months he will learn enough foreign languages. Such an idea is absurd. All the boy learns is an acquaintance with habits he is very much better without. No, there is an awful lack in English educational methods.

. . . I have been a ploughman and that's more than you'll ever be. I have also (like the dear Vagabond) shovelled manure for a living, and curiously enough, manure smells just the same in the South Seas as it does in England.

Island of Ambrym,
November 2nd, 1913.

SINCE I wrote my last long letter to you I have been without a fixed abode and have scarcely had time to write even had the inclination been there. Let me explain myself and excuse myself a bit before beginning my real talk. I told you in my last letter that I was chucking the Joint Court business and was going to start on a plantation on the Island of ——. Well, that deal, like all business which involves French law, has been a lengthy one and is not yet settled.

There are two law-suits involved, which, though I am in no way interested, prevent me from closing my deal. However, I am hoping to get everything finally fixed up in a month or two. In the meanwhile I had chucked the Court and Vila to my own great mental satisfaction, and it was necessary to do something in order to live. Consequently I have turned surveyor once more. I knew there were lots of folk who wanted their land surveyed, so I made a trip round the islands and booked orders. I didn't quite expect the rush that really happened. In spite of refusing everybody who was not prepared to put down the ' ready ' in advance, I have contracted to do over 80 properties scattered round the group and involving about 150,000 acres of land. This means heaps of money. I shall stick to it just as long as it pleases me, and then sell my contracts to some surveyor bloke from Sydney, and retire to my property. I like the life too. I have a small caravan of niggers, tents, gear, etc., and move from place to place in a small cutter which I have purchased. I am my own master and there is just enough wildness in the life to make it mildly exciting. I have been at it two months now, and so far have only been in the more settled districts (*i.e.* where the natives are really no longer cannibals). Very soon, however, I am off to Malekula right into the bush, and there I expect some fun. I am arranging to get five or six 'boys' from the French Loyalty Islands as a body-guard. They are fine big fighting men and hate Kanakas like poison. I shall give them Winchesters and orders to shoot at anything brown that shows itself in the bush. My own niggers would run like curs from a bush-man because Christianity tells them they must not shed blood— for no other reason, of course—but fortunately Christianity has not been caught by the Loyalty boys to any harmful extent.

I am taking on a partner in January—the chief engineer of the ——, a Scotchman named Fraser. He has wandered pretty well all over the world, including a little trip on his own up the Amazons, where he left half an ear and various other bits of anatomy. He has done a lot of railway surveying and is a very handy man with a spanner. I saw him tackle his Arab firemen with one and it was really a masterly performance. I always thought a spanner was to hit with, but Lord no ! You hold it half-way down and poke with it straight at the solar plexus. You see down below in a small steamer there is no room to hit, but one really good dig with a spanner makes any kind of nigger so sick. Between us I think we ought to persuade the gentle cannibal that the land we want to survey does really belong to a white man. I grant you that nearly all the land was pinched originally, but that is much too abstract a question for me. M. Chose tells me that he has 5,000 acres of good land somewhere in Malekula ! He has never seen it, and has unfortunately lost the title-deeds, but he is willing to pay me £150 to go and find it and survey it, while he on his part will look for (and most assuredly find) the title-deeds after he has seen my plan. I pick out a nice chunk for him with as much sandal-wood as possible, survey it, and leave the rest to him. It's nothing at all to do with me whether he has rows with niggers or with the Joint Court. It is quite unreasonable for the niggers to try and stop me surveying the land. If I am surveying in the wrong place, well, it's a mistake anybody might make, and they can't expect me to move my camp just for the silly reason that it is pitched on their land. I shall doubtless have arguments, but never mind. As I say, as long as the job pleases me I shall stick to it. I ought to make enough money to afford a trip home shortly, but that is in the future and I am chary of making too many plans. At present I am close to a trader's where the steamer calls once a month for copra, so I am taking the opportunity to get letters written and left here against the time when the tub really does come. The mail in these outlying spots often misses a month or so because the wind is in the wrong quarter. You see you can't anchor near a coral reef except under very exceptional circumstances, and, if the wind is wrong, lying-off without anchors down means a very large hole in the bottom of the steamer. Hence one's mail is a bit erratic. The steamer people are very good and always try and put your mail off somewhere. But the gentleman who lives there may take it into his head to have a three weeks' drunk, and then take at least another week before his nerves are steady enough for him to venture out to sea. That is exactly what happened with your letter this time. However, I got it eventually, so what matters ?

I have just looked up from my letter and outside the tent there are a score or so of brown folk without one stitch of clothing amongst them. There is a ' school ' (= mission church) not far away and these folk are on their way back from ' divine worrrship.' The natives round here are in the half-way stage. Usually they are nude and picturesque. On Sundays they put on Christianity in the form of a lava-lava for the men and a smock for the women, but once outside the school off come the signs of grace, to be hidden carefully in the bush against the ' time of the evening sacrifice.' In the meanwhile they are happy in the surf, with no thoughts of ' predestination and election,' nor yet of ' grace abounding.' They have heard that there is a ' big fellow master belong gevernment' who lives in a ' house calico' and does strange things with machines. By and by they will come and bring me yams and coconuts and sit down for a talk. Slowly the missionary pest is killing picturesque savagery, but from the nature of the disease its spread is slow. Gaudeamus igitur. No, this life is better than ushering—much better. You have no idea how hard it is to realise High Street, Kensington, from here. I have caught the ' Pacific languor,' and it is impossible to make sharp pictures of anything. And then it's so hot. Everything conduces to a kind of misty wondering, and nothing to movement of any sort.

THIS letter will at least be begun under peculiar circumstances. Please note. I am in hourly (even minutely or secondly) expectation of being invaded by a pestilential and mortiferous flow of lava from a volcano. Let me try to explain:

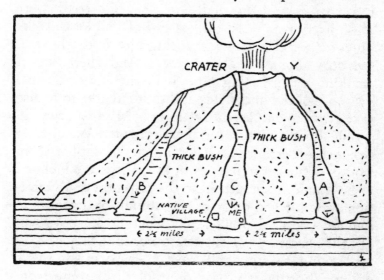

The eruption began yesterday morning. A and B are steep gullies cut by previous lava flows. They are already full. The bush is on fire from B to C and from C to A, but the wind is blowing towards the crater. C is a gully at the mouth of which I am encamped. Interesting question—will the gully C also be invaded. Observe that escape is impossible except by sea. I have no boat; my vessel is away being repaired. Observe also that XY is a kind of subsidiary ridge which runs up to and past the crater. It may be high enough to stop the flow down C. On the other hand it may not. In the latter case you will not get this letter. I spent last night sitting on a camp-stool on the sand watching the finest sight that man could wish to see. It was bright moonlight. The surf was thundering on the reef in a broad patch of gleaming white. The bush fire roared and howled and the big trees were crashing down. The gullies full of hell looked like gigantic fiery serpents creeping down to the sea, twisting about for their prey. And there was I smoking a comforting pipe, drinking my occasional glass of whisky and water and quite unable to realise that I was in any kind of danger. My boys were in a blue funk and but for the sight of a Winchester would have escaped by swimming. I wanted them to stay because the natives in the village are inclined to be fractious and attribute the eruption to observations which I had made of the summit of the volcano two days ago. I don't know whether my boys will fight if necessary. I am afraid not, but they're jolly well going to stop and have a share in all that's going. Fortunately they none of them come from this island, and are therefore just as much disliked by the villagers as I am, and perhaps more so. For this reason they may prefer to remain with the man who has got the gun. This supervision of my camp is the only worrying part of what might be a most interesting situation, full of possibilities. You see I don't like to sleep at night. Were it only for the volcano and the niggers of the village I should enjoy a peaceful rest to-night. If the lava comes, it comes and I can't stop it. I know the New Hebridean too well to fear that he will attack me by night. He is too much afraid of the devil to venture out. But my curs are so frightened that they'd go and drown themselves in the sea just to spite me. And then who would carry my baggage ?

Island of Pauma,
December 12*th*.

I'VE been having such a time. I shouldn't care to go through it again for a good deal. Ever since I stopped this letter on Sunday last I have been running and dodging that beastly volcano. Fortunately I did it with conspicuous success, and have brought myself, my boys, and my baggage safely to this small island with thirty miles of sea between us, and that hell from which we escaped. The only ill result is that I have got dysentery, but I am comfortably installed in the house of a very decent missionary and being properly doctored, so I hope that I shall get off lightly. Now to go back a bit. I can't hope to give you a lucid account of all that has happened. Much of it has been simply a nightmare. When I left off on Sunday I was watching that creek C and wondering whether the lava would come. Well, it came. About eleven o'clock in the morning I spotted it with my telescope coming, and coming fast. There was only time for desperate remedies. I reckoned that the lava would reach us in about an hour, perhaps less. I ordered tents down and everything bundled into bags and the caravan to move off towards A. The natives thought I was mad as the fire had been coming down

there since Saturday. However, I drove them on
vi et armis. I had surveyed that creek and I remembered its formation. There was the possibility
that the lava-flow had got blocked and had not yet
reached the sea in very large quantities. So on I
went, and much to my relief found that my prognostications were correct. There was only a small
stream of lava coming through, and by dint of walking in the sea up to our necks and swimming a
bit we got across. The sea-water was terribly hot,
and the surface of it inches deep in hot pumice
stone; but we got through. And then for three
miserable days the game went on. As soon as I
reached what I thought was safety, a fresh outbreak
would occur. New craters were apparently opening
everywhere on the mountain and there was no
safety. I and my boys were dead beat. We had
been overtaken and met by hordes of ' bush '
natives flying anywhere, naked and mad with fright.
The shore was a foot deep in ashes mixed with dead
and boiled fish, turtles, birds with their feathers
burned off and other cheering road-material. The
natives that we spoke to told stories of awful
happenings to white-men's stations, loss of life and
so on. I began to despair of ever getting away.
Each night I kept watch myself for the chance of
a boat, but it was not till Wednesday that the chance
came. It was about midnight when I thought I
heard the teuf-teuf of a launch a long way out. I
set fire to a whole tin of kerosene and let off the nine
shots of my Winchester. And the launch came in.
It was my old friend G., going back to his home on
Pauma after having been out three days saving

people higher up the coast. There was an awful
swell on, but G. is a sailorman, and after about two
hours' struggle we got my caravan safely on board
and headed for Pauma. Half an hour later his
benzine gave out and we had to beat up against a
head wind, taking eight hours to cover about 20
miles. But we arrived. G.'s house was full of
refugees, so I walked round to the mission station
and dropped. I was absolutely finished and done,
and could only lie like a log. However, bar the
dysentery, which I hope is only going to be mild,
it is over. This place is full of folk who escaped
earlier in the week. The wreckage has been fearful.
One place where I was surveying about three weeks
ago there was a large trading station with nice
house and garden, a big missionary hospital with
about 60 patients, and three or four native villages.
Of all this now there is nothing to be seen. Everything buried thirty feet deep in lava. You remember my big basket that went to Cairo with me
and has since been round the world ? Well, that
has gone and with it all my clothes (except camp
clothes), fifty pounds in good red gold and my
despatch-box full of papers. Of my boat (cost £100)
I have heard nothing, but I fear it will have gone.
I used the place as my headquarters, but fortunately
as I was out in camp I had got nearly all my stuff
with me. The loss is a distinct bore, but I might
have been frizzled up myself, so I suppose I ought
to be thankful.

. . . You say that you would like a tramping
tinker's independence of time. But how could
anyone in England disregard time ? They may

not have to catch the 5.34 to keep an appointment
at 6.11, but everyone is bound just the same. Here
—to the natives at any rate—time is less than
nothing. Of course, on a plantation one has heures
fixes for beginning and finishing the day's work,
but that is all. Even the white men after a few
years of island life become extraordinarily vague
about time. Up till a short time ago my natural
stodgy fussiness made me rave about the slackness
of people here. Now I am beginning at least to
tolerate it. I am bitten by the lotos. (That is not
really 'mixed.' The juice corrodes.) Time is
getting more and more for me to be considered
merely as a convenient index of natural instincts,
but in no way a governor of them. I thought that
among the Dagoes I had found the depths of artistic
procrastination. Here, however, people have pro-
moted procrastination from an art to the grade of
an instinct. A small example—some years ago
Ashby at Mosquito Bay had a bright idea for saving
time on the plantation by using a cart for bringing
in coconuts instead of the usual bag on a Kanaka's
back. After months of thought he ordered a cart
from Sydney. It duly arrived and was landed on
the beach. Obviously, roads had to be made before
the cart could be used. That cart (or its remains)
is still on the beach where the steamer people left it.
The inter-island trading vessels captains when asked
to fix a date for coming to collect copra can never
get more definite than the probable number of
weeks—and they are never right in their guesses
even then. Even the Sydney steamers—with a
printed Time Schedule—are just as bad. The

Messageries Maritimes boat is already 6 weeks behind her scheduled time this year. One trip she makes up a week and comes to catch everybody unprepared with no ' boys ' to unload cargo. (The work is done in —— by bush tribes who come down for the day.) The next trip she will be a week late and the ' boys ' have all got tired of waiting and gone home. Just imagine such methods in England.

Have you ever lived amongst goats ? In two places in these islands I have camped in goat-infested parts—goats which have gone wild from some planter's herd. I have heard them and seen them in the bush at night. You wouldn't believe how extraordinarily human they look when standing on their hind legs to chew bark, face peering round a tree at you in the moonlight. There was one old Angora (white) billy in particular on an island named Lanour who would have passed as a satyr anywhere. He looked positively ghastly in the bright moon. You can imagine the effect of such apparitions upon superstitious peasants in ancient Greece. The natives here hate wild goats and wouldn't dare shoot one for any money, although they will eat them fast enough if a white man shoots them. " 'Im 'e all same devil-devil. Me feller fright longa shoot 'im."

When I was in Vila, two enterprising fellows ran up an iron shanty and installed a cinematograph with the idea of astonishing the Kanakas at a dollar a head, and making a fortune. The first night a few natives rolled up and were not in the least impressed. " Something b'long white man," was the contemptuous verdict, and the promoters had to declare themselves bankrupt in a month. My heart rejoiced exceedingly. It is the unemotionalism of the Kanaka that makes me like him.

1914

I AM seated—covered with a mosquito net—on a bag of copra upon the indescribably dirty floor of what a hopeful house-agent would describe as 'a one-roomed weather-board cottage with galvanised iron roof.' I don't know what a ' weather-board ' is, but I presume it implies some kind of wood which allows you to appreciate the weather without going outside. If my presumption is correct, so is the description. ' Galvanised ' obviously means that crinkly kind of iron with a lot of holes in it. Outside the weather is working up for a hurricane. The rain has poured down for 48 hours ; the barometer has done the same, and things are looking ugly. Everything I have is wringing wet, but I have managed to rig a tarpaulin over enough of myself to sleep more or less dry. I have been marooned in this lonely spot for three days. I arrived with the idea of surveying the fairly large property here, but without the idea of living here. There is a very dear little ' small-island ' just outside the reef and it was there that I hoped to dwell. On the said island there is a commodious house belonging to a missionary who is away on furlough. I, considering that a surveyor is a kind of missionary, borrowed the house. I installed all my gear, had my ' boys ' tents put up and prepared to spend a pleasant two or three weeks. I came over to the mainland on Monday to have a preliminary look at the property to survey, got a dose of fever which kept me busy all Monday night, and then by Tuesday morning this beastly weather had sprung up making a return to the small island impossible. Fortunately, I had brought a small bag with me in case of accidents, and as this weather-board, etc., is a ' store ' (visited once a week or so), there is a sufficiency of tinned meat and biscuits to last out the siege. My small bag contained, oddly enough, a bottle of whisky ; so things might be worse. Some natives offered to take me over in a canoe yesterday ; but as I had seen several canoes upset, and had also seen several particularly hungry-looking tiger sharks close to the reef, I politely declined the offer. These Kanakas don't care a damn for sharks. When one has dynamited a shoal of fish the sharks simply swarm up, and I have seen the natives actually disputing fish with a beastly shark. I suppose the stink of a brown man is too much even for a shark. Anyhow I don't intend to let the brutes take me as an object-lesson in one phase of the ' colour ' question. By the way, isn't the ' White Australia ' cry amusing ? The very men who come out here and produce half-castes by the score and then treat them as equals won't allow their own children into Sidnee. Ugh, you have no idea how these half-castes make me vomit. The New Hebridean Kanaka is about the last word in ugliness, filth and depravity, but one can tolerate him as a useful beast of burden. I look on them exactly as if they were camels. The fact of a white man mating with a female of such a kind of course argues depravity and shocking bad taste on the part even of an Orstrylyun, but after all it is a purely private and personal matter. The product of such mating is, however, quite another thing. I consider that they ought to be done away with as some sort of pathological impossibility—or possibly preserved in spirit in a hospital museum. And yet here (and in New Caledonia) they are treated exactly like white men. I can't make Frenchmen understand my views—I fear the French as a nation are very far gone on the downward track—but I have imposed myself on all the Anglo-Saxon mob with whom I have come in contact. I simply point blank refuse to sit at table with half-castes or niggers. Even at ——, where the ' boss ' is married to a Kanaka, I persist ; and in consequence Madame feeds in the kitchen and incidentally enjoys it. There are only three Englishmen (as distinguished from O——ns) planters in the group, and, curiously enough, they are entirely at one with me. There is actually a missionary's widow (white) in the group, who has lately entered into the bonds of holy matrimony with a Kanaka. I am waiting for the day when the hubby reverts to heathendom (they do periodically), and little wifey will have to crawl on her hands and knees past any man of the tribe and feed with the other squaws off what hubby throws over his shoulder, if she can crawl to it before the dogs. Suchlike treatment and a daily beating over the head with the butt-end of a musket will perhaps teach the lady the real value of her black brethren.

I broke off here to have a much-needed drink and have my dinghy pulled even higher up. I must tell you a lovely instance of missionary influence I came acoss the other day. I chanced to be passing two Sundays ago through a native village. I knew that there was a ' big-fellow school belong make him Christian ' (= baptism) on, and I was not surprised to find dungarees and ' trade ' print dresses substituted for bamboo boxes and palm leaves. Neither was I astonished that all the population of the village was perspiring in their hideous galvanised iron ' school ' (= church) howling ' What-kin-wash-away-my-sins.' . . . What did surprise me was to find a young maiden aged about 14 sitting in a state of nature in front of her hut looking very disconsolate. As I happened to know her by sight—her father being one of my boys—I addressed her and held converse as follows :

' *Spearman* ' (Surveyor). Which way you no belong school ? (which way = whit wey = how, why).

Waivira Kilu-Kulu (= little red flower) Oh, me pall. (p = f.)

S. You pall ? Which way you pall ? You sick ?

W.K. (quite proud of herself). No, me pall last night, me no sick. (I didn't tumble to the language. I thought she'd fallen and hurt herself.)

S. Yes, but which way you pall ? You sore some place ?

W.K. (a little petulant). No, what name. You cranky ? You no sabby ' pall ' ?

S. No, me no sabby.

W.K. (delighted to explain). Oh, me pall. Tom

he been humbug belong me last night and me speak him 'yes.' Missy he speak, 'Suppose one woman make him all same he one ' pallen women,' he no sabby go belong school. Me one pallen woman now.

S. Oh ! ! !

Is any comment necessary ? Think of a black, naked, 14 year old Magdalene proud of her isolated position, but angry at not being allowed to go and sing Sankey's hymns with her fellows.

At present I simply long to be in London. I am fast coming to the conclusion that fireside travel is much more pleasant than the reality. There are fewer disillusionments and one can pick one's company. Here, for example, life might be tolerable if I had a decent soul to speak to occasionally. Life is free—all that there is of the most free ; but one's fellow-creatures are unspeakable. The other day while I was still at —— I heard that Mowbray was on a visit to a neighbouring island. I borrowed Bernhardt's launch and hied me away on a six hours' journey on a rough sea merely to hear a voice that was neither Scotch nor O——n. I found him staying with a missionary, but I didn't care. We waited till Missy and his mate had gone to bed, then we sneaked two glasses and a water bottle and went down to the shore. There I produced a bottle of Pernod Fils and we talked the whole moonlight night through—by arrangement our sole topic was Oxford. It was largely undergraduate nonsense, and often maudlin, but, my God, it did me good.

. . . What I want out of places is charm, and I am sure that no such thing exists in reality. Whereas if one sits comfortably with a comfortable pal and reads and looks at maps and charts one gets all the charm most perfectly and free of all expense. And one is not disillusioned. If I had been content with reading Stevenson I should still believe in the paradisaical charm of a coral reef and a coconut tree. Now the one is a thing that stinks like Billingsgate market and knocks nasty holes in expensive boats, while the other is the produce of 1/100th of a ton of copra which also stinks. Even the rags of romance that still fluttered round the South Sea pirates disappear when one has seen them vomit in their soup and go to sleep with their heads in it. No, it was foolishness ever to come to the S. Seas. So goodbye to one more poor little romance. It is like losing a child. I have still left to me the mysterious East. It is probably perfectly matter-of-fact and exceedingly beastly, but as long as I don't go there I shan't know. For me it is going to remain a mystery and the home of all mystery. Beauty and mystery are the only gods for a sane man to worship, but like all other gods they must not be sought after, they must be conceived and nurtured solely in the imagination.

. . . I have heard sentimental folk describe a landscape as surpassing human imagination, which of course is absurd. It is only because sentimental people have no imagination that their breath is taken away by what a very commonplace artist could improve with ease.

March 13*th*, 1914.

YOU curse me for not writing, but I'm sure you wouldn't write as much as I do if you had my life to lead. I get up each day before the light. I am out in the field by 5 o'clock and remain there in the blazing sun, hacking through tropical virgin bush till sunset. Then I draw my plans until I cannot keep awake any longer. That, barring Sundays (when I am generally calculating), is my daily life, except for the days when we are shifting camp. Then I am captain, mate and everything else of whatever craft I can requisition—generally a native whale-boat now that my own craft is gone. Add to this that I have the provisioning of a fairly large camp under circumstances that are not exactly easy and you will see that my leisure time is exceedingly limited. Of course I am my own master and can take off any time I like, but each day costs me £2 dead loss, so naturally I don't often indulge in such luxuries. Now, however, my partner (the aforementioned Scottish spanner-wielder) has just joined me, and I shall get more free time. Also my deal for the plantation will probably have been concluded before this reaches you. I shall be able to retire there for a month or two at a time to see to the making of my copra, and I shall have heaps of time to write and think. Also there will be, I hope, a considerable monthly sum coming in from the plantation which will allow me once more to hatch plots of a rush home.

Malekula,
May 17*th*, 1914.

I AM hoping in a week or two that Bernhardt will
turn up with his launch bringing mails from
Mosquito Bay. We have pushed on a few miles
higher up the coast, chiefly to try and regain a
little health. Both Fraser and I had had about 10
days' continuous fever, which has to be experienced
before being understood. I won't try to describe
the condition of a wretched being down in camp
with fever, the miserable longings for home, the
nausea, the dragging of one's limbs from bed to
look after camp and safety. The whole state is too
vivid for me at present. . . . We have got to, I
trust, a better place now. We are camped at the
mouth of a big river where there are quantities of
fish and wild duck, and the fresh food will help us
to pick up. I foolishly essayed a swim last night
and paid the penalty by fainting as soon as I came
out. That will give you an idea of my condition
when ten strokes make one behave like a silly
school-girl. Oh, I am sick of it. I simply must
come home, if only to get some ' guts ' again. I
haven't got a looking-glass, but I can imagine the
sight of my bony yellow face covered in dirty
whiskers ; my head crowned with a battered helmet
that was once white, all underneath the helmet a
tangle of filthy-looking elf-locks. I should love to
have myself photographed for you.

May 24th. Same camp.

IF ever man deserved salvation for a single act,
you do for the writing of that letter which I
received yesterday (the letter I mean 'accused
reception' of my volcano epistle and enclosed a
charming sketch of the oak chair). I was feeling
miserable, sitting at my tent door in the cool of the
evening, gnawing my nails and cursing everything,
looking lazy out to sea with no hope of seeing even
a canoe. In the failing light I saw a speck, a lump
on the water, an excrescence, masts and no sails.
It must be a launch. It must be Bernhardt, because
no one else ventures up this wild coast. I got up
and ran a good mile to where I knew he must
anchor and got there as he came ashore in his dinghy.
He had got my mail, a great fat parcel of it—incidentally he had got my tobacco and I had been smoking 'trade' for a week—and there sticking out in the
most obtrusive manner was your letter. I shook
Bernhardt warmly by the hand. He thought I was
drunk (as he was), and ran back to my tent. I had
to be alone. I felt the envelope and it was so thick,
and then (don't laugh !) I kissed it. I got back
to camp, threw Fraser his letters and told him not
to come near me till the morning. And then I
opened and read solemnly and conscientiously my
other letters—dull nonsense about surveying from
lawyers. Then I filled myself a mighty pipe of
Baron, mixed a corresponding whisky and started
to read. . . .

After my rotten go of fever at —— I had picked
up in health. I had shot many sleeping duck (tell

your cousins this). I had dynamited much delicious
fish. The diet combined with a strong trade wind
blowing through my tent had filled me with enough
strength to long. I had lost the languor of fever and
was craving with an indescribable force for what I
could not define. I know what it was now.

Why weren't you here yesterday ? I have had
such fun. I got thus far with my letter when a
wretched, bleeding and half-dead Kanaka turned
up to my tent and moaned out a piteous tale. He
came from a store about eight hours away and the
store had been attacked by bushmen. He was
shot through the calf, and his master (a white man)
was either dead or nearly so. Fraser was away,
having gone down to our base with nearly all the
boys, to bring up supplies. Within half-an-hour I
had provisioned and armed a punitive force of four
—three Kanakas and myself. Our arms were two
Winchesters, two Colts Police Positive Special
revolvers, two Browning automatic pistols. I patched
up the wounded man and then set off. We got to
the store about 4 o'clock in the afternoon, found
the white man—an absinthe-drinking libéré—more
frightened than hurt. He had a bullet in his thigh
which I skilfully (he will probably die) extracted,
and having put him within reach of his Pernod Fils
we started off for the bush village. Near the store
I captured a native who ' volunteered ' to guide us
to the village about four hours further into the bush.
Of course it was pitch dark before we got to the
place. The walking was awful. I slipped and cut
and bashed myself every ten yards, and got more and
more furious. At last after about 6 hours going we

got to the village about midnight. We crept in, but it was no good ; the birds had flown. They had probably heard us for hours. I was just about dead-beat, so it was just as well that there was no fighting to do. We kai-kaied (= fed), and then I turned in to the least filthy of the huts and slept till daybreak. I knew jolly well that ' man-bush ' would be shivering with fright of the devil-devils somewhere in the bush. In the morning my rage was greater, so I did what I could to annoy the swine. We burned their village, cut down their ' God '-tree and then found their gardens and uprooted and stole all their yams. That means that they will starve during the winter. They had driven off all their pigs and not one could we find. However, I guess I've ' made them sabby.' And so (as Pepys occasionally remarks) back to camp, which we reached just after dark. I have had a bath, a feed and a drink, and now I am going on with this letter until I fall asleep. I was lucky enough to find in the chief's house his great dancing mask, and I naturally purloined it and am sending it to you. It is, of course, supremely hideous, but they are practically unprocurable. It is garnished with real human teeth extracted from the pièce de resistance. The tusks are from the chief's own pigs which it is death for any lesser man to touch. If a woman looks at the mask she becomes sterile, so tell —— to be careful. The colours are all from native plants. I have tried and tried to get the secret of them, but can't.

I suppose if the Government get to hear of my goings on there will be a row, but I shan't tell them,

and I don't fancy ' man-bush ' will either. I do
wish you had been with me. All the time when I
was stumbling along to that village where every
tree might hide a dozen cannibals, I thought of
your joy in the fun of it. I don't mind telling you
that I should have been very glad of any reliable
companionship. My force of three was ready to
bolt at any minute ; and I knew that if we had
found ' man-bush ' at home it would have been
myself against the crowd. But if I had had you, we
would have hunted the swine. As it was, I didn't
care to run the risk. My guide would have bolted
and I might have found myself ' bushed,' for no
white man could ever find his way alone through
this jungle. Old Fraser was furious when he got
back to camp and found out what he'd missed. He
wanted me to set out again and ' massacre some of
the beggars,' but 20 hours' walking inside 36 hours
has left me without any wish to move again for days.
I was rather pleased to find that spite of putrid condition I had a little reserve strength handy for
emergencies. I shall have to send my boys with a
stretcher to get that Frenchman in the morning. I
feel no sympathy at all with the man. He sells the
niggers grog and Winchesters, and then wonders
that he gets shot. He, of course, being a Frenchman, wants to go to the Joint Court with his case.
I don't want him to, as it may lead to complications.
Anyway, he can't read or write, so I shall have no
difficulty with him. I can't keep awake any longer.
I have been to sleep three times already over
this.

    . . . Oh, England is a beastly place. Just think

of the rules, the chains and fetters of brass. In London one can be ' Bohemian ' only by dint of living an absolutely lonely life, suspected by the police and stared at by the rabble. Do you think there is one person in London who could like or even tolerate a really free man and an unconventional life ? And then, when one thinks of the country— sacré nom d'un nom d'un nom ! . . .

. . . Curse and expose the people for their beastly prudery, for their foul snobbishness, for their loathly cult of hide-bound respectability. Curse —— and hoc genus omne. Blast the haute bourgeoisie, the petite ditto. It is high time that some Nazarene arose in England. He will most assuredly be without honour and will probably be crucified.

Away to hell with art for art's sake ; the Church of England, full of snobbery, which the petits bourgeois enter as a respectable profession. Butt against missions and missionaries. Damn violently English education both of boys and girls. Curse the ignorant parenthood of all classes of English people, who leave their boys and girls untaught. . . .

Think of the joys of a wandering caravan life. With a very small outlay a caravan can be bought, cosy, tastefully bedecked and watertight. What more can man want ? For the rest, for your smoking-room, your library, your dining-room, you have whatever parts of the world please you best. You pay no rent. You follow the sun. If a place bores you, you move on. Once resign yourself to keep in touch with the ordinary, how do you hope to get out ? Think of the thousands upon thousands of books in many languages that are published every day, all of them excellent in their way, but oh, so ordinary. And why ? because their authors haven't the pluck to tear themselves from the accepted.

. . . When I arrive at some village that pleases me I shall halt and live there for a bit. I shall scrape acquaintance with all and sundry. Then I shall cultivate the padré, the cura, the curé of the place. I love them for their childishness, for their gossiping, for their very gluttony. In Uruguay I found them veritable mines of gossip. Even here the Marist missionaries are the only folk worth speaking to. They get £30 a year and have to build a house out of what they can save. The natives love them ; for the father speaks the native language, eats native food, encourages them to dance, and has never even heard of John Knox and the shourrrter cat-echism.

. . . The shores of Maggiore compared to the streets of Maida Vale—Como and Kilburn—the architecture of Grenada and that of the Edgware Road. And Cricklewood—I once went there— fancy voluntarily allowing a child to grow up with impressions of Cricklewood stamped upon his brain cells. I should really love to go into a ' retreat ' for two whole years to wipe myself, to try and get my mind free from my beastly body. If only such places existed without the interference of some nonsensical creed I would go. I want to live. I want neither to be blamed nor praised. I lost my Dante, but fortunately had committed to memory lots of things that pleased me. One was these lines from the *Inferno* :

> Ed egli a me : Questo misero modo
> Tengon l' anime triste di coloro,
> Che visser senza infamia e senza lodo.

> .   .   .   .   .   .

> Questi non hanno speranza di morte,
> E la lor cieca vita è tanto bassa,
> Che invidiosi son d' ogni altra sorte.
> Fama di loro il mondo esser non lassa,
> Misericordia e giustizia gli sdegna :
> Non ragioniam di lor, ma guarda e passa.

That is the life of the ordinary person, and he owes it to his childhood when the ordinary, the even, the accepted were forced upon his helpless mind. On Monday we do so and so . . . every Monday. On Tuesday, etc., ad inf. You mustn't do that—no reason given. . . . The child grows up ruled in columns without reason. The poor little creature is stamped into the grotesque modern man-shape by a pitiless machine. He soon grows to accept his little world as the all ; and hence his limited mental horizon in after years. He never sees even any changes in people's costumes except with the varying hours of the day. From this springs ' all the best people wear. . . .' He only hears one language, one form of speech : therefore, God speaks in English and is distantly related to the Duke of Wellington and the Prince Consort. Groove, groove, groove ! nothing but groove from the cradle to the grave. True, that in after years some sturdy spark may be fanned into a flame, and the child may begin to think for himself. But then

think of the useless lumber he has to get rid of and
—the most foul part of all—some lumber that he
can never rid himself of. Some—the great majority
—of those brain cells, those tendency makers,
are indelibly stereotyped. Others are hopelessly
atrophied.

I am no crank. It is all sound uncommon sense,
based on science and not on tradition and evil sentiment. I will stop and have a drink, for my brain
is seething. The spirit has begun to move me, and
that is uncomfortable. I am calmer now. I have
filled my belly with duck and finished the repast
with wild honey which I like to think came from
scarlet hibiscus. Anyhow it's very lovely and quite
unlike any honey I have ever tasted before.

Malekula,
June 14*th*, 1914.

. . .

IS it not rather the very best thing that you can do
for any child to teach him truth, real values and
independent thought in lieu of binding him down to
'proper,' 'right,' and conventional. From the
basest point of view, what profit do 99 per cent. of
the 'proper' slaves make out of their properness?
They crawl and cadge and intrigue; and what does
the successful man care or do for them? Would not
a true man with sound ideas unfettered by convention stand a better chance of beating these
worms in the battle? The world hates originality,
but originality plus force will always beat the world.
And how is a child to escape infection if he is

brought up in daily contact with every kind of
mental and moral disease ? Once send a small boy
to a school kept by a man like ——, and in 5 minutes
he has caught 50 diseases. At the end of his first
term he will be quite ' proper,' quite ' right,' a
seething mass of convention germs. And so the
culture will go on. . . . Think seriously over my
madness. There is really the deuce of a lot of
method in it ; and, after all, sanity's only the home-
made test by which we approve our own actions
and condemn those of others. (I must have a drink
after that. It took a lot out of me.) (I have had it.)

Mind you, I am not butting against certain conventions such as ' manners,' for in the main they are
founded upon what is really good. All that is
really gentle, all that springs from true chivalry,
from unselfishness, from consideration for others,
from truth, I hold noble. All conventional ' politeness,' all snobbery, all ' doing the thing that is
done,' all false appraisement I hold ignoble and vile.
A conviction, however radically wrong (and who is
to be the judge of radical right and wrong ?), is
infinitely finer than a host of inherited and accepted
opinions. The child that is not forced, who is led
to form his own convictions, will be a man. The
child who is formed with ready-made opinions will
only be a mannikin. Of course, I do not believe in
lack of discipline. The child may be wisely guided
into the proper methods of thought ; but between
that and imposing ideas with which his reason has
had nothing to do, il y a un monde. It is the same
with the assimilation of knowledge. Guide a child
and leave him free to asimilate by heuristic methods

of his own.   He then gets a fully developed brain.
Force tasks upon him for which he sees no reason,
save through fear and necessity, and you get a
phonograph.

> Mosquito Bay,
> *October 12th,* 1914.

I HAD a singularly unproductive stay in Sydney.
I spent many pounds and much time with the
dentist and feel much comforted.   For the rest life
was more or less a blank.   I lolled in comfortable
chairs, had many baths and consumed much passable food.   I searched the city high and low for
something to hear or something to see which would
content me a little, but my search brought forth
nothing.   Of architecture there is nothing that is
not clamorously vile.   The one and only picture
gallery is filled with copies of old masters by
O——n artists and just a few of the horrider
crimes of Marcus Stone.   Of music there was
absolutely none.   Organ recitals in the Town Hall
(genus Imperial Institute), where the programme
consisted of fantasyers on national anthems inter-
spersed with gems from Handel and Gounod, were
advertised in the papers, but did not, curiously
enough, attract me.   At every street corner are
representations in bronze of worthy patriots in
trousers, but as I had never heard of any of them I
was not even amused.   For the rest, the place is full
of foul electric trams, movies, quick-lunch bars and
saloons for the exhibitions of professional pugilists.
The harbour is lovely.

November 15th, 1914.

YESTERDAY I took a stick and a toothbrush and set out for a long mad tramp through the bush. I walked all the afternoon and evening and arrived after dark at a house that I knew many miles from here. The house is that of a widow who lives with her likewise widowed sister. The women are the only gentlewomen in the New Hebrides. (Am I snobbish and petty ? But they have nice speech, and nice linen and china.) Most important of all there are two kids there, twins, aged just under 2. I received a hearty welcome and was understood without having to explain myself. I demanded to spend the whole of the next day alone with the kids. It suited admirably. The sisters wanted to go to Mass, which entailed a twenty mile ride through the bush and a whole day's absence. I simply revelled. I fed the kids. I played with them, bathed them, put them to bed and talked to them.

. . . I send you a rondeau of Charles d'Orleans. I find it charming—oh, you shall have two of them, both precious—

> Laissez-moy penser à mon aise,
> Hélas ! donnez m'en le loysir.
> Je devise avecques Plaisir
> Combien que ma bouche se taise.
>
> Quand Merencolie mauvaise
> Me vient maintes fois assaillir,
> Laissez-moy penser à mon aise,
> Hélas ! donnez m'en le loysir.

Car afin que mon cueur rapaise,
J'appelle Plaisant-Souvenir,
Qui tantost me vient resfoüir.
Pour ce, Pour Dieu ! ne vous deplaise
Laissez-moy penser à mon aise.

Allez-vous-en, allez, allez,
Soussi, Soing et Merencolie,
Me cuidez-vous, toute ma vie,
Gouverner, comme fait avez ?
Je vous promet que non ferez ;
Raison aura sur vous maistrie :
Allez-vous-en, allez, allez,
Soussi, Soing et Merencolie.
Se jamais plus vous retournez
Avecques vostre compagnie,
Je pri à Dieu qu'il vous maudie
Et ce par qui vous reviendrez
Allez-vous-en, allez, allez.

The English words that strike my ear are chiefly :
blahdy, boi croipes, petreotism, Kichnur, and ' the
boieys.'

December 6th, 1914.

THIS firm has offered me the management of
their plantation at ——, the place where
I was before. I may accept the offer and settle
down to plant cotton. The pay is ludicrously small,
but at least I shall live and eat and sleep and per-
chance have some time to devote to myself.
    . . . Surveying, though strenuous, is interesting ;
and the natives amuse me. I had to stop this letter
and get up and barter for yams with trade tobacco,
and even now the gentle Kanakas are in front of my
tent howling with laughter at a quite unwritable

jest that I shouted at them 10 minutes ago. If it weren't for mosquitoes and fever I could live like this for a year in camp. I would only need one servant, and about £20 in money would last me the year for provisions. I should spend the whole day reading and writing and nothing would worry me. But there are too many mosquitoes and too much fever to make the idea possible.

Later.

... I have decided to go and run the plantation. I shall there have a house entirely to myself. Muller is giving me absolutely carte blanche as to furnishing the house and making it livable. I have ordered suitable furniture, a bathroom, mosquito-proof doors and windows, and other necessities which no one else has. I shall be able to snatch odd hours during the day-time, and shall have every evening alone and with not too unpleasant surroundings. I shall hope to resuscitate myself somewhat.

1915

THERE is nothing thrilling about a plantation life. At least, if there is, I have become familiar and contemptuous. At any rate, it is free. I am my own master, with my own hours and no one to interfere with me in the slightest. I have servants (some 100 odd) under me. I say to this one . . . and in fact perform all the traditional acts à leur égard. I have nine horses upon which I can ride ; but there is nowhere to ride, save to and fro on the plantation. I have two cows which give me much milk. I am inaugurating a poultry farm from which I hope to get many eggs. I have built a small hospital and surgery in which I spend two hours per diem treating many things from malaria to elephantiasis. I have bush-felling, cotton-planting, road-making and 100 odd details to superintend. In short, from 4.30 a.m. till sunset I am very busy. At sunset I bathe and discard the planter, and spend the evening in reading of pleasant things pleasantly written in a pleasant tongue. At present one is perforce largely a vegetarian and entirely a teetotaller ; but I am hoping for better times. If the present dearth of alcohol continues I shall make a still and manufacture spirit from bananas and pineapples. There is always kava, but I don't care for it as a drink. Tobacco I have on the plantation, and it is foul muck. I am trying a new way of curing it which I hope will make something better. If it is successful I will send you some of the product. Yes, curious as it may appear to you, I am going to be happy here. At present my house is deplorable and would shock you terribly even in a description. But I have got a large order arriving in March, and then I hope to make a dwelling which will be comfortable and at the same time eye-pleasing. I have already started a nice garden containing crotons, hibiscus, flamboyants, red lilies and many other things, all of which come out of the bush. The total effect will be a gorgeous mass of colour.

. . . Sunday is my only possible day for writing letters, because I can only write in the early morning. I get up about 4 o'clock, have coffee, and then settle myself comfortably in a deck chair, and with any luck, can write till 11 o'clock. At 11 I lunch and from then till about 6 it's a damn sight too hot to write. In the evening mosquitoes make life quite impossible except under a net. And I can't write lying down. I don't know why. I hope shortly to have my house mosquito-proof, but until it is you mustn't expect me to write in the evenings. I am absolutely hardened to the bite of a mosquito, which no longer even makes a mark. But the things annoy me. Also, all the mosquitoes here are a species of ' anopheles clavigera,' whose bite means a fresh infection of malaria every time. I have suffered too much from fever in the past to neglect precautions now. At present I am fairly free—I only get a dose every two or three weeks—and I want to try and keep free. There is a particularly alarming fever complication going about in this district just now in the shape of a mouth disease. One's teeth ache like fury individually and collectively. One's mouth grows moss like any tombstone. The teeth eventually drop out. Several of these mouths I am treating at present. Just figure to yourself the excitement for me and the agony of the poor niggers who have never known toothache before, and whose front teeth are usually strong enough to husk coconuts. I have actually seen them open a tin of meat with their teeth.

I think my infirmary parade would amuse you. All natives who have not answered to the roll call have to parade in front of the hospital for preliminary diagnosis and inspection. There are usually a dozen or so every morning. Now, you must remember that Biche-la-mar does not admit of finesse or polite euphemisms. It is a direct language and a nasty, having been originated by aforetime pirates and other sailors, *e.g.* the common, vulgar words of our school-days are the only ones with which to indicate certain portions of anatomy and certain natural functions. Let me try (inserting blanks where necessary—although the very nicest of white women has to use the nasty words here) to give you an idea of a very ordinary parade.

> *P.* = planter.
> *N.* = native labourer, male or female.

P. You sick long what ?

N. Me pever master. (Thermometer then brought into play while *P.* passes on.)

P. You sick long what ?

N. 2. No. (This is placatory and apologetic.) Belly belong me, me hear him he no good. Me think belly belong me, he run out, finish.

P. You bin kaikai what name ?

N. 2. No. Me kaikai rice no more.

P. You no bin kaikai crab ?

N. 2. Yes. Me bin kaikai one crab. (This means that he has eaten at least 20 scavenger land crabs.)

P. (to native ' infirmier '—a civilised fellow from Nouméa) Toi, donne du sel d'Epsom à ce boy.

P. You sick long what ?

N. 3. Arm belong me he swell up me hear him he strong (= hard and hot).

P. (to himself—Hell. Another abscess to cut). (To *N.* 3) All right. You go along house. By and by me put him on medicine. Then to-morrow night after to-morrow, him not very good, me cut him arm along you.

N. 3. All right master. Me think very good you cut him.

(They have no fear of the knife and are extraordinarily stoical. If I did not cut abscesses, they would do it themselves with a piece of glass. As their cutting invariably results in mixed infection and sinus formation, I prefer my own inexpert methods and have put tabu on all self-cutting.)

And so the parade goes on. The diseases are few. Fever, diarrhœa and abscesses are the most

usual daily list. Of course there are skin diseases
innumerable : elephantiasis, lupus, leprosy are all
represented.

I had rather an amusing example of the delicacy
of speech of a native who has learned that decent
white men don't use Biche-la-mar words among
themselves. My horse-boy—who was for years
in Queensland—came to me to say that my stallion
had escaped and got into the horse paddock. I
naturally enquired whether the boy had seen
' Cloudy ' misconducting himself with the fillies—
and I used the usual Biche-la-mar word. Charlie
looked at me very reproachfully for forgetting his
superiority and replied : " Yes, me bin look
' Cloudy ' he want *breed* long black-horse-where-
he-woman (= mare), but him he no want him."

April 15*th*, 1915.

THERE are rumours of strikes and civil war
in Australia, and, in consequence, steamers
are not being loaded. I suppose our scanty supply
of provisions will be cut off altogether now. Fortunately, I have been gradually making myself independent of food-stuffs from the outside world.
At present flour is the only thing that I must import
for myself. If it came to a pinch I could make a
kind of flour from maize, but the bread is rum stuff.
Germans might like it. I make my own bread,
butter and cheese. I have plenty of fowls (thanks
to an incubator), goats, of which I share a herd with
a neighbour, and there are enough cattle at Mosquito

Bay to keep us going for two years. We have not started seriously to consider ourselves besieged yet, so we have accumulated supplies.

. . . All I know is that no one is going forcibly to arouse in me qualities at which my subjective self mocks. I have tried forcing sentiments before. I think I have told you of the curious psychic phenomena which always attended my real earnest efforts to practise a pseudo-catholicism. I was devout, exceedingly devout. I had my moments of delicious exaltation, quite comparable with those of the early Fathers. But there was always present a mocking, subjective self, who urged me on to greater efforts. " Go on. Put your head lower down. Sign yourself more vigorously. The sensation will be accentuated." I suppose if I had been a real, unsophisticated saint I should have recognised the Evil One and promptly had recourse to flagellation and standing in a tub of icy water. My zeal was not, however, sufficient. I could not help laughing and my faith expired. I know that the same thing would happen if I turned patriotic or courageous or devoted or even earnest. It's a bit unsatisfactory, isn't it ? But you have got to take me tel quel. My only honest belief is in je m'en fichisme. And there you are. I suppose an alienist could refer my case to some exceedingly obscure cerebellar lesion. I think I shall leave my head to a French hospital. I only hope they will appreciate the legacy.

. . . Don't the sheep-like habits of people really make you laugh in your for interieur ? One fool baas and says " When I baa, it's being patriotic."

And then they all baa and say " We are patriots ;
we must be because we've baaed." And then all
these noble, high-minded young fellows with no
prospects who join Kitchener's billions, are they
really noble and courageous or are they merely
sheep ? I am only asking. If one of them had a
grain of imagination would he be so noble ? War
is a side-splitting farce when one looks at it dispassionately.

. . . I am really quite glad to be in the impossibility of taking any active part or interest in
this war-business. You have no idea how awfully
remote one is here. True, we suffer inconveniences ;
but one gets used to them and they might have any
cause. For the rest we are isolated. It is quite
possible, then, to look at things dispassionately.
Anywhere nearer I could not do it. Even here I
occasionally feel waves of hatred against Germans
surge through my silly little self. Then I have time
to think : " Well, I have known many Germans,
and they were just as harmless and just as silly as I
am." And the rage passes quietly away. Also one
is free from the pernicious influence of the newspaper, which instils its poison even into the most
strongly constituted mind. One is bound to think
the stuff one reads. It is a psychological law
that cannot be broken. And the more one reads
the more one is bound to lose one's independent
judgment, which, even if entirely erroneous, is
more precious than reams of newspaper-inspired
paragraph ideas.

August 8th, 1915.

. . . .

TALKING of judgments reminds me of the Joint Court. And that again recalls the Anglo-French entente. And what humbug and rot it is ! I saw a leading article in a newspaper with the heading 'après la guerre.' Are these three words untranslatable into English ? And in the same number of the same paper I saw the word 'solidarité' used. . . . The affectation of these modern fools, who can't find enough words in English to express their great ideas. You may retort to me that I sometimes err myself in using French words where English would do. Guilty. But I am writing usually against time ; and you must remember that for three years I have scarcely ever spoken English.

And how impossible any near friendship between English and French really is. I give you two examples : (1) here is a little story (or what I can remember of it) given as an example of ' l'esprit français ' in a French book on the subject :

Madame X. (parvenue) en bordant Monsieur Y., ambassadeur distingué a une réception publique quelconque : Ah, cher monsieur, je vous aurai vu avant quelquepart.

Monsieur Y. (à haute voix) Chère madame, c'est bien possible. Il arrive que j'y vais quelquefois.

Now translate that into English and you will see what I mean.

(2) I saw a New Hebridean contingent of

young Frenchmen leaving Vila for the war. I saw two fat bourgeois attired in frock-coats, bowler hats, and white trousers, both decorated with the Mérite Agricole, with their arms round one another's necks, weeping and condoling with one another over the departure of their respective sons. To them approached fat bourgeois No. 3—" Ah, messieurs, du courage ! C'est pour la France."

Do you think you could write a book which would shake the Englishman's faith in his newspaper ? What fun it would be to have a campaign against Fleet Street. I am afraid that the obstacles would be too heavy for anybody except a Carnegie. The book would have to be privately printed in your own cellar, the machine protected by an armed guard day and night. Every copy of the book would have to be personally delivered by you into the hands of the recipient. And then, of course, there would be the countless lawsuits which you would have to defend in person ; for no barrister would dare to appear for you. Why, the very idea is worth writing about. And within the idea—the power of Fleet Street and the world—there are wrapped up numerous other possibilities—who rules the world ? Who rules England ? Why does publicity rule England ? . . . Je t'en fais cadeau.

August 23rd, 1915.

I GOT thus far yesterday when I was interrupted by the arrival of one of my masters. I had to put a good face on it and entertain him for the day ; but may the Lord pay special attention to the edges of his liver before long. I had no letter from you last month, but nowadays that means nothing. I think that only about half the proper amount of mail ever reaches us, and during the war the fraction is reduced to a quarter. What happens to the rest, I cannot say. I know for one thing that all my letters are opened by the French postmaster in ——, because I am suspected of being a secret agent of the Commonwealth Government. Par exemple ! Mowbray and I correspond in cypher when we have need of exchanging written news. Ordinarily I send word to him by the natives, whose smoke-talk beats me utterly. Mowbray is the only white man for whom they will use their smoke. I think he has some kind of juju hold over them. I have very serious thoughts of buying an island close here. I know one that is for sale. There are only about a dozen natives left on it, and it is about 2,000 acres in extent, quite large enough for me to walk about in. Having bought it, I shall plant yams, taro, manioc, and other life-sustaining vegetables. I shall build myself a grass house, and live the life of a self-supporting hermit. Seriously I am thinking of this. It is only thus and in places like the New Hebrides that one will be able to live at all if this fighting business is to continue much longer. Even if England does not become a part of the Hof-kaiserlich dominions, there will be no living in the place when this war bill is being paid. The same may be said for any of the combatant countries and their colonies. The money business in England cannot possibly have been realised by the great majority of the dear people.

. . . What fools, what swine men are. To think of this ghastly insane business going on while I write. . . .

I imagine a cartoon done in the very gross style : the Almighty is just recovering from a side-splitting bout of laughter brought on by reading the Hague Convention. He beckons to St. Peter and says, " Here, take this and show it to Satan. It will amuse him. But be sure and let me have it back quickly. I wouldn't lose it for worlds." (And how wicked of those vile Yankees not to let us pull their leg. . . . Just as if the Yankees hadn't played Poker long enough to detect that silly little boys' bluff.)

October 26, 1915.

. . .

I FOUND out many things at first hand, and you have the better part in that you only imagine them. I know the exact value now of a roving life either on or off the rolling sea. I have suffered on many kinds of craft in many kinds of weather. My valuation of coral islands would be brutal but correct. When I hear the dear sentimental ones sighing about palm trees, I shall chortle. Of such things as O——ns, tropical diseases, niggers, half-castes, iron houses in the tropics at midday, tinned food, scabies, fleas in herds, nerves and jumps, and the wonders of solitude, I can speak in an authoritative manner—and I wish to God that I couldn't. To hell with your Blue Mountains.

Something had to be done, or it was a case of exit me and entry a certain beachcomber.

I may tell you that I have very seriously considered the advisability of a return to the beast. The plans are all cut and dried and I could do it to-morrow. Muller owns an island far away north beyond the Santa Cruz group. He would sell me this for a song. I should charter one of his boats to go over there, taking provisions for a few months to last me till my yams and taro began to grow. I should then be quite, quite lonely and unworried for the rest of my existence. There is a tribe of natives on the island (I have been there and surveyed it for Muller) who would keep me in yams and dry my tobacco leaves for me. I should have nothing, nothing, nothing to do all the live-long day and month and year. And the flies would crawl over my sores and feed on the crust around my eyelids. And the sea would boom on the coral reef outside and the palms would wave gently in the trade wind and the brown folk would laugh and chatter and scratch themselves quite in the proper R. L. S. way. And I would get up and look lovingly at my dear little Webley and Scott and wonder when I would have pluck enough to do it. And I never would. Sperat infestis, metuit secundis. Damn and blast Mr. H. Flaccus ; because when he wrote that he formed the character of a certain [the writer] —not yet born. I got a ' prize ' for translating that into English verse . . . just think of it and laugh. And about an hour ago I was scraping dirt off a tuberculous Kanaka in order that I might lance an abscess and prolong his beastly existence for a few weeks. La diddle di iddledy, umpty i.

. . . If you want to know about the British

Empire, listen to me. The British Empire is the product of the sweat and blood and tears, not shed but only suffered, of the poor beasts that have suffered as I have suffered. And it isn't only the British Empire. The French and the German and the Dutch and the miserable white man's empire everywhere, where the white man has been driven out by his instinct for land and space. The pimps at home have nothing to do with the white man's empire. (But I really couldn't develop that idea without growing serious—and I must never forget that I am a happy hedonist.)

November 21*st.*

I AM sure you can't get any real impression of loneliness—and I am equally sure that I can't give you one.

If I were satisfied and whole in body, I might succeed as a hermit with plenty of books. But here I am horribly unsatisfied. I am ill. Reading is almost impossible. One can't concentrate one's mind while sweat is running off chin and nose on to one's book. At night after the day's glare and heat my eyes are too tired for reading.

I fill my day as far as ever I can with the to me peculiarly obnoxious details of plantation life. But always there is the horror beside me saying : " When there is nothing more to do or when you are tired you will have no one to speak to. There will be nothing new, nothing new anywhere." I rush out and stare at the sea and the horizon. I know every detail of it by heart. I know that there never will

be a boat to break that ghastly line. And yet I
stare and stare and sometimes I scream. I have a
cow that I talk to and a young foal. The foal butts
me in the chest when I tell him that I am very
unhappy. It seems to help me a little bit.

Don't think I am hysterical. I am more phleg-
matic than a good many people, but there are limits.
I know that there are people who manage to live
isolated in savage parts. I have met some of them.
One or two were scientific cranks who were really
interested in their surroundings. The rest—and that
includes all the planters, traders and others in the
New Hebrides—were simply animals. I don't
want to pose as an ' ultra-intellectual,' but, really,
eating, drinking and sleeping will never satisfy me.
I neither know nor care anything about Plato,
Aristotle and Co. Ψυχὴ ὀρεκτικη and νοῦς ποιητικὸς
convey nothing whatsoever to me. They are as
meaningless and uninteresting as ' Salvation by
faith,' ' original sin,' and all the other catlap. I
do know that, be what they may, go where they may,
give 'em any fancy names you like, I have certain
desires and tastes apart from those so neatly and
chastely described in text-books of physiology.
And here not one of these my tastes and desires is,
or ever will be, satisfied.

. . . Why did you and I ever talk sentimental
nonsense about cocos nucifera and madreporic
formations ? I had a pal years before I knew you—
he does something in your line—with whom I used
to talk South Sea swilge. Our idea then was to have
an enormous harem and a couple of typewriters and
combine fat living with high thinking. It is many

years since I heard anything from the chap—he was gross, but he had rather a nimble wit in the Oxford-cum-Bouverie Street manner—and I wonder whether it was he or you who determined this exile for me ?

I think this imprisonment has done a good deal for me—in fact I am sure it has. I got too damn near being a drunkard at Montevideo. Not that I have any inherent moral objection to drunkenness. Under certain circumstances I look upon it as almost praiseworthy. But it means ' finish,' and I am nowhere near ready to finish yet. If ever I do give up hope it won't be alcohol to which I fly. I know too much about it.

December 5th, 1915.

. . .

MOWBRAY and I had an amusing idea of a little party of murderers. Owing to the recruiting season being in full swing the party could not be large, but we got five—three Frenchmen and two Englishmen. They were pukka murderers —not mere nigger-shooters, but men who had killed their friends. We gave a dinner at the Cercle and engaged a special waitress for the occasion, a native lady named Nguna who had just stood her trial for murder. Her master had flaunted a white wife before her and had gone to the unreasonable length of tying Nguna to a chair so that she might see for herself. . . . She shot the gentleman and his wife that night and owing to the eloquent pleading of Mr. Mowbray escaped with a fine. Of course we did not explain to our guests the motive of the feast. We merely let the news circulate that the food would be good and the liquor abundant. Both Mowbray and I enjoyed the sensation. Another little picture from the ' Blood House,'[1] with the Melice Brittanique—silly niggers in khaki—solemnly patrolling the road outside, I have seen recruiters playing poker after a successful season. The drink is champagne (Cliquot—demisec) ordered in cases. The regulation method is to shout for a case, kick the lid off and open the bottles with an 18 inch knife. The stakes are merely the recruited niggers who are ranged solemnly round the wall of the room and who change hands many times a night. All this in spite of the Anglo-French Convention of October 20th, 1906, many joint labour regulations, Pacific Orders in Council, and other such amusing flummery. Fancy the excitement of a jackpot with four stalwart male niggers and two female (total value £92) in the pool. ' Years of labour ' is a unit of currency here. For example, when I bought and resold my property there was a 7 ton cutter which I withheld and subsequently sold for twenty ' years of labour,' *i.e.* five boys engaged for three years and five for one year or any other equivalent combination. I have some of the price still working for me here. In the open market a male Kanaka indentured for three years fetches £17. If you are a Frenchman it is cheap ; because you keep him for nine or ten years, and then send him home without paying him. If you are an Englishman you are naturally more superficially honest. At the end of each three years you supply

[1] Pet name for the hotel at Vila.

him with a new wife (generally your own cast-off), and then, when he insists upon going home, being tired of wives, you pay him in ' trade ' at 10 times its cost price and throw in a Bible as a make-weight.

I was held up a few months ago by having a big cotton crop and not enough labour to pick it. I went off into the bush and persuaded an old chief to bring his tribe (men, women and kids) down to pick my cotton. They were quite an unsophisticated lot of niggers and could only talk their own gibberish. At the end of the picking I paid them cash. A few days ago I learned that some of my knowing hands —returned from Queensland—had introduced the gentle bush tribe to the intricacies and joys of Euchre, and had taken every sou from them. What about the universal brotherhood idea ?

You will notice that I have become tainted with commercialism. I sell calico and gaudy vests (called singlets by the O——ns for some reason) to Kanakas now and am becoming quite expert in forestalling and even creating my customers' needs. It rather pleases me to harangue them in the most approved Selfridgian manner, much to their astonishment and alarm.

December 19*th.*

JUST a few lines excusing what I have written above. With December came the hot weather quite suddenly. For three weeks the temperature has been 100-104 in the house by 8 o'clock. The sun has not shone. The walls of my iron hell have (spite of their heat) trickled with warm water inside.

My clothes have been perpetually wet, and my boots, books and other trappings have been covered each morning with an interesting mould or fungus. Sleep has been practically impossible. That will probably continue till the end of April. For the last week, in addition to my ordinary work (which is no sinecure) I have been fighting an outbreak of dysentery. Perhaps some gifted war correspondent can convey to you what an outbreak of dysentery means in the midst of Red and Victoria and other crosses, with doctors, nurses and all the modern aids and appliances. This week I have tended single-handed 28 cases and buried five under conditions which even war could not beat. My means and strength and time are all quite unequal to the need. The filthy things that I have had to do would be nauseating in a cold climate and among civilised creatures. Here they are unspeakable.

1916

. . .

I AM not a crank. I have really no high-falutin notions about democracy, universal brotherhood or any such big and dull subjects with capital letters and paid secretaries. Sometimes owing to the depressing circumstances of a lonely life the worm gnaws at my throat, and then I, being debarred by high principles and the French Government from killing the worm, foam at the mouth. Some of the foam splashes on the letter. . . . For the rest I am a mild enough creature who spends his days (and often his nights) doing medical and surgical things to Kanakas because I am too soft to 'let the beggars die.' This, incidentally, is foolish from a Darwinian point of view. The Kanaka ought to die, and is dying out under the glorious shadow of the Tricolunion Jack just as fast as every other aboriginal race has. It is only mistaken fools like myself who try and stop the inevitable. Then I do funny things with cows and cotton and coconuts. At sunset " I put off my country habit, filthy with mud and mire, and array myself in royal courtly garments ; thus worthily attired, I make my entrance into the ancient courts of the men of old, where they receive me with love, and where I feed

upon that food which only is my own and for which
I was born. . . . For hours' space I feel no annoyance, forget all care ; poverty cannot frighten, nor
death appal me." The words are a translation of
a letter written by one Niccolo Machiavelli to
Francesco Vettori.

April 9th, 1916.

MAN, I'd give you three weeks to be sick to
death of the most lovely island that ever had
sea round it. I have read gushing descriptions
written by steamer trippers of the wonderful, etc.
(you know the adjectives) beauty of the New
Hebrides. Thank you. I have had some. At
the present moment I feel that I should love to be
in the Club Uruguay at Montevideo (it is about
apéritif time) with the atmosphere thick with the
smell of Brazilian tobacco and absinthe and some
joven distinguido with a shocking accent reciting
Verlaine. Of course that wouldn't last long. I
have no real love for decadents and never had very
much. Only some ' decadent ' people are distinctly amusing ; as long as one doesn't probe.
But no more nature unadorned for me. Given a
really nice climate and heaps of books and leisure,
I could easily do without other folk. I may say that
I detest other people. But solitude without health
or wealth or books or cooks is not compensated for
by the marvellous beauty of a palm tree hanging
over a coral reef. Wait till you've cursed the sun
for sinking to an empty horizon minutes on end ;
till you've felt excited at the approach of a canoe

with two or three dirty natives from somewhere else—a glimpse of the outside world. It is the knowledge that one is ' right up against it ' that is so appalling ; that one is bound to go on living this rat's existence for months if not years to come.

[At about this time Asterisk took to himself a native woman. He made the announcement in a letter which is not printed here.]

April 25th, 1916.

MOWBRAY paid me a visit in his launch about two months ago and we sat up for two nights talking the only pleasurable talk that had fallen to my lot since I left Vila. Cheered by much wine (brought by Mowbray from France), we got very confidential and recited our poems to one another. Mowbray topped the bill with some really nice translations from Pierre de Ronsard which he had set to music. We sang them with infinite pathos. I then confessed my temerity and gave examples, only to be capped by Mowbray who quite unblushingly owned to a spare time translation of the Odyssey ! He recited both the original and his own version at much length, causing us both to weep. Onéla Kohkonne was all the time sitting at my feet smoking innumerable cigarettes, rather frightened because she thought that we were both drunk and would shortly begin to fight—whereupon she would undoubtedly have stuck Mowbray with a knife. It makes a pretty picture, doesn't it ?— even when one throws in the moon and the palm trees and the spicy garlic smells. Oh well, it is better than Whitechapel or Deptford anyway.

I have given up trying to teach Madame Biche-la-mar, and I am learning Aobese (her tongue) instead. The method is quite Berlitz, and it is really wonderful how quickly one learns from a sleeping dictionary. I grieve to confess to you that the thing is rather growing on me. The oddness and quaintness of the little person appeals to me. I didn't believe Kanakas were capable of affection; but I have had two rude shocks lately. One was when the lady hit a lady friend over the head with an axe for trying to steal a handkerchief of mine from the wash. The other I got only last Saturday. I had to go round to Mosquito Bay by launch, being sent for to try and save the life of a white man there. I spent the night at Mosquito, and, having occasion to rise in the middle of the night, was a little astonished to fall over Onéla, who was asleep on the mat outside my door. She had come round on foot, braving the four hour walk, and all the devils that 'steal 'im-woman 'long bush' in order to make my coffee in the morning. It is a dangerous path I am treading, but I am not really afraid. The islands are so full of illuminating examples of the end of the journey that I am only going as far down the road as I please. In the meantime 'I learn about women from her.' I have built a grass house on the other (the weather) side of the island where the trade wind blows spray in the verandah. The floor of the house is crushed white coral covered with native mats. There is nothing European in the house from start to finish. Onéla and I go round by canoe (she paddling to show her servitude) on Saturday evening, and come back at dawn on Monday. We splash about on the reef—she stark naked, I clad in lava lava to protect the non-sun-burned parts of my body—spearing fish, catching trocas and generally playing the Kanaka. We roast yams and bread fruit and wash the kaikai down with water from green coconuts. There is not a living soul within miles of us.

One thing this game is doing for me—it is helping me to refind youth which was fast disappearing. Also it is making my exile more tolerable. Gaudeamus igitur.

At present I look on all writing as utter vanity. I fill the whole of my spare time by reading Italian and things of Italy. What I read makes me hate the thought of writing.

. . . I was afraid at first I had got blackwater, which is in season just now ; but I have dispelled that fear at any rate. You see I have to be my own doctor and nurse without the possibility of help or advice ; and it is rather awkward when one is more or less off one's head, and moving is excruciating pain. However, one may as well be as cheerful as possible. I ain't dead ; and that's always an asset. When I re-became sensible I felt that something must be done for my vile back. I was too bad to move and couldn't shout over much. After about an hour's effort I made my house boy hear and come to me. " Go take 'im mustard he come." After about an hour's absence he came back but said : " He no got " (there isn't any). That meant that I had to send to Mosquito Bay, which took a whole day. Then I had to make the poultices and put them on. You see, it is harder than telephoning for a doctor and having a nurse. It is so rotten lying helpless and knowing that one could die and putrefy long before even another white man came near. We buried a white man round at Mosquito Bay on my last visit (mentioned ci-dessus). He died about midnight, and when we took his coffin in next morning we could scarcely get into the room for blow-flies, and had to brush the ants off him with a stiff broom.

May 4th.

BETTER, but still groggy. In justice to my wife I must tell you that she is away on a visit to her own island to show her finery to envious relations. Otherwise she would have nursed me tenderly, that is to say, she would have sat on the floor and smoked and played on a mouth organ. When their own folk are ill they leave them absolutely alone just as do the healthy members of a herd of cattle. If a sick person dies, there is terrible grief and wailing for quite a whole day and then— 'sorry he finish.' Widows are not considered to have behaved decently if they marry in less than a week after hubby's death. But their relations are too bored to mourn for more than a day. Perhaps they are more honest than we.

July 1st, 1916.

IF a German (or even an I-tal-ian) were to hurt anybody that I loved, 'frightfulness' would not satisfy me. I am quite certain that the fons et origo of French patriotism is simply revenge, brooded on for forty years ; revenge for wounded pride. Of course there are many people in France to-day who have got actual personal debts to wipe out from the old account. I will tell you a true story of an old man in Vila. The story has little body and no ending, but it is suggestive. The old chap was an Alsatian and had fought in the great débâcle. The tide of battle took him near his father's farm. His belly urged him to make a surreptitious visit by night to the dear adored parents. He found them both, together with some sisters, dead and nastily mutilated. He found hard fixed in his mother's skull a German sword. He forced it out with bone and hair attached. That sword hung in the old chap's house in Vila. He had lived in France for nearly thirty years, keeping in the army as long as he could, waiting for his chance. He had seen France apparently forget. He had watched the Germanisation of French commerce, the intermarriage of French with Germans, and had grown sick and tired. He emigrated to the New Hebrides. After a dozen or so years of hardship, of fever and illness, after losing his wife and both his sons killed by the Islands, war was declared. The old man—he was only about 65, but wrecked with malaria—did all he knew to try and get sent to France, and (such is the power of sentiment amongst them) would probably have succeeded had he not died of dysentery in Vila. That, of course, ended his silly little story. Now that wicked, revengeful old man, cherishing for nearly 50 years a desire directly opposed to the teachings of Christianity,

was not a patriot.   He would talk for hours, inspired by many free ' consommations ' of his dear
France, of his lost Alsace.   He never mentioned
the sword and decaying remnants attached to it.
He was a little pitiful, but au fond extraordinarily
human.

July 10*th.*

I AM alone in my abode of love for the week-end.
It's too damn windy to write properly.   The
joy of this place after the stuffy, mosquito-ridden,
galvanised iron horror of (the plantation bungalow)
makes me very peaceful.   I am content to lie on my
verandah idly looking at what must be very nearly
perfection in a sea scape.   I can't describe.   The
sea is deepest blue.   The foam on the reef is bright
white.   In the distance (about 7 sea miles) are
two islands, Pauma and Loperi.   Pauma is high and
bush-clad.   I know (and loathe) that bush from close
quarters.   At this distance it is an ever-changing
impression of wonderful tints, which have nothing
to do with green.   Loperi is an active volcano,
almost perfectly conical in shape, some 4,000 feet
high.   The tracks of the lava reflect and refract
light in the most astounding way.   Every now and
then it gives a weirdish growl and crash and a great
bubble of smoke forms and bursts, and one can see
the shining snake of lava traced out down to the
blue.   At night the volcano is a little too Drury-
lanish for me in the darkness.   If there is a big
moon to challenge the red glow, the effect is very
pleasing.   In the background like some monstrous

sea serpent are the undulations of the island of Ambrym with its heavy fall of volcano dust through which the setting sun does very nice things. Quite in the foreground is the reef, ugly in itself, but the cause of delightful sights and booming sounds. And round me are quaint tropical trees, coconuts, pandanus, rosewood, nambanga, croton and hibiscus.

Later.

I had got thus far when my wife arrived. She had gone away for the week-end, but could not support a long absence from me. Oh, Lord, I am fed-up. Unfortunately I don't see my way to getting clear, either. I very much fear that there is a half-caste en route, rather complicating matters. Out of sheer curiosity I want to see it, but I very emphatically don't want to acknowledge it. Once born, the kid and its mother shall go back to Aoba, where —— junior shall be brought up as a native. These islands teem with half-castes brought up 'white,' and I hate them individually and collectively. Why does one hate half-castes ? The Aobese are very fair-skinned and light haired, their features being good also. They are obviously a Malayan people rather than Papuans. . . . I could wish that I had never ventured into this galère, but it was a question from saving myself from a growing morbid insanity. This week-end playing the savage is not all beastly, and I am beholden to it for a much saner outlook on life than was mine of a year ago. . . .

The ' missis ' is at present roasting yam for our dinner. You don't know what a yam is ; so don't pretend that you do. It is *not* a sweet potato.

Properly roast in the ashes of a wood fire and pro-
gressively scraped with a shell as the exterior
blackens, the cooked yam is like a very well-made
soufflé. It beats roast potatoes into fits. Then we
have a large clam which is likewise roasting in a
lap-lap of grated plantain, the whole enveloped in a
plantain leaf. I must confess to liking native food
and cookery. The ' solid viands ' will be washed
down with coconut water. It pleases me to go the
whole hog on this occasion. (You may think the
expression is too apt.) I even feel anachronistic in
writing to you, but mails will not wait on sentiment. . . .

I am off to the bush to-morrow to recruit women
and children for cotton picking. I shall have nearly
100 tons this year, and, as I get a percentage of the
proceeds, I don't want to lose the crop. Last year
a fall of volcano ash ate the lot.

. . . No one could have been more sentimental
than I in my quest of lovely tropical nature. Well,
I have got it, and three weeks sufficed to show me
what a fool I was. I tell you I have seen descriptions
of the New Hebrides by tourist-journalists which
a few years ago would have made me ache. They
make me ache now. Even the great X.Y.Z. says
that ' the New Hebrides far surpass the tamer
charms of Samoa and Papeete ' ; and you know what
a wealth of adjectives Stevenson squandered on the
loveliness of the Eastern Pacific. Seen for a few
months with a nice hotel and a comfortable liner as
your G.H.Q., tropical islands may be delightful.
Go and live in one and see what you hanker for.
Think of the people. Think of the prevailing style

of architecture. Of course, in a bungalow near Kingston [1] you will probably have creature comforts such as one never even dreams of in the New Hebrides. You scoff at Devon.[2] Do you imagine that bananas and bananas and bananas are more exciting than mangel wurzels or foxicide ? I know I shan't convince you, but I should like to think that your plots for the disillusioning of yourself will never pan out.

. . . I know about Henry James and have even read some of his exercises. One could read modern German psychology translated into English as an exciting recreation in the intervals between struggling through chapters of Mr. Henry James. I ain't clever. I ain't up to date. I can appreciate beautiful prose for its mere beauty. I cannot admire an olla podrida of commas and long-winded periods faltering and limping to no conclusion whatsoever. When I read a novel, I do so for respite. If I want to do a dull patient task of Sandow exercising with my mind, I don't go to the novelists. That is not their métier at all.

. . . One redeeming feature of Sidnee is that the place is a kind of Venice. One travels almost as much by water as by ' car.' The city is built all round the harbour, each bay being a separate quarter. That is rather nice at night. I used to go about a good deal by dark, and by means of shutting one's ears to the accent (which is honestly terrible) and losing the vulgarity of the sky-scrapers in the gloom of night, the harbour was refreshing. A propos of the accent, the following is perfectly true.

[1] Jamaica.   [2] Not at all.—ED.

My ex-surveying partner, an Aberdonian, was 'calling' at the house of an eminent Counsel in ——, who was the agent for the O——n Government. The Eminent Counsel's wife is, in Sidnee, in what is known as the ' Government House push.' Here is the conversation :

Eminent Counsel's Wife. Mr. Fraser, *do* you know
    anything about ile ?

Fraser. Oh, yes, Mrs. A. It's part of my job. Do
    you mean heavy oil, lubricating oil or what ?

Eminent Counsel's Wife. Mr. dear Mr. Fraser, I
    didn't say ile, I said ile. I have got a recipe
    for home-brewed ile, but I can't make it work.
    . . . (confusion of the very bashful Fraser).

The same lady once remarked in my presence to the wife of a French doctor : " Aow, j'ime lay petteezongfongs." I interpreted rapidly (too rapidly for Mrs. A's O——n French) to the poor puzzled mother, who thereupon beamed cheerfully upon her hostess and expatiated upon the charms of her marmot in a speech of which the O——n lady could not understand a word. She ejaculated " Aow, wee " at intervals and looked sympathetic. Why is it that the simple French affirmative is invariably the shibboleth that betrays even the fairly well accented Englishman ? And why do they always—but the French never—preface it with an Oh ?

July 30th, 1916.

MY Polynésienne is away on a visit to some of her fellow-savages at Mosquito Bay. So I am alone in my grass humpy for the week-end.

I realised quite suddenly last night what an absolutely deafening noise the surf makes perpetually here. Why does one not notice it or feel annoyed by it ? When I was in Sydney the rattle of the trams and ' autos ' made me rave. I used to lie awake at night cursing the fiendish noise. I found, too, that I had become a proper savage in my fear of speed and mechanism. I went out to the ' stadium ' at Rushcutters Bay one night to see whether I still liked the acrid reek from a pugilistic ring. To journey there I hired a taxi-cab. I was in a condition of sweating funk for the whole drive, and, but for the fact that I could not have found my way, would have stopped the thing and walked.

. . . So K. of K. has gone to join Joshua, Sennacherib and Alexander. I can imagine the shop that will be talked down in that seventh circle ; how Joshua will explain how *he* would have taken Verdun, maintaining the superiority of trumpets to modern artillery, pooh-poohing cavalry and extolling the German ideas of putting to the sword all civilians after the capture of a city. " When I had taken Jericho, my boy, there were no subscriptions made in Egypt for starving Jerichoans." . . .

. . . Let it be sufficient to say that I play the most absurd practical jokes, howl with laughter over their result like some boy and literally get the fatter for it. I have really never had anything like this in my life before. I have always been too earnest, too intense, too damn self-sufficing. It is funny that I should have had to wait for a Kanaka woman to drag me out of my tub. You see, these people are exactly the same as four year old white children. Well, just picture the grafting of a very womanly instinct upon a child's entire indifference to all theories of right and wrong. Once having over-come her shyness and fear of me, my woman is a constant source of joy in her naïveté. I am very careful never to hint at ' right ' and 'wrong '—(I couldn't, because there aren't any native words for the idea) so as not to spoil the charm. What she wants, she asks for. She surprised me the other day looking at a picture of the Farnese Hercules, and was very interested in his anatomy. Yesterday she came in and started looking round my room. I asked her what she wanted. " I am feeling very sad. I want to look at that big man on the paper. . . ." What would —— have said to her ? I very nearly laughed, but I am glad I did not. I just gave her the book and she sat down on the floor and purred like a cat. Can you wonder that I feel younger ? ' The cult of savagery . . . spells dim-inished physical vitality.' To Hell and Hell. Should I like such direct simplicity in a white woman ? What an absurd question. In a white woman it would spell unspeakable nastiness ; because it would be quite affected. In a very few years the missionaries will not have left any heathen ignorance even in these islands. The damned apple will have been eaten and the serpent will be clothed in fig-leaves and say ' shocking.' The only ' teacher ' who had been working for me came to me t'other day and told me he had ' sinned ' with a woman and felt that he ought to marry her. I hurt both of my feet and one hand on him and ran him off the place, and told him I'd shoot him if he ever came back. Fancy a Kanaka ' sinning,' and ' feeling that he ought.' But I should like to have a free hand with missionaries just for one month. The news of my sinful life has got round the islands and the local ' missy ' no longer calls in on me on his way to instil the shorrter catechism into his faithful.

I say, don't for God's sake tell —— that I liked his guide book. I didn't. It is the most dreadful tosh and written for ' automobilists.' I said that he had made a useful list of places at the end of the book and that in the list he had omitted all comments. That pleased me. The rest of his book is the very worst kind of muck. I tried to count the number of times he used the adjective ' glorious.' I got tired at 500 and gave up.

August 20*th*, 1916.

THERE was a big dance and kaikai last night to celebrate the wedding of my boss-boy, and, as the infernal row lasts from dusk till dawn, I always absent myself on such occasions. Madame, of course, remained for the show. These women would not miss a dance for worlds, and even walk miles on a Saturday after work to be present at one. They carry all their finery in a bag and change their costumes various times during the dance. Of course, a white man's woman has the pull over her virtuous sisters who earn 10s. a month and rarely get it. Monna Onéla has been fleecing me for weeks for this dance and intends to create a record in the quick change line. She will coo for months over the discomfiture inflicted upon her dearest friends, as she had a pièce de resistance—or rather deux pièces—in the shape of a real dress from Sydney, and—to knock 'em in the Old Kent Road—a pair of knickers with frillies which she wears with no other embellishment.

Naturally the women are not allowed to take any part in the dance except that of spectator. In most of the islands they are not permitted even to see the men dance; but the ' civilising ' influence of a plantation breaks most of their customs. The islands of Ambrym and Malekula still preserve a most complicated caste system, which the dear missionaries do their utmost to destroy as heathenish —are we not all buruthers? They even appoint chiefs from among the ' soundly converted ' plebeians and generally have so improved the condition of the heathen that from a virile, strictly virtuous, fertile set of fighting cannibals, they have evolved the filthy, cringing, lying, lazy, sterile Kanakas who have been steadily vanishing ever since they heard the name of God. I managed to get an unspoiled gem from a district where the Gospel has not dared to penetrate. Some inflamed ass on the plantation had jeered at her because her tribe were not ' school ' (= Christian), and because she had not even heard the word God : so she came to me to know whether such an omission was really a social stain.

Five of my nodding acquaintances in this island have pegged out since I wrote the above. One was knocked on the head by ' Man Bush ' and eaten, together with his four children ; one was drowned

while out recruiting ; two succumbed to an epidemic of dysentery which is cleaning out the group
—the third epidemic in a year. . . Nothing, of
course, to you people blasé with war slaughter, but
five out of a total of 15 is overdoing it.

September 1916.

. . .

I REMEMBER when —— had his first tea with
me à deux upon our arrival at Mosquito Bay.
I had poured him out his tea very carefully, and was
proceeding to drink my own, when I saw him get
up and start looking round the room. " What are
you looking for ? " " The bell. There's an ant
in my cup ! " Ye gods ! After a month in the
New Hebrides I never even bothered to try and
fish 'em out. I only draw the line at cockroaches.
Incidentally, this very night I caught and slew over
30 fleas inside and outside my trousers. I didn't
try and count the host that escaped me. No, if one
is going to be a rough traveller, it doesn't do to be
finicking. The essentials (body lice and so forth)
are all that really matter. Of course, I don't mean
that you should buy fleas and make pets of them. I
used to think that Cairo was bad for fleas, but this
place in the dry season beats Cairo hollow. It is
simply impossible to keep free of them. They
swarm everywhere. That's why I don't keep a
dog. The poor brute's life would be one long
martyrdom. Young Ashby at —— keeps Irish
terriers, and I have seen the poor things with their
bellies literally black with fleas. When I was

staying there I tried to give the doggies a bit of ease. I washed 'em in carbolic, smothered them in Keating's powder and kept them close cropped. Ten minutes after their bath they would be as infested as before and nearly mad with rage. And you know that a terrier can stand a goodish number of ' touches of eczema ' without worrying.

You still keep your faith in the charm of the Marquesas, Gilberts, and so on as far surpassing the New Hebrides. Why ? I have met scores of people who have been round and round the whole Pacific. One or two of them (*e.g.* Muller) have been appreciative folk, or if not appreciative at least intelligent and observing. I travelled for a week round these islands on the *Pacifique*, one time in company with a certain Major ——. He was a delightful old retired boy, a bachelor with just enough money to toddle round and round the globe. He comes out to New Zealand every year for salmon fishing, and then spends three or four months going about on these odd inter-island steamers and staying a bit here, there and everywhere. He had been in all the well-known groups and in most of the others. He had stayed for two years in Papeete and for several months in the Cook group. He was a very keen and very good photographer, and had over a dozen huge albums full of South Sea pictures. From what I saw and from what he (and Muller and many others) told me, there is practically nothing to choose scenically between these islands and all the others. The Major man had never seen the Nlles. Hebrides before, and his opinion was that aided by active volcanoes and high moun-

tains they are distinctly more beautiful than anything he had seen. Of course the majority (but not
all) of the New Hebrides natives are surpassingly
ugly. Muller tells me that the Tahitians are fairly
beautiful, but entirely and absolutely spoiled by
hideous clothes. You never see even a woman
now in island costume. In Papeete they wear
hobble skirts and high-heeled shoes. Of Tongans
I have seen a good many, but they also are quite
' white men ' now. If the New Hebrides had been
written up by a sentimental Stevenson or a gushing
X.Y.Z., they would be as much on the lips of the
sentimentalists and gushers at home as are the other
places. If you want scenic beauty, what island in
the whole world could compare with a view of
Derwentwater either in summer or winter, or with a
view of Wastdale and Wastwater from Scafell Pike ?
—the former view being the very acme of gentle
loveliness, the latter an exquisitely proportioned
scape of savage grandeur. No, you are a senti-
mentalist who invests the unknown with charms
which exist only in your imagination. What have
I said before ? I repeat it. Touch not, taste not,
handle not. Keep your distance and you will keep
your enchantment. Mind you, I am not saying
that the islands have no charm. I know the way
that in spite of all the drawbacks they grip me. I
remember my feeling of absolute pleasure when I
first caught a glimpse of Vila on my return from
Sydney. When I finally leave them I shall doubtless get the true perspective. They will call me
back and I shall become ' Romanesque ' once again
about them. Be prepared for this, and don't accuse

me rashly of being a turncoat in days to come. I don't suppose there is anywhere in the world where I could support loneliness as I do here. There is an ' ambiente ' which refuses to be defined. I am afraid that I have really eaten too much lotos already. The effects show in the deterioration of one's morals and one's mentality. I realised the other day when she was ill, how absurdly and disgustingly attached I have grown to my little brown woman. And what is she ? A little nut-coloured savage less than five feet high. Her body certainly is beautiful in its doll-like tininess. Her face and hair are quaint. She behaves to me just like a very nice Persian kitten or a terrier pup would behave. She won't sit on a chair but always snuggles up at my feet and purrs and sings her little croons quite regardless of what I may be doing. It is only when I find that she has stealthily filled up my shoe with sugar from her ever accompanying tin that I realise what an absolute baby she is. I hate scolding her because she weeps for hours and does the most absurd things. The other day I cursed her for chucking cigarette ends everywhere about and called her a dirty pig. She wept bitterly and ran out of the house. That night she didn't come back, and next morning when I went out to muster the labour I found her in line with the working women, ranged up with her pet abomination, the really dirty Maewo women, smoking a clay pipe and with a hoe in her hand. She had smeared woodashes over her face and limed her hair. I had to carry her bodily into the house and smack her bottom well before she would hear reason. She spends the whole afternoon

in the sea swimming and diving, and in every way
is much cleaner than a good proportion of the white
women I have ' met.' And yet six months ago I
was lampooning her to you as a savage beast.

But do you think I could tolerate her in civilisation ? Not for a week. That is the difference that
the islands make. I am afraid that I bore you with
these trivial details of my domestic life. Of course,
I solemnly ask pardon of —— for writing about
such an immoral subject. She must pretend to skip
these passages. Curiously enough, I don't feel
immoral at all. I feel (and look) more of a man
than ever before in my life. I suppose that means
that the brute man in me is rejoicing that it domin-
ates over a female, even though the female be small
and brown and savage.

For five solid weeks I haven't seen a white man
and have spoken nothing but Biche-la-mar and
Aobese. Can you expect me to be fluent even with
a pen ? Since I came to the plantation I have only
had an opportunity on Mowbray's two visits of
talking to anyone who could understand even a
little. Then we scorned bed and talked the livelong
night.

I like to make an occasional balance sheet of what
years and places do for me. Besides mental benefit
and general experience I can leave the New Hebrides
with a knowledge of three useful things learnt :

    (*a*) the French colloquial tongue.
    (*b*) surveying in virgin country.
    (*c*) tropical agriculture.

All three of these things are useful assets to a man,

though of no use to an usher. Against the profit I suppose I must write a certain amount of wear and tear and damage to constitution. That is easily repaired if not allowed to go on too long. I have lost my hair, and mounting a tall horse shows me that some of the spring has gone. But I am still devilish solid and a bracing climate would buck me up to my fine normal in no time. I miss my meat, you know. It is exactly 10 months to-day since I last tasted fresh meat. One gets so damnably sick of ' singe ' that I go for weeks without tasting any flesh at all. That might tend to keep one pure in thought—it has no such effect on me, but what would ?—it certainly tends to dyspepsia. Before the O——ns grew patriotic, *i.e.* before the Sydney stock of German delicatessen was exhausted, things weren't so bad. The German tinned foods were honest and eatable. Now we have to exist on what the O——ns make. You should just see it.

It was amusing of you to tell me to ' read my papers a bit more.' The truth is that my newsagent has been a bit slack lately. The boy rarely comes round with the papers before 8 o'clock, by which time of course I have put on my bowler hat and am chastely sitting in my tram. Read my paper a bit more, forsooth. You wait till you have experienced the arrival once a month of a three-months-old newspaper and see whether you will read it a bit more than I do. Remember that if by chance I comment to you upon European events, such events are probably six months old before you read my comments. At the pace that Europe is living at present, that must seem like a short lifetime to you.

Don't forget that I am the veriest old Rip Van
Winkle as ever was. I sometimes get chance bits
of news from passing recruiters which they have
picked up at Vila where the wireless station sometimes (but not often) works. Such chance visits
only happen about once every four or five months ;
so I am for the most part dependent upon my
mail.

You might wonder how I find time to write such
a lot every month. The explanation lies in the fact
that I like writing to you. I don't bother about
dates. My letters are written chiefly in scraps, a
little bit at all spare moments in each day and a good
big whack on Sundays. My savage never attempts
to interrupt me when I am writing. She is quite
content to sit at my feet and bask in the presence
while I am performing the mystery. She knows
your photograph. . . . Of course to her you are my
brother and therefore hers. . . . Conversation on
these points is a little delicate, because her ideas are
quite natural. They never dream of enquiring into
the paternity of a child. The woman who carried
him is obviously the mother ; and that's all that
matters. They take it for granted that some man—
either the father or another—will look after the
woman. If no one else offers, the child and mother
are ipso facto a part of the chief's household and
care. Under these circumstances it is practically
impossible to trace relationship. ' Brother ' simply
means friend. A man will suddenly change his
name, give and receive presents and adopt four or
five new brothers. They even adopt parents. When
it used to fall to my lot to cross-examine witnesses in

Biche-la-mar in the Joint Court I had often some
knotty problems to solve. If you want to know
whether Jack and Tom are brothers in the native
sense or otherwise, you ask : " One mamma 'e bin
carry you two feller more Jack ? " Then, if it is
necessary to find out whether the twain are full
brothers, the language has to be more explicit still.
There is one word and only one word which is
understood in Biche-la-mar to express procreation,
and that is the word you dislike so. And so does
Mr. Justice —— dislike it too. " Erm, Mr. ——,
can't you teach them a more polite word than
that ? " The fat old President and the French
judge who understood the word—and a very few
other words of English or Biche-la-mar—used to
chuckle aloud every time I had to say it. I strongly
suspected the President of deliberately laying traps
for me.

Tell me, if you consider the question of sufficient
interest, how Biche-la-mar strikes you as a vehicle
of inter-communication, basing your opinion on
the specimen I sent you last mail.[1] Of course,
not knowing the language, you can't appreciate its
difficulties. For one thing, it has to be pronounced
in the native way and not according to the English
origin of the phrases. Then you must remember
that there is only one possible way of expressing one
idea. Circumlocution or the slightest change in
the order of words makes it quite unintelligible.
Some few natives who have been in Queensland can
vary their speech a little, but they are in a very
small minority. It really requires a good ear and a

[1] See Appendix.

certain amount of mimetic intelligence before you
can really talk to natives. The majority of English
(*i.e.* O——n) people here talk Biche-la-mar very
badly, just as hopelessly as the average Briton talks
any foreign language. The English judge, who has
had to hear Biche-la-mar spoken every day for the
last eight years, cannot speak two sentences. I once
heard him remark to the wife of the French President
—" Ceci n'est pas la place pour moi." You can
supply his pronunciation at discretion, but you
cannot see the look of utter bewilderment on that
lady's face. He was merely trying to impress the
good woman that his sweetness was wasted on Vila's
desert air. Another of the same gentleman's famous
sayings was in interruption of a speech by the Haut
Commissaire who was tactfully referring to ——'s
high office. "Vous, monsieur magistrat" ...
"Pardonnez-moi. Je ne suis pas un magistrat.
Je suis un juge. ..." That is a pearl of great price
to Frenchmen, and they are never tired of
repeating it.

Young Brooks in our interview with the Governor
of New Caledonia was rather sweet too. I had
absolutely forbidden him to utter one word as I
knew his propensity for ' gaffes ' ; but the family
loquacity overruled my command and he came out
with " Mais, Monsieur le Gouverneur, est ce qu'il
y a beaucoup de cocottes (v.d. cocotier) en Nouvelle
Caledonie ? " " Ah, monsieur, je regrette que
d'office je ne suis pas à même de vous renseigner.
Ces affaires ne sont pas de ma competence." What
could have been nicer ?

I have just been fire-fighting. These wretched

Kanakas will start lighting fires in their grass houses, which at this time of the year are as inflammable as an 18 year old boy. The fire broke out this after-noon while all hands were away at work. In less than 5 minutes six houses had gone and the flames were spreading to my own 'case' and to the produce shed with several hundred pounds' worth of cotton therein. By heroic efforts we saved the whole caboodle, but I can scarcely see out of my eyes and have got a thirst which needs serious attention. So I close.

. . . I grow more inarticulate every day. It's the result of not talking. If, as happens occasionally, my wife is away, I often go the whole day long with-out uttering a single word of any sort. My servants are experienced enough to do my behests in silence. I have trained a native overseer to supervise the labour when I feel too bored to do it myself. I should grow into a horrid old crank here were it not for my 'little bit of brown stuff.' I miss her horribly now when she goes away. Before many months are out I shall have the mixed delight of seeing the métis that I announced to you as being already on the way. I wonder whether I shall like it, or want to drown it. It's sure to be male. These Aoba women always throw colts from a white man. There is only one known half-breed filly in the islands, but scores of colts. One thing is certain. He is going to be brought up 'native.' No snuff and butter coloured citoyen français for me. I really believe that the English are the only race with proper ideas on the colour question. The French are quite unspeakable. When I was in Vila, as

Vice-President of the Cercle de Port Vila I had the joy of black-balling irretrievably two of the most noted colons of the place, one a Néo-Heb. métis, the other a pure Martinique nigger. There was an awful row and the French called a general meeting of the club, but I whipped up all the English members and beat the égalité beggars on the post again. Since my time they have altered the rules of the club, and now the aforesaid niggers swank on the verandah and drink their consommations with the white men. All the English members have, in consequence, resigned. That is all by the way. I am over in my little grass house for the week-end, the wind is fresh from the sea, I have defied the sharks and had a good swim.

... I read a short time ago a Spanish novel entitled *La Ciudad de la Niebla*, by Pio Baroja. It is one of the most extraordinarily clever books I have ever read. It is quite short and does not contain a ha'porth of story or plot. It's simply a series of thumb-nail sketches of London by a foreigner. The man is a consummate artist, and picked out essentials for his pictures with amazing instinct. I don't believe that the heart of London, those things that we all know but can't describe, has ever been portrayed like it before. I fear the book would not translate well—Spanish is too subtle for translation—or I should be strongly tempted to try it. The book is worth studying by every novelist.

October 27*th*, 1916.

. . .

LIKE all other things that have grown up with time and by natural selection, class distinctions are not going to be lightly destroyed. I don't deny the exceptions. All natural laws are at best approximations. Nature may (and does) produce a very few ready-made gentlemen. On the other hand, some gently born may be, by some mistake of breeding, vulgar cads. These exceptions are to be expected, but do not break the boundaries one little bit. I don't think that many more gentlemen will be made by Nature. The spread of democracy is all against the process. The old stock will remain, because their traditions go back to times when transitions were impossible. . . . I am not now talking about ' Government by, with or from the people.' I presume that the march of events must bring the able and able-to-shout to the front rank in politics, quite irrespective of who they are. I am thinking chiefly of the social life which, after all, counts for more than laws. I am sure that the really lasting phases of a country's development come from the country—not from the town. The great machine of town life, with its grinding and levelling of classes, produces quick-changes and frothy formulae which deceive the superficial observer and lead him to think that there alone is progress, that London and Manchester and Birmingham are really all-important to the hub of the universe. They are wrong. The spirit of the country is born in the country. Show me your

country gentry, and I will show you your country.
That is an idea worth developing. Don't mention
it. I make no charge whatever.

November 5th, 1916.

. . .

THESE women are entirely devoted to their
man, but they are as little ' vicious ' as one
could imagine. Yes. Aoba is one of the Nlles.
Hébrides. The English name of it is Leper Island,
but the accusation is based upon the inability of the
old black-birders to distinguish a harmless leuco-
dermia from leprosy. There is plenty of leprosy
in the group, but none in Aoba. The Aobans are
freaks among the Kanakas, being Malayan rather
than Papuan. Their complexion is light ; their
hair yellowish and long ; their features are good.
I should not call the women classically beautiful,
but they are very pleasing and petite. Also they
are worshippers of bodily cleanliness, spending the
whole day in the sea. They are quite established
in the N.H., and in a good many other groups, as
white men's ' keeps.' The men are still cannibals,
though only occasional ones. My dear confesses
to having just tasted a teeny weeny bit of a roast
hand when she was a little girl. As she is only about
fifteen now, it couldn't have been so very long ago.
I fancy I know whose was the hand.

1917

I SIMPLY must shift from here. I have mis-calculated the effect of lotos eating; I mean of my last meal. That wretched little brown slut has tied me up a dam sight tighter than I could ever have imagined. It won't do at all. If I were to give way now, it would mean the renunciation of all that I really love. And I'm not such a fool as that.

. . . There should be no need for me to tell you that I hate the mockeries of modern civilisation, but between hating them and hurting my poor head against them il y a un monde. We simply can't help being respectable Puritans. It isn't our fault. A fat duck who set the Mendelian clock back a few hundred years and proclaimed itself a wild bird of soaring flight would be justly laughed at by the rest of the poultry yard. No, the family is a product of thousands of years. Those who try and upset it only hurt themselves and make themselves ludicrous. That is what I meant when I stated my preference for the 'latter day Christian womanhood.' By 'Christian' I obviously did not mean Anglican or anything else like it. I am averagely ignorant both on the subject of ethics and philosophy, but I do really believe that as a nice, sound, workable philosophy the essentials of Christianity are very hard to beat, at least for Occidentals. You see, we are only the product of the best part of a hundred generations who have lapped up ' Thou shalt not commit adultery ' with and after pap. Naturally, then, when we do try and commit adultery we can't do it with any kind of ease. It is only a backstairs, French-comic-paper performance at its best, and at its worst something even beastlier.

I apologise for having accused you of a desire to be a Squireen. That was only a touch of ' bilious remittent.' I am sure, though, that you would like to be wealthy. I should like you to be so, at any rate ; for then I would come home and live on you. I don't want you to be Croesy. I merely want you to be perfectly free to say—" Blast this place, it's getting on my nerves. ——, go and pack the bag. We'll catch the 9.17 to Sicily." I should have no shame at all in reaping the benefits of your spondulicks. I should be extremely useful to you as a handy man. I could cut your hair, mend your 'auto,' cook, and do a host of, well-menial services. I shan't be respectable enough to settle down with you for a long time yet. I don't mean to say that you are respectable by choice. I believe you are entirely disreputable at heart. But you know what I mean.

I see that —— is still booming himself. In a recently arrived number of *Punch* I saw that he had " laid down his pen with a sigh having just completed seven novels with one —— fountain pen. . . ." Rather amusing when one knows the gent.'s dictatorial methods.

February 5th, 1917.

MADAME has learned from the other women to talk Biche-la-mar quite fluently; but she will never talk it to me unless she is very offended. The other night I was annoyed with her and ejaculated : " God damn you for a harlot." Immediately came : " What name Godama " . . . (a tolerable imitation of my phrase) " Me tink you talk no good 'ere. What name frarlot ? Me no frarlot." Curious instinct, eh ? Forgive all this pettiness, but I am enjoying this part thoroughly.

Now I'll tell you how this letter was interrupted, and how the interruption caused me to play another part which I enjoyed. About 8 miles from [the plantation] ' cross bush ' lives a family of whom I have spoken to you before. The father-planter is a rough New Zealand ' back-blocker,' but quite the whitest man I've ever met. The mother is a scioness of extremely ancient Swedish nobility—and looks it. Her pa was proud and very poor, and took to whaling and subsequently sandal-wood trading. Hence her New Hebridean upbringing. They have a pair of lovely twins aged 3½—'twas the twins that I tended and bathed some two years agone. Pa (en secondes noces and not the father of the twins) is at present ' out recruiting ' Kanakas. Three weeks ago one of the gemini fell ill with what might have been an abnormal dysentery or possibly a more serious thing. I was sent for and prescribed. For about three weeks all went well. Daily bulletins were sent by native post and the kiddy seemed to be improving. I was too busy to go over and advised by correspondence. Beginning last Saturday came more alarming reports twice a day. Sunday morning's was very bad and I had made up my mind to ride over on Monday. I had just started to write to you about sundown on Sunday when a breathless Kanaka arrived with the news that I had dreaded. I was slacking in pyjamas and slippers. From —— to [the plantation] I ran in that costume. Arrived at [the plantation] I howled for my Kanaka groom to catch and saddle ' Cloudy '—the plantation stallion. He had been unridden and maize-fed for three weeks with a view to stud duties, so I knew he would carry me as quick as I wanted to move. I got into riding gear and was in the saddle just as dark fell. Then the fun began. Within two minutes I was drunk with the madness of speed. The horse seemed to catch my mood and went like a good 'un. I fairly revelled in the ride. It was a case of face down on his neck all the way, pitch dark, a narrow bush-track, up hill, down gullies, great ropes hanging all over the track. My hat went in the first minute, then my whip. Both hands were cut and bruised with warding off branches, and only a colonial saddle (if you know what that is) saved me from dislocated knees. I took two of the loveliest tosses as ever was, due to the fact that Cloudy has only one eye and shies very disconcertingly every time an obstacle crops up. However, he behaved very well, and I have learned enough rough horsemanship to fall clear. I should have liked that ride to last for a day. It seemed about five minutes. Actually it was 32 minutes by the clock for a ride which usually takes me an hour and a half by daylight. Cloudy was simply gorgeous. When we sighted the lights in the house at ——, and were doing the last half mile—along the beach—he let out with a whinney like any trumpet. It's true that there was a mare in the —— paddock ; but I am certain he was shouting his joy of the run.

I found the little girl suffering dreadfully and in a very critical condition ; so I decided at once that we must get her to a surgeon quick. In view of this possibility I had told my ' groom ' to follow me on foot. We waited for the moon to rise—about 2 a.m. and then I sent him off on a three hours' ride to Mosquito Bay to try and get a boat. It was only a chance that there would be one of the launches at home ; but Fate was kind and by 6.30 a.m. the launch was at anchor at ——. These Island people are like that. Spite of all their beastliness, when it's a case of help for the sick, they never wait. Cost, loss of business, risk are never counted. It was an awful job getting the mother and the kiddies on board. —— has no ' passage ' through the reef, so the launch had to anchor about half a mile out. There was a filthy sea and nothing but very smart seamanship saved the dinghy from being capsized or smashed against the launch. However, I got 'em on safely and then came ashore. I could do nothing by going to Vila with them. The mother is born and bred of the sea, and, if necessary, could have sailed the boat herself. The captain is a splendid sailor ; so I left them to him and came ashore to think things. That poor woman would have a voyage of anything between 12 and 24 hours in a 24 foot boat, burned by the sun, drenched

by the sea and chucked savagely about all the time.
When I told the mother that it was a case of Vila,
she never made a murmur but started to pack up
for the trip. She had not had her clothes off for
four days and is seven months ' gone.' And so
back to the plantation on foot, very tired and sore.

. . . Only don't let me get lotos-poisoned. Before
I took a woman my chaste life kept me sufficiently
fidgety. Now there is more danger. There would
be more still if a single one of my fellow inhabitants
were a lotos eater. But they are not. They
are merely vulgar Orsetroylyurn failures eking a
miserable existence by swindling Kanakas. Every
man of them, if he were clever enough to make any
money out of swindling Kanakas, would leave
to-morrow for Sehdnee to live in a suburb of that
place the life of the suburban O——n. The
French people are just as bad. They would be
podgy petty bourgeois in Marseilles or else con-
seillers municipaux in Nouméa, which is worse.
You seem to think that the French colon is better
than our colonial. As a matter of fact, he is ten
thousand times worse, infinitely more vulgar and
infinitely more bombastic. I hate yappers; and I
have never met a Frenchman who didn't yap. You
know what I mean. They carry into private life the
phraseology and live in terms of Royal Messages
and such like fatuities. C'est pour la France !
Ah ! ma chère France ! Oumpluich ! They have
a catechism in the Ecole Laïque at Vila which
begins : Qu'est ce que ton papa fait la bas ? Il se
bat pour la France et pour le drapeau . . . etc.
They suck up this emotional flap-doodle with

their mother's milk and ooze it out of every pore all their life. I got a sickener of that sort of thing among the yellowbellies in South America ; but there it had its comic element. The children can all recite the stirring history of La Patria, la Banda oriental, Meestro pais hermoso y magnifico. It takes about ten minutes to recite the lot. No : I am an Englishman and be damned to all foreigners. True, I like foreign languages. But I hate Frenchmen. That's very largely due to my being a bit bilious at present. . . .

Yes : I was very bilious yesterday. Took some calomel last night—quite well to-day, thank you.

How would you like me to tell you a story in Biche-la-mar ? I don't care how you would like it : I'm going to do it for fun. Remember that Biche-la-mar is not only spoken among natives and between whites and natives, but is also the Esperanto of a large proportion of the English and French for intercommunication. I don't know a single Frenchman who can talk English. None of the English (except the Néo-Caledonniens who are bilingual) talk French. You can't imagine the effect of hearing two apparently sane, adult white people talking pidgin to one another. Of course the French people talk it much better than we do, because they learn it purely by ear and the words to them are only Biche-la-mar words and not perverted English. I am quite sure that you wouldn't understand a single word of the spoken stuff at first. I used to think that the niggers were talking their own language. Well, here's the story. It's a true tale of a local happening. It has little

interest except for the language. I write it more or
less phonetically, but cannot convey the queer
native sound values. (They can't pronounce J—
they make it T. They can't pronounce initial F :
it becomes a kind of Mp, like a Zulu click).[1]

I have put it in dialogue form as the only possible
thing to do. . . . I append a few notes and also
enclose you the pièce on which the story depends.
It was a ' dying declaration ' taken by me and then
not used because the wounded man lived long
enough to make another in Vila. Le nommé ——
eventually got six months, which meant that he
was confined at night in the offices of the British
Residency. During the day he was on parole,
fed at the hotel, had his missis with him, and all
other comforts.

February 25th, 1917.

SINCE sending off my last long letter I have
heard from the man —— in Sydney. He had
registered his letter to me and therefore the Post
Office people overlooked it and sent it on by a
trading cutter. That is their way. My professor
is not very hopeful about jobs in Sydney, but he
will press my claims hard.

Through his good services I am actually a candi-
date for the Professorship of Chemistry at the Govt.
Agricultural College. I shouldn't mind that job a
bit. The pay is good and the long vacations would
give me a chance of voyaging round to some of the
Pacific Islands (*e.g.* Aitutaki), which I feel that I

[1] See Appendix.

ought to see before coming back, if only for the
sake of laughing about their beauties. . . . Now
that there is a chance of getting away I feel curiously
reluctant. You can say what you like (or rather, I
can say what I like), but there is a subtle charm
about this island life in spite of its many horrors.
I am really thankful that chance took me to a malarial
part of the Pacific instead of to a healthy one. Were
it not for the beastly fever and dysentery, I should
find it very hard to leave even the New Hebrides.
I am afraid that Kultur has entirely done for some
of the places of which Stevenson raved. Muller
was staying with me a short time ago, having just
completed on one of his schooners a very compre-
hensive business voyage round the Pacific, y inclus
Tahiti. He told me that at Papeete every four
natives own a motor car, and that the Kanaka wharf
labourers ride to their work on ' autos.' The combined perfume of benzine and lotos must be charming. In contradistinction there is the Lord Howe
group (*not* Lord Howe Island, which is near
Australia) which is of the most primitive. Marriages
are performed in public. . . . As soon as the people
perceive that the maid has been properly initiated,
they proceed to shower their wedding gifts upon the
pair, who then eat their wedding breakfast and
leave for a short honeymoon behind a tree. What
could be more charming ? The Chief assured
Muller that weddings were very contagious, one
being always followed by a crop of others. Not
really surprising.

In the Wallis group the laws of hospitality
demand that, when a distinguished stranger arrives,

the first woman who tickles his fancy shall be ceded to him for the duration of his stay, even if she be the wife or daughter of a chief. The law is never broken, but, as the woman is usually killed upon the departure of the stranger, it is as well to be careful if one wishes to return to the group. In the same islands a chief is always buried in a large grave with his living wives and with two heralds who sing the praises of the dead chief even while the earth is being shovelled on to them. There is no mistake possible, as the other mourners roll an immense coral boulder on to the filled-in grave, and keep watch there for a week. There is no doubt that the Wallis Islanders rate women and reporters with some shrewdness. . . . Here one is too unhealthy physically even to attain to a modest condition of mental activity. I don't really know how I have stood such an existence for five years. The black whoring part has amused me because I have treated it merely as a source of amusement. It has tickled me to give long harangues in English to a little brown savage who has sat with wide-opened eyes apparently awe-struck the while she, unknown to me, has been carefully secreting my tobacco, matches, etc., in various parts of her person. You must allow that the subsequent screams of childish laughter and the rough and tumble were not all piggishness. I don't want to be a pig, but rather that than be a prig. Always supposing that there is a Scheme and a Schemer, it seems absurd to believe that the aim of man is to subdue and mortify those parts of him which au fond tend to propagate the race and perpetuate the Scheme. Why then this insistent desire for such mortification ? Is it disease ? Or is it that man's life should be naturally divided into periods, a period of preparation for propagation, one of propagation, and then a retirement for the development of the other part or parts of him ? If so, have I reached the third period ? My performances in the second have been rather inappreciable. Am I then called to the third period earlier ? . . . Morals and religion I don't bother about. We (Europeans) are all Christians. We can't help it, any more than we can help having white skins. Our morality is as much a part of us as is our gall-bladder. We may or may not adhere to some particular sectarian idea of our occupation in a future life. That is all quite unimportant. The important thing is that no living sane man denies the possibility of something after physical death. And in view of such an admission it behoves us to try and enter that condition decently prepared. If one knew for certain that Mrs. Blong-Ponkin was going to ask one to dinner on the nth, one would make an effort to have one's shirt back from the wash by the n − 1th. Well, I fancy that we are all certain. . . .

March 1st.

MY evenings are passed in solitude now because I have built Madame a little nest of her own. She passes her time there making the most impossible bungles and botches which she is pleased to call ' calico b'long bloody picaninny b'long you.' She produces several of these things each morning giggling for my approval, which I duly give. I don't know where she got the idea of sewing for the yet unborn. It is quite certain that her ma never did anything of the sort. She probably feels that it is required of her as the mother of a half-caste.

Later.

I like the thought of ——— having written a book on fox-shooting while he was a wretched prisoner. His views on ' foreigners ' are nice too, as also his opinions on scenery. However much superior folk play at despising the ——— type, they know jolly well that they are sound chaps, men to have near you in a scrap against odds, en fin the Englishman of tradition, but very little seen in these days. To people of ' artistic temperament ' and degenerate tastes, the ——— is frightfully annoying, because he simply does not regard them. He knows that long-haired, sensitive-souled, Cubist-minded oddities exist and even flourish, but he smiles in a quietly superior manner and knows that his way and his sort are really what matter in the long run. Which would you personally prefer, L. M. N. sucking maraschino in a Soho café and enthusing about the purple tints shed by some female's hat on a dirty marble table, or ——— sighing inarticulately over the moon the while he notes where he is going to shoot his fox in the morning ? And I believe that the great Victorians were men of the ——— type. Certainly Browning, Thackeray and Tennyson were. They were clean, decent-minded gentlefolk, and sound scholars even if they did worship tradition a thought over-much.   At least they did not invent jig-saw puzzles in colour and words and hawk them, screaming shrilly, as art while spitting venom and newspaper froth on all who can hold a pencil and scan a line.   I have a theory that all these absurdities and vulgarities in the way of freak-arts come from U.S.A. via Germany, and are simply part of a subtle scheme to make the modern Englishman what he is fit to be rather than what he should be. . . . Is a man a physical and mental failure, does he lack the elementary senses of eye and ear, has he to boot a dirty, degenerate dwarf-mind, overflowing with self-conceit ? Then let him pour scorn on what he is incapable of doing and become a super-artist, a very apostle of Futurism : or, let him have his behind well kicked and learn humbly to tend well and thoroughly a closet for his betters.

I HAVE just been indulging in somewhat acri- monious correspondence with ——, who has taken the strange whim into his head to play the lawyer and pester me for a payment of wages to a boy that I kicked out very summarily some months ago.   —— is not a bad sort, but he has to learn. . . . The boy in question had the effrontery to pay quite unwelcome attentions to my slut in my absence. I was forbearing enough on my return to give him three minutes' grace while I went to the house for my Winchester.   I quite enjoyed seeing him run, and it was only because Onéla commanded me to do so that I fired a parting shot after him—nowhere near him. —— talked very big about 'attempted murder,' just as if the affair had happened (as I pointed out to him) in Houndsditch. Anyhow old 6s. 8d. didn't get any change out of me. I dam nearly did kill a boy the other day. The brute was jumping on his wife's neck and hammering her indiscriminately with an axe. When I arrived on the scene, he, to my great surprise, did not attempt to run. He chucked his axe into the bush and put his fists up quite à la old-time pug. That was cheek and riled me more even than his wife-beating, so he got it proper. I only got in two on him : my left landed right on his squat nose and split it and my knuckles, but my right fetched plunk under the heart. I thought the swine was dead, but by expending much time, drugs and energy I got him round. Muller had come up by then and promptly ' signed on ' the creature for three years.

April, 1917.

. . .

GOOD wine needs no bush, but bad wine must be labelled Château something or young men wouldn't enjoy it. Muller told me that he once ' descended ' at a famous pub in Paris in company with one of the Catalans. They spent a week working solemnly through the carte de vins, and were, of course, presented with a colossal bill. Then Monsieur Catalan introduced himself to the manager and told him exactly how many casks (I think three) of his own wine had been necessary for

the production of that long list of Château this, that
and t'other. They finally paid three francs a bottle
all round for their wine. It was a bit ' commercial '
but rather a knock to the man who is very ' sound on
wine.' I don't think I ever did affect that particular
snobbery. It's true that I prefer dry champagne to
the lemonade variety, but I don't like either except
as a means of getting drunk.

It has just flashed upon me that I never spoke to
you about the time that I lived at the Bermondsey
Settlement and helped to ' raise the masses.' There
was a guild of cripples in connection with the
settlement called the ' Guild of the Poor Things.'
The members of the guild had a counter-sign and
secret handshake. They greeted one another (when
any guild official was within earshot) with ' leeters
sorty meer—'appy in me lot.' Isn't that rather
sweet ? . . . I was finally ejected from the settlement for being caught in an embarrassing position
with Titania when I was supposed to be acting as
prompter. I explained to the Warden that I was
doing my best to raise the masses, but he missed
the point.

Probably before this letter goes the half-caste
brat will have arrived too, and they are such pretty
little devils when they're young. It is the thought
of the adolescent and fully grown métis, however,
that steels my heart. I broke the news to her the
other day of my impending departure and had an
awful scene. She vowed she would kill herself and
the kid, etc., etc. Fortunately I knew my Kanaka
too well to be seriously troubled. An hour later
she had put a crab in my bed and was pretending to

be asleep till I put my foot on the horrible creature. She will marry some native buck a week after I go and be perfectly happy. However, it will be a memory. I had to give up trying to speak her language. I hadn't the time to learn it properly. Now we talk Biche-la-mar savoured with a whole collection of English oaths and lewd expressions which she has learned from me. You should hear her recite ' My Mary Ann's got legs like a man.' It's all very silly, but it has been gorgeous fun. Of course, none of the white swine here could understand my joy in the little creature. It has made me that most gorgeous of all things, a grown-up child again for a short time. Let's leave it at that.

21*st May*, 1917.

JOHN-JAMES-FRIDAY salutes you from a great distance. The poor little girl had an awful bad time with the parturition, 48 solid hours of it instead of the two or three that they usually get off with. The mid-wives, two ancient wise birds skilled in all magic, predicted twins and possibly triplets. In reality it was only a super-enormous one. Heaven save you from ever having to play doctor-accoucheur to your woman. Those two nights made me old. Twenty times I thought the poor little mite was dead—and she would have been but for me. You see, they are not built for great labour and she's only about fifteen. I had to fight myself not to use chloroform and interference. I had everything at hand but would not use it. I

was madly determined that short of killing Topsy
I was going to see that child born safe and sound.
I should most certainly have killed it by my amateur
surgery. I seem to have struck the right mate as
far as breeding for size goes. The average native
infant weighs three kilos—I have weighed a good
many—but this prodigy weighed just over six
kilos an hour after birth.

Poor little Topsy looked absolutely frightened
when she came to and saw it. Her first words were
to me : " 'Im 'e bald'ed all same you." Then to
the nouveau-né : " My word ! You you fat too
much. I tink you like place where you been stop
before. You lazy too much longa come down."

Hope I don't bore you with these obstetric details.
The experience was quite novel for me. Topsy as
a nursing mother is a joy for ever. She literally
spurts milk and shakes with laughter when her son
gets a shower bath of it long before he has made his
grab. But, talk about the essential mother. If ever
I lay so much as a finger on the child I can feel her
eyes on me like a cat's, and I'm sure she's ready to
spring. It is primitive (and therefore, I suppose,
beastly), but it appeals to me. I quite expected
that she would be as happy-go-lucky over her kid
as she is over every other thing. But, Lord no.
She has imbibed all that I have told her from
my store of book and family wisdom, and nothing
is too good for Man Friday. He is bathed and fed
by the clock, and woe betide the handmaidens if
they are slack with him. " 'Ere, you man-bush.
You no sabby piccaninny 'ere 'e b'long white man ?
You tink 'e all same b'long dirty boy ? "

... I had to give a huge kaikai (feast) and dance in honour of Man Friday. Not only were new songs invented, but actually a new dance. Topsy translated the words to me. They were a little bit ' free,' in fact almost licentious, but they flattered me no end. The dance began at 5 p.m. on Saturday and stopped at 8 a.m. on Sunday, and that only because the bullock was already cooked and the yams were getting overdone. Topsy was in the seventy-seventh heaven at the honour. She hung on to my hand and every now and then rubbed her head against it and gurgled " O, bald'ed ! " I tell you, the sensation beats having your mother-in-law and a few friends in to lunch, sneering at your electro-plate and talking scandal or art.

May 26th, 1917.

WHEN I came to the plantation, I found as dwelling-house an iron and weather board four-roomed cottage with verandah in front. There were four rooms, two 14 by 14, two 14 by 9. The outside walls were galvanised iron, the inside undressed w.b., I am a bit of an old campaigner, and set to work to try and make the place habitable. I knocked the two 14 by 14 rooms into one. I papered the top half of the walls with ' lignomur ' (a kind of lincrusta paper). I painted the bottom half with Hall's Sanitary Distemper pink. Between the white lignomur and the pink distemper I ran a narrow skirting and painted it dark green. I then built a verandah on the back of the cottage. I then enclosed back and front verandahs with mosquito gauze and made mosquito doors and windows of gauze for the whole house. Part of the back verandah I partitioned off and called it the bathroom. In that I hung the shower bath. Further, I stained the floor of the living room and bought some native grass mats. The total result is that the cottage is very tolerable to look at. It is hellishly hot on account of the iron and also because the mosquito gauze shuts out any breeze that there might be. But it makes sitting at night possible. You owe most of my letters to that gauze. Nearly the whole of the work I did with my own hands.

I am certain that I can never be English again. I carry my own breakfast apparatus, to wit, an Austrian coffee-maker, a Thermos flask for the hot milk, and a tin of sugar. That is the result of seven years' absence from England with its family gathering round the greasy bacon dish and its morning face rubbings. I breakfast immediately I get up, then bathe and dress fit to meet the world. Even the comparative cold of Sydnee and the cooking in a nice hotel couldn't convert me. I tried breakfast the first morning, but the sight of a man stirring honey into a basin of porridge was too much for me. I boiled with hatred of the man and cleared out quickly. The only thing that worried me in Sydnee was that I couldn't get lunch at 11 o'clock, but I soon found out that sandwiches were free; so I stuffed at the expense of a small glass of lager beer and found I could still manage the 1 o'clock meal.

About three years ago I was doing a survey at a place called —— Bay in this island. The bay is the most fever-mosquito ridden place in the New Hebrides. I stuck it in my tent for about a week and then shifted on to a small island about two miles out in the bay. The small island is delightful, swept by the trades and absolutely free of mosquitoes. Naturally enough in such a delectable spot there is a mission house. The local missionary (who lives elsewhere) had given me permission to occupy the house, so I proceeded there by canoe after an awful hot day's work in the bush. The house was complete with linen, plate, etc., so I took only whisky with me. By the time I got to the island I had a really remarkable thirst, and ordered my valet-de-corps to mix me a long whisky-lime at once. This ' boy ' is the product of my own genius. He attached himself to me in Vila and has been with me ever since. He is a first-class valet, cook, boatman, etc., etc. In addition he talks real English and hates missionaries like poison. His father and mother were harried out of their island by a missionary because they refused to ' be married ' or ' join the church,' and so this boy lost the only thing that a Kanaka really prizes—his ancestral bit of land. I was rather astonished that Jimmy was so long in mixing my drink and went into the kitchen to see what was up. I knew he would sooner forget his own gun than my whisky.

"There isn't a glass in the bloody house, sir, and you can't drink whisky out of a tea-cup." We hunted everywhere and at last I was successful, finding the enamel-ware tumblers all dirty and sticky inside and out.

" Here you are, Jimmy, but what in the name of
hell have they been used for ? "

" —— if I know, sir. Oh, yes, that's ——,
raspberry jam and water. You know, the stuff they
drink at Christmas "—at the yearly communion.
In the Presbyterian Church the elements are carried
round by the deacons for the delectation of the
faithful who remain seated in their pews in order to
show their friendliness with the Deity. To your
(doubtless) correct Anglicanism these stories may
savour of blasphemy. To me the missionary is the
real blasphemer. You should just read the canting
flapdoodle that they write in their local missionary
magazine.

" The spirit was very manifest in its movings in
—— last month. Many gave themselves to Jesus.
The catechism class is a saving means of grace.
The collections were, perhaps, not as good as they
might have been, but these poor people are passing
through a time of spiritual and material stress, etc.,
etc."

In reality that month a French grog-seller had
visited —— and done a roaring trade. The whole
population, men, women, and kids, were blind
paralytic for weeks. Many died of the spree. The
missionary shut himself up in his house with his
wife and —— with fright, all their house-servants
having joined in the orgy. That is a very good
sample of the real good that missionaries have done
and are doing in the New Hebrides. It would be
very hard indeed for an unprejudiced enquirer to
find any good at all done by missionaries in this
group. Of course they claim to have civilised the

New Hebridean, to have weaned him from cannibalism, etc. That claim is quite without justification.
The abandonment of cannibalism, the utility of the
Kanaka as a labourer and other such effects have
come about naturally with the advent of the planter
and the trader. The proof of this is that the island
of Malekula (the largest in the group), being too
mountainous for planting and containing too few
wild coconut trees to tempt the trader, is as frankly
cannibal as it was a hundred years ago. Only this
year they routed two Government punitive expeditions armed with machine-guns, hand grenades and
other forms of Schrecklichkeit, killing and eating
many of the far-famed New Guinea Police and also
a few Anzacs. Needless to say no missionary is to
be found in Malekula. No; the missionary is
found in the coast villages among the Kanakas
already ' civilised ' by long years in Queensland or
Fiji. There he fills them with cant, encourages
laziness and discourages recruiting in order to
have a large tally of converts to send home. The
missionaries (*i.e.* the Protestant ones, *not* the Frères
Maristes) have abolished all tribal customs, all
feudal notions, all very salutary Levitical habits.
The chief—who in the ' heathen ' villages is a
veritable father of the tribe—has in every case
been deposed in favour of some glib-tongued lazy
swine of a ' teacher ' from their training college.
Dancing—the Polynesian's great form of exercise
and almost his raison d'être—has been banished
entirely. Polygamy—with its Levitical abstentions
always rigorously observed—has given place to
Matrimony. In consequence it is only in the

' heathen ' villages that one ever sees piccaninnies. It would not be fair to attribute all the decadence of the Polynesians to the missionary, but he has been very largely responsible for the wiping out of hundreds of villages by disease, for the vanished birth-rate, for the general lazy, care-about-nothing condition of the natives. All his old occupations are tabooed (including the ' tambo ' itself), and nothing except yowing mission hymns (which don't suit the plain-song-singing Kanaka a bit) has been given him in return. They have not even been taught cleanliness. The ' mission boy ' in his lice-ridden, never-changed-till-they-rot-off clothes is loathsome. The heathen with his 'nambas' is as clean as any other wild animal. Even the sanitary condition of the ' heathen ' villages is ten thousand times better than that of the mission villages. In all that I say about missionaries you must understand that I refer to the present lot and not to the ' old school.' The early missionaries may have been mistaken fanatics, but they had guts. When one reads about the pioneers who landed from a small whaler on Erromanga in the 'seventies, that they cleared the bush, built their own house and stuck at their job among a crowd of real savages until they were finally killed and eaten, one may pity their mistaken views, but one must grant that they were men. The present-day missionary is quite another affair. He comes to a comfortable house—some of them have 3 or 4—built always in a fever-free district. He receives £300 a year and £12 for each kid. He travels free on the Burns Philp steamers, and receives all his goods free of freight.

Every one of them has a fast comfortable motor launch, which incidentally he is generally too lazy to use. He gets 6 months 'short leave' every two years and 12 months once in five years. In very many cases they add to their income by 'trading,' which, apart from other prejudices, is grossly unfair to the ordinary trader, who has to pay enormous freight on his goods. The missionaries receive every month large consignments of 'clothes for the poor heathen,' etc., from the busibodies at home. These are invariably sold for the benefit of the missionary's pocket. There is one very flagrant case here of a missionary trader (more flagrant than most) which has caused a certain amount of trouble lately. The missionary, ——, is the trade rival of a very worthy fellow named, say, Robinson. Mr. Robinson protested to the Presbyterian Synod till he was tired. Then he said : "All right, you compete against me. I'll return the compliment." So Mr. Robinson built an iron church and set up as a missionary and very soon emptied the rival tabernacle. Things got very lively, and Mr. Robinson was finally foolish enough to put a firestick in his rival's church, store, etc. For that he got six months' 'jug.'

Of course the missionaries wage bitter war against the French and the war is very heartily reciprocated. The two parties are not likely to come to a better understanding, for they cannot understand one another even if they wanted to. There is not a single missionary—and they call themselves educated men—here who can speak a word of French. Even the doctor in charge of the Mission Hospital

at Vila when he has occasion to consult with the
French Government doctor does so in Biche-la-mar.
You can imagine the ease with which one would
discuss in Biche-la-mar the fine points of an operation. The reverend sluggards profess to know the
particular native language of their districts (there
are over 30 totally distinct languages spoken in the
New Hebrides), but there is not one who can really
make himself understood even after 20 years of
' labour.' They spend their time translating the
Bible into native languages. One old cove has been
over 30 years translating the Epistle to the Ephesians
into the Nguna language, which is spoken by at
least 30 natives, all of whom will be dead long before
the work is published. That tells you something
about the intelligence of people who actually try
to translate the terms of Paulinism into a primitive
native tongue which has not even reached the stage
of having names for separate colours.

The Frères Maristes are infinitely wiser. In
their schools (like good Jesuits they don't even
pretend to make adult converts, they baptize the
children, seize them and educate them) the kids
are taught to read and write nothing but French.
The Catholic missionary lives a very different life
to his John Knoxian brother. He gets £30 a year
all told. He generally lives in a grass hut and feeds
on native food until he has made his plantation and
made it pay. They encourage the natives in all
their old customs, and have much more influence—
despite their poverty—with their flock than do the
Presbyterians. They are the only people here who
know anything about the folk-lore and old customs

of the natives. The Presbyterians dismiss everything of that sort as ' heathenish.' Consequently,
they have only succeeded after 40 years in grafting
a spurious, artificial Christianity on to a stock that
they know nothing about ; and the graft is naturally
a thing of very short life. The repetition by Kanakas
of Wee Free cant phrases is sometimes amusing,
sometimes not. In the herein-above-mentioned
island of —— (area about 300 acres) there are
three villages, one of which is Christian, the other
two stolidly refusing to accept ' the benefits.' The
inhabitants of the said islet come to the mainland of
—— to make their gardens and keep their pigs.
Their territory adjoins mine, and I am often annoyed
by the depredations of their beastly pigs. Not long
ago I rode over to hold a court about some such
damage. I found on the beach a crowd of youngsters,
mixed Christian and heathen, the heathen in shining
brown skin, the Christians in filthy shirts and
dungarees. As the heathen can't speak Biche-la-
mar I started to interrogate one of the Christian
kids as to whose pigs had been loose during the past
week. " Oh, he no pig b'long me feller. He pig
b'long —— " (here followed something I couldn't
locate as Biche-la-mar). I made the boy repeat
slowly what he had said. Then I understood " pig
belong those in darkness." Wasn't it lovely ?

26th May.

I SAW the absurdity of what I had proposed to
myself. I was going to be worse than a missionary. I was going to say to a quite primitive

savage : " You are fit mate and equal for complex twentieth century me." It would have been hopeless. Our conflicting ideas of how children should be reared and educated would have killed her, the weaker antagonist. The child could only loathe her or me. She, poor little soul, in her great faith in me, would have struggled on and died silently, longing for her savage life and for the kid that she had borne. It's true that plenty of ' white men ' here have lived happily for many years with Aoba women and have brought up half-caste kids. But, to begin with, the white men were the mental and physical inferiors of their brown wives and, to end with, their kids were unspeakable. That was no use to me as a comfort. I could never grow native.

You will surely understand my madness. I had longed so intensely for paternity that the gratification of my longing blinded me to all else. I forgot I was sentencing myself to burial—literal if not actual. Anyway, I have remembered in time. I don't quite see my way clear far ahead yet. The Topsy and Man Friday question I can solve by sending them back to Aoba. She will weep her heart out till the anchor's up and perhaps have wistful half regrets for even longer. There is a quite nice French half-caste who lives close to Topsy's passage. I shall arrange with him to take the pair into his ménage. Then if after a year or two Topsy forsakes the kid—as the Aoba women generally do—Monsieur Métis will adopt him and he will become a citoyen français. If Topsy sticks to him and he grows up to be a ' man Aoba,'

he will probably be much happier. I am afraid that
I have spoiled her, but the spoiling is less than
skin deep.

   ... I had occasion a short time ago to exchange
letters with a very official official in ——. For two
letters I did it properly, but the third was too much
for me. I just slipped in an ' Oh ' into the correct
end form which then read :

> " I am,
>   Oh Sir,
>   Your most obedient servant."

I don't suppose the addition was appreciated. The
gentleman with whom I was rash enough to jest
was originally a Tommy—in the very old days
when they were pariahs. Now he is all kinds of
high officials rolled into one. He was much offended
a short time ago by a drunken old ex man-of-wars-
man beachcomber who was arraigned before him
for a breach of regulations.

   " Now what have you got to say this time,
Bill ? "

   " Wot I've got to say, ex-private ——, is this :
one day you was cold in London and 'adn't no
customers, so yer sold yer blackin' brushes and
joined the Ormy."

That is literal truth. Bill got a month, but I
fancy he enjoyed it. I don't suppose my " Oh "
redundant hurt Mr. Official a bit. He probably
ascribed it to my innerance.

   ... Once away, glamour is sure to raise its
deceiving and malicious head. " There's no times
like the old times," and " Ah, you should have

sailed in my last ship, mates. She was something
like," will most certainly be my epistle and gospel
before I have been long out of the islands. I believe
that poets and others have enlarged upon this
peculiarity of humans. It's curious what acute
powers of observation these artists have.

Later.

Ashby took it into his head—may it foster lice—
to ride over because he thought I might be lonely.
He has just gone, but the day is ruined. Yes :
that little girl got better. But three weeks ago I
had to repeat the ride, the sending to Mosquito
Bay for the launch, and so on for her twin. Unfortunately the result was not the same. The poor
little kid died on the launch half-way to Vila. I
knew what had happened when I saw the boat
coming into sight just about sunset. I rode over
to —— and got there just afterwards. The poor
mother was absolutely done for. I had to do everything (no need to insist on what that implies). I
got the coffin made and nailed the poor little chap
up and then buried him about midnight. It was
more ghastly than I can tell you. I was really
awfully fond of the kid, because I love all little boy
children, and this little nipper was the only baby
in all my life here. Then I had to stay on and nurse
the mother, and, finally, to break the news to the
father. I don't think I should say anything about
that if I wanted to persuade people to come to the
islands. Of course to our war-hardened veterans
the occurrence would rank with the catching of a

rat, but I had never laid out a four-year-old kiddie before, or made a coffin, or read the Burial Service at midnight before. I don't think I should make a good soldier.

Just fancy what would have been the plight of that poor woman if I had chanced to be away even for the week-end. She would never have allowed anybody but me to do what I did; and I write it down as something to the credit of Providence that I was there to do it. It's the last job of the sort that I want, though.

June 2nd.

THE trade wind season began yesterday—about a month late. For two days I haven't sweated. For two nights I have slept wrapped up in nice thick blankets. The sea is gloriously blue. Topsy and Man Friday suit the colour scheme to perfection. And I hate you for taking me away from all this back to your grubby, grimy, sordid land of 'Défense, forbidden, verboten.' How nicely those words sum up the situation.

June 11th.

BY last mail I sent you pages of gush about my brown baby and drew you a touching picture of him accompanying me round the world. Well, he is not going to do anything of the sort. You can see for yourself from his photograph that he is a sweet little baby, jolly and amusing as a baby could well be, and it is true that I love babies. And it is

true that I would give the hell of a lot to have one
of my own, a man baby to bring up. But—but—
I do know that this one won't do. And the sooner
I get rid of him the better. It is not that I am afraid
of growing too fond of him. Au contraire—you
understand. I told you at the end of my last letter
that I had been out recruiting. The captain of the
launch was a half-caste, good-looking, well educated
(in the Australian manner), intelligent; probably
a dam sight better man than I in most ways. I
studied him carefully. I said to myself " That is
your son, my boy. Go and touch his bare neck
and see whether you shudder." You follow? So
I withdraw and apologise for that ' insular ignorance '—or whatever the phrase was. I have been
fighting hard to convince myself that I had no
' colour prejudices,' but I chuck up now. You see,
qua baby and my baby I have been and am fonder
of that little brat than I could express to you in
English. Surely then it is wise and surely righteous
for me to let it rest at that, both for his sake and
mine. Mind you, I am going on enthusing about
him and enjoying thoroughly both him and my
pictures of him. In years to come you and I will be
very sentimental about him. . . .

. . . The affair of finding a home for Topsy and
the offspring is close on settled. I think I told you
that I knew a very worthy French métis who is
married to a ditto; they are a very respectable
though childless couple and are exceedingly keen
on adopting my Bilbil. The man is wealthy and has
a nice plantation to bequeathe; so Bilbil will be
much better off than if I had stuck to him. Mme.

Métis iş an old bosom pal of Topsy's; thus the arrangement is really excellent. I feel a most awful cad over the whole business. I know the feeling is silly, mais que veux-tu? The kid is not old enough to care a damn either way. I am sure that Topsy will really be infinitely relieved at being free again. And yet I feel a cad. And yet I should be a bigger cad to stick to them. Then I should make both of them and myself very unhappy for a very long time, until finally I did something desperate. I should only have pandered to my own mistaken desire for respectable self-satisfaction—a hideously selfish form of unselfishness. No; I made a horrid mistake in ever making that kid; but the only real way out is to end the whole business before it goes any further.

. . . Then I can begin to look round for a way of escape from these islands. I don't see at present what I am to do. I fear it will mean Australia for a bit at any rate. But I am a pretty good hand at getting about, and once I am on the road again, I shall be able to get steering way on. At present I am only drifting.

There are enemy craft again between here and Sydney, including sea-planes which many very frightened natives have seen even in these islands. Jap warships are all about and escort our mail steamer. Incidentally they have surveyed every harbour and anchorage in the group, so paving a nice little way for the Yellow Peril, I suppose. The only beer I could find in Sydney was Japanese. What further need have we of witnesses when the yellow man makes beer for so-called Britons? I received a few weeks ago a request from the local secretary to join the Overseas Club. I have taken some care in the composition of my reply. It had to be translated into the vulgar tongue (O——n), but I think it has lost very little in the translation.

August 26th, 1917.

. . .

I FANCY that personally I should, in preference to collecting old furniture, like to spend my time and wealth in encouraging the making of good new furniture. There is so much lovely wood in the world and there are still handicraftsmen even in these days of LABOR. Here in these islands there is timber that makes one's mouth water. One in particular—I call it black rosewood for want of a better name—I am sure will defy centuries and even white ants. When skilfully polished (in the native manner) it is very lovely. The boat-builder at Mosquito Bay, although an O——n, is a man who loves making nice things. Between 8 a.m. and 5 p.m. he is a zealous Unionist, but after work hours he seems possessed with the spirit of some old carver of stalls and fairly gloats over his cunning hand. I saw a dresser that he made from the afore-said black wood the other day. It would not have shamed an ancient monastery. To my vulgar mind such a piece (its lines copied if you like from some good model) would be more satisfying in modern Łondon than a harshly transplanted thing of old oak.

I agree with you about O——ns, in so far as I

know them. In prosperity they are apt to be insufferable, but they are dam good friends. You see even the oldest O——n families have not forgotten their settler days when every man helped his neighbour as a matter of course. They are like that here, as I have occasionally pointed out to you. They would really and truly be bitterly offended if you were in trouble and did not call on them for help. One has to get away from the hub of the universe nowadays in order to find examples of the primitive Christian virtues. For a' that, I can't help liking my guinea to be stamped in a pleasing ornamental fashion, even if the stamping does necessitate the introduction of a little base metal. I suppose that is because I am a snob and degenerate.

I still like my café-au-lait baby ; in fact, I like it enormously. I like all babies ; but he is the jolliest, most contented prodigy of fat strength that I have ever struck. I wish to God he were pur sang. . . . At three months old he had two teeth and could sit up unsupported—which, I believe, is unusual. You must certainly think me an old fool. Je m'en fiche—I am an old fool ; but I am experiencing keener delights than I have ever known in my life. Also I am being a little bit unusual and am distinctly ' misunderstood.' Should I not, therefore, be completely happy ? Sometimes I have the ordinary futile longing for the soul mate, for the wife who could be all in all to me (and probably ditto to some other man while I was away at work), for the life intellectual à deux. More often now I understand that I am better off with my nut-brown savage who, two minutes after a storm of

tears because she thought her baby was dying
(when he was merely flatulent through his own
greediness), was choking with laughter over " Simon
says thumbs up," " Allez, go on. Again. Me want
win 'im you." She will play for hours at these
nursery games. Do you remember playing ' pat-a-
cake ' with your nurse ? Topsy loves it. Many a
time when I have been aching for sleep she has
kept me up with " 'e no time 'long sleep yet. Allez,
you me two."

Thank heaven I can still howl with laughter and
forget my age and pomposity upon suitable
occasions. I trust that I shall never develop a sense
of the fitness of things. One is always fit to be a
fool, no matter what young fools may think.

November 2 5th, 1917.

I HAD a short letter from you by last mail. You
told me of ——'s narrow escape from being
shelled on a bus. Words fail me when I think of
these abominations. Man is vile without a doubt.
The familiarity with the neighbourhood of the
occurrence brought the affair very vividly to my
mind. So stirred was I from my usual disgusted
boredom that I opened my packets of ' Times
Weekly ' to see if I could find further lurid details.
While hunting for the report my eye was caught
by the word dysentery. As that is a subject in
which I am presently and painfully interested I
read on idly. What I read was the evidence of the
medical witnesses as to the arrival of two lighters

full of dysenteric patients from the campaign in Mesopotamia. It was a pleasant story. The Germans for not being entirely prepared for the reception of hundreds of thousands of quite unexpected prisoners, are called all the vile things that press-scribblers and politicians can invent. The English show criminal folly and wicked laziness and ignorance in making preparations for a tiny affair, so that their own people suffer ten thousand times worse hell than any German ever conceived.

There is a foul epidemic of dysentery happening on this plantation just at present, and I am nurse-doctor day and night to the loathsome wretches. You ought to try a bad attack of dysentery when you are isolated amongst savages just to let you know to what depths an habitually clean white man can sink. I have had it twice badly in the Islands, to say nothing of several minor attacks, recurrences and so on. I am taking no risks this time. Fortunately I had laid in a stock of disinfectants. Oh, those poor beasts in Mesopotamia. What I feel most is being separated from Topsy and Friday. I daren't go near them for fear of carrying infection. Shall I ever get back to a clean, cool, healthy life.

. . . Every little tuppenny thinker imagines that he is a prophet; and every little ha'penny newspaper makes therefrom its profit. It makes one wish for the appearance of Elijah, were one not certain that London would be immediately placarded with

> 'Moving Movie Drama at Brook Chereth
> —Baal beaten—Front Seats 2s.
> Bring your best Gurl.'

Having viewed these last three years of Europe from a leisurely remoteness, I must say that I prefer Cathay. That is the fact of it. It is hard to express in words, but I am possessed with a loathing for civilisation and its humbugs and mockeries. Here I have practically no contact at all with the sham. Here I have what elemental man needs, a woman (who is not a lady), a man-child (who has doubtless got enough of his father in him to make an interesting subject for experiment, and most certainly has not inherited any love of convention), food, shelter, earth to be buried in. Do I want anything more ? Yes, I do. I want friendship—with my intellectual equal.

... What does it matter that my son is only a half-caste ? As long as he stays in the islands that would never be thrown in his face. I flatter myself that I can train him physically and mentally so that as a man he will be a dam sight better than his father. At any rate he won't be a Complete Gentleman. You know quite well that I have been itching for a real child to train up entirely on my own plan. Now I have got it. Naturally Topsy won't interfere. I am her god and her heaven and her earth. From her he will inherit bouncing health, a corrective to my ungainly form, a love of mirth and an entire ignorance of ' what is done.' That's very satisfactory.

I am a crank. I know it. I have now got in my hand most of the elements for an unordinary life— a little savage mate, a fat baby, the ' Island life ' where I can't starve or want, a cynical pleasure in flaunting before all the respectable Kerlonials, tastes and fancies which I hope to transmit to my heir, an opportunity for determining that at least one child shall not grow up in damnable ignorance of nature, shall not from babyhood be loaded with the barnacles of convention. All that interests me enormously. A return to Philistia does not. I have got an unique chance now. If I were to throw it away I should deserve whatever might befall me—even an usher's job at —— or the necessity of writing vulgar things in a vulgar paper for vulgar people.

If I could come to Europe, pick my woman and be free and independent to raise my kids in my own way, there would be something over which to hesitate. I realise the risk in experimenting on a métis. But the alternative is denied me. What woman—except such an one as I should loathe—would marry me, middle-aged, penniless, bald, ugly and cranky? I have not got—and I thank my own god for it—one feature that would redeem me in the eyes of such a bourgeoise as I could marry. Fancy me being even as respectable as you. . . .

I have had the seed of vagabondage buried in me for very many years. It has germinated now and I am proud of the plant. One of my unknown ancestors must have been a tramp. It is possible that many of them were. Don't imagine that I am a crank of the nut-chewing, sandal-wearing variety. If I were, I should come home and live at ' Hygeia,' Golders Green, or somewhere like that. No; the flat-chested, Garden Suburb girl does not appeal to me; neither does what she stands for. That is as effete and beastly as old oak in a modern jerry-built tenement. I don't despise flesh-pots, but I hate the kitchens of civilisation.

December 23rd, 1917.

I AM still busy physicking—and burying— Kanakas. I am still enormously fond of my fat baby. For the rest, this is the season of prickly heat, dhobie's itch and other delights. I am having my full share of them all. I cannot, however, expect you to be vastly interested. After all, altruism should remain quietly with charity and look after the ' alter ego.' Neither of the virtues would probably notice the trivial substitution of ' ipsissimus ' for ' alter.'

The missionary ship is at present anchored at Mosquito Bay and is beating the adjacent Islands for a huge Christmas Day meeting for intercession. Shouldn't I love to go ? Think of the hard cases, shell-backs, beachcombers, grog-sellers and other varieties of the New Hebridean whitish population meeting to pray at Mosquito Bay. For they'll all come. They are of the class that loves meeting even for prayer. And the praying can't last very long. And there is sure to be free beer in the store when once the manofgod has got safely back on board.

December 30th, 1917.

YOU say that you have got anarchy. So have I. The etiology of our complaints is, however, not the same. I contracted mine through a taste of freedom, you yours through a taste of slavery.

The resultant manifestations are very similar. It is not law and order to which I so much object as interference. I must be perfectly free to be good or bad, as long as I don't interfere with my neighbour's goodness or badness. The thought of the militarism that reigns surpreme now and the Socialism that will be the inevitable sequel in England makes me rave, see red and become a conscientious objector to allowing any bureaucrat to remain alive. That is, more than anything, what attracts me in the islands. We have laws, Conventions and Kings Regulations here, but, very fortunately, the executive is, and must always be practically absent. I couldn't commit many violent murders here without being brought to book. I could commit a very large number of quiet poisonings without anyone being the wiser. Up to the present I have felt no such sporting desires. But I can do hundreds of things that you can't. I am free from a thousand shackles which you obediently and all unconsciously wear and which chafe you. That is what I mean when I say that I have my woman, my child and my daily bread. My own individual existence is bound to be less hampered here than in, say, London. Why should it necessarily be brutish because it is not British ? I look upon the woman and the daily bread as necessary incidents and no more. Topsy is far less of a bore to me than would be a white woman. She does not expect ' attentions,' and would not understand them if she got 'em. The thought of the upbringing of the child in my own free way pleases me tremendously. As you suggest, the colour question does loom, but not quite in the way that it used. One loses through experience the petty prejudices born of generations of insular ignorance. My fear is due to my ignorance of what really composes Friday's distaff half. I know little enough of my own congenital gifts ; naturally, I know still less of Topsy's. Of some things, however, I am certain. From his ma Friday will not have inherited snobism, gluttony, Christianity or any other of the sweet legacies to which we are victims. At present he shows rather frightening precocity both of mind and body. The clay is very promising. I am itching to have it on the wheel.

If I could select my white woman, guaranteed free from affectation, spite, femininism and vulgarity, I should prefer to breed a pur sang. I couldn't ever hope to make such a selection, therefore I prefer the métis that chance has given me. In the Islands no distinction is made between half-castes and pure white. The President of the Conseil Générale of New Caledonia is a half-caste. In that way Frenchmen are true to their national motto. It is only the man that counts ; and if he has the makings of a good bureaucrate in him, a half-caste can succeed as well as another.

An Australian aboriginal half-caste came here about three years ago and tried to start a Union among the Kanakas. He met with no success whatsoever. The Kanaka is above all things an individualist. " Me fellow wanta work. S'pose Jack 'e no wanta work, all right ; 'im 'e business b'long Jack." The gentleman retired to the more congenial atmosphere of Norfolk Island.

If I had known one-hundredth part of what I

know now, I should never have come near the islands.
Wherein, doubtless, I should have been the loser
in many ways. But I was single and unattached.
I came here more or less by chance and couldn't
get away. Obviously I had to make the best of a
bad job. Of course with means, even modest ones,
a long stay in the Pacific à la Stevenson might well
be delightful. It need cost very little too. But
you couldn't do even that in the New Hebrides.
The only possible way here would be to adopt my
plan and charter a small vessel and cruise lazily
around. Then when you got tired of the sea, you
could beat back to New Caledonia and wait for a
vessel for Tahiti and the Marquesas. Before the
war there were vessels doing the round trip every
month, either largish trading steamers or else
' auxiliary schooners.' Doubtless they will begin
again some day. On such boats you would avoid
the tripper element altogether and even the Sydney
bagman. You wouldn't get ice, but the ' tucker '
would be good and the accommodation clean even
if somewhat scented with copra and sandalwood.
I can't speak for other groups, but I have met
several wandering scientists and such-like folk
here and in New Caledonia whose living and
travelling cost them nothing. Every solitary white
man is only too delighted to have a guest for absurdly
long visits. When the guest is tired or tiresome,
the host passes him on either on horseback or by
sea to the next reasonable place. ' Island hospitality ' is notorious and much lauded—which is
absurd. You might as well canonise a thirsty man
for drinking.

——, headmaster of one of the prep. schools where I ushered once, asked me if I would mind telling my mother to write to me on rather better note-paper (she was very poor just then) because ' the boys notice these things.' I, like the cad I was, didn't smash his ugly mug. I remember one of the ' awfully nice ' boys asking me whether Turner (him of the paint-pot) was ' a gentleman.' Poor little chap ; he wasn't to blame. —— had the pedigrees and stud-books of the country by heart, and rolled the word ' aristocratical ' round his bearded old chops like a dog eating buttered muffins. The school was small but very select. There was only one boy who was not quite ' nice.' He was the son of a rich manufacturer and had at home con-tracted a huge friendship with the son of the 69th Baronet, the local squire. There was no parting the two lads ; so —— (doubtless for double fees) sank his aristocratical scruples and admitted the plebeian. The boy was a fine kid, the life of the school sort-of-thing, but —— never spoke about him to me without prefixing the adjective ' poor ' to his name. When any parents came, the boy was carefully warned not to mention the paternal shame of boots. He eventually went to Eton which, I I presume, saved him. . . .

I wish I could have you here with me for a few months. Even with what you could see from the plantation as a centre you would get enough for a year's writing. I would guarantee to keep you free from malaria if you came in May and went away at the end of October. I have got this place so cleared now that it is only in the bad season that the

Anopheles mosquito appears. In the wet season the water lies thick everywhere and one can't stop the brutes from breeding. I would have a small cutter à la houseboat moored just inside the reef and, to make assurance surer, you and I would sleep on that. It would be too hellish hot there in the day-time, but the Anopheles only appears after dark, like the lurking swine that she is. Just think of a full tropical moon, the water like glass, and admitting a view into its depths for all the world like one of those kaleidoscopes of our childhood ; every now and then a fish leaping out of the still blue and its splash echoing all round ; on shore a few natives monotonously chanting Lilió-liliou-lilió, while one one of them beats very quietly but very rhythmi-cally and insistently on a hollow bamboo ; on the reef coconut-leaf torches flashing as the nightbird natives fish : Topsy exclaiming : " Me wanta swim now," throwing off her dress and diving in one motion, her brown body looking black in the silvery coral depths ; you and I too lazy to follow her example, pelt her with pieces of biscuit and cry " Sark 'e come " to make her struggle back on board and yell with laughter at our ' gammon.'

Turn it over in your mind and see whether the prose to be amassed outweighs the cons.

I have recently had as labour some real bushmen from Santo, naked and unashamed. They were refugees from a big cannibal raid who had escaped to the sea and on to the first recruiting ship that turned up. They can't talk a word of Biche-la-mar, and I conversed with them in signs. The other day when visiting them—the poor brutes have all gone down with dysentery—I found in their hut a perfectly made Pan's pipes. I know most native instruments, but had never seen this. I held it up and looked interrogation. One old chap got up smiling and began to play it and danced their stampado—and if he didn't look like a satyr, I've never been to the British Museum. One other curious little point. I noticed that when I was medicining them a man invariably shifted his position so that I was at his right hand. Sometimes this irked me and I tried in vain to shift him. My boss-boy, a very superior fellow, told me that in heathenish Santo anything that comes to you from the left-hand side is ' no good too much '—sinister in fact. A bit odd, isn't it ?

In a way I am extraordinarily fond of my petit métis, and I can't help doing everything possible to ensure for him at least a decent start in life. If I weren't such a damned sentimental fool the problem would be easier of solution. But I am not—and never was—a light libertine. . . . Now that I have got a delightfully amusing little savage woman and —what I wanted most in all the world—a baby, bone of my bone (one can't help that, spite of virtuous cynicism), the problem is horrid. Living here in this happy-go-lucky way it is almost impossible to realise that ' it won't do.' And even in my thoughtfullest moments—' not guilty ' to your accusations. I don't suppose you've passed so many sleepless nights in your life as I have done during the last year. I can't make up my mind that you are right. Is it not possible that I have, more or less, found the right ?

Is the complicated rule-life of civilisation man's highest and best expression ? If so, what about its culmination, this war and Prussianism ? To what is the modern world tending ? To state Socialism, to compulsory Ruskinism, to absolute loss of freedom and simplicity, to the very antithesis of nature. That bogey is to me more loathsome than the foul fiend of Prussianism. It is more subtle, more beastly ; but the result is much the same. It is no use saying that such social tendencies will not affect you. They will ; and you cannot help it except by fleeing to the uttermost parts of the earth. And I am sure that there will be no spot in Europe where you will be allowed to play the gentle Arcadian. If you really and honestly want to cast your chains and avoid those that will presently be loaded upon you, you must make up your mind to come out here (= Pacific Ocean) immediately the war ends. I can't believe that you are au fond in earnest. That is why I slightly jeered at you in the earlier part of this letter. If you aren't in earnest the thing isn't worth discussing. If you are in earnest, I am with you to the last ounce of my capacity and experience. But I can't believe it. Think of the promise. With a little bit of capital and a tiny income one would have no need to be a planter. There is no money in planting either. One could easily combine a lucrative occupation (*e.g.* pearl shelling, trocas shelling, trading, etc.) with a not too strenuous life. Thus you would have nearly the livelong day in which to write.

My mind still turns to the Cook Islands and to an islet in the Aitutaki Lagoon in particular. These islands are gloriously healthy and although populated by New Zealanders (million times better than Australians), there are so few of them that one could be as isolated as one wished. Moreover, Muller tells me that they are excellent from an island trade point of view. Scenically they are, I believe, a first rate article. But what rot I am talking. Fancy you at your time of life (do you remember Herbert Campbell ?). Fancy your position, tradition and estates [1] being thrown into the pot to make a life. Fancy H. not having the educational advantages which his ancestors had. Fancy his not having the chance to wear a pink, yellow and majenta cap and know cricketer's initials. Fancy too his missing the chance of being inscribed in the State register as ' XP 43218, bred by A. G. 9172 out of V. L. 92365. Previous education—nil. Home influence—unsatisfactory. . . . Male parent twice convicted of eating mustard with bacon, breach of reg. Lp. 4271 (nourishment). Female parent convicted of breach of JGr 114 (hygiene female), offence aggravated by her declaring that she would ' see the commonweal in hell before she would wear flannel nightgowns.' Mem. child to be removed and attached to State institution B.R.Y. 69 to be trained as hairdresser. . . ."

Yes ; fancy—idle fancy. But you told me to make a plan and I've made it.

Life in the Pacific (barring the absence of disease and cannibals) is pretty much the same everywhere. And, mind you, I talk with people who know, not

---

[1] I don't understand this word. It must be Biche-le-mar for something wholly reprehensible.—ED.

with journalists and novelists. I spent a month
surveying with a man who was for many years in
Raratonga and afterwards in Tonga Tabu, whence
he eloped with a Tongan princess. He is a planter
here now and has as fine a family of half-caste sons
as you would wish to see. The Tongans are magni-
ficent-looking people, and their manners are highly
superior to most Britishers—' quite nice,' in fact.
It is in that respect that the Aobese (Topsy's people)
are so different to the other New Hebrideans. Of
course their code is not the same as ours, but they
are very strict. I used to be annoyed at the way
Topsy received gifts, I looking for the " Oh, thank
you *so* much, darling ; where did you manage, etc."
That was my ignorance. Gifts should be presented
in the most utterly careless manner and received
with the most stately indifference. It is only the
vulgar, ill-bred, missionarisés who deviate from this
rule. The inner meaning of the manner is that
friendship ought to be quite independent of gifts.
And gifts must be returned strictly ad valorem. I
have known Topsy, when some of her pals were
going home after completing their engagements,
use one dollar for ' Goodbye-shake-hands ' for at
least half a dozen friends. She presents the dollar,
and ten minutes later the recipient returns it. Its
journey then re-begins. When you think that these
women earn 10s. a month, and that the thieving
traders rook them 10s. for a trade print dress (cost
price about 1s. 6d.), you can see that a dollar is
' some gift.' It is only the very dignified Aobese
who would risk the chance of the dollar not coming
back.

Oh Lord, these child-women do make me laugh —and they do laugh themselves. I have got eight women attached to my household now, and I often have to go out and smack 'em all round to stop their row. I found 'em the other day all holding down the oldest (aged about 125), and forcibly feeding her out of Friday's feeding bottle. " 'Im 'e all same Friday. 'Im 'e no got tooth " was Topsy's excuse for the row.

1918

MAN FRIDAY'S record at seven months = 12 kilos (26½ lbs.) and eight teeth. Oh these fond fathers !

DON'T you realise yet that for months on end I don't see a white man and, even when I do, it's only a little Sydney cockney who glibs about ' cheap lines ' and ' how much they stood him in ' ? Don't you see that even my mind gets stocked with cartridges ? Where shall I fire them ? At my Sydney cockney ? And it is so with lots of the charges that I bring against you. The charges must be brought against someone who understands their nature. Only this morning while drinking my 5 o'clock a.m. tea I prepared two more darts which by hook or crook would have been shot at you in my next letter if you hadn't. . . .

There is no need for me to repeat that I am torn asunder. You know all about that and the opposing forces. But it isn't Topsy. I have tried to convey to you that our parting would be but the sweet sorrow of an hour or so. No ; I can fix Topsy to our mutual satisfaction and—I confess it—to my

real relief.   Topsy at the plantation is just the thing.
Topsy elsewhere would be miserable and quite unsatisfied.   But I am not going to part with Man
Friday.   (By the way he has been rebaptised.   He
is now Bilbil the Bulbul for obvious reasons.)   I
could not possibly bring Topsy to England.   It
would be murder.   There is, however, no earthly
reason why I shouldn't bring Friday.   He is going
to have a beak like mine.   He has got long, very
silky black hair without the suspicion of a kink and
he will be by some inexplicable freak of nature a
rather extraordinarily pretty child.   It only shows
what cross-breeding will do sometimes.   I have got
an old mare here—part Clydesdale—who throws
colts like herself with bumpy legs and big heads, but
her fillies are for all the world like thoroughbred
racers.

But let me rave a little about Bilbil the Bulbul.
It will do me good and will lead to the desired end.
He has slowed down in physical development and
has turned his attention to mental functions which,
unless all that the psychology books say is utter rot,
are little short of phenomenal for his age.   Little
wonder then that I don't want to part with him.
The poor little mite caught the prevailing plague
of dysentery a month ago, and I have had to fight
like hell day and night to save his life.   You may
have gathered from Mesopotamian disclosures what
a foul thing dysentery is in the tropics.   And
imagine a ten-month-old baby with it and a savage
mother to tend him.   Poor Topsy has behaved like
a brick, but the utter incapability of these women
is beyond imagination.   She could only sit on the

floor and howl while I was irrigating the poor little man's colon. Of course it was horrid agony for the poor mite, but it saved his life even if it nearly killed me. He is practically fit again now, though I still have to weigh, measure and sterilise all his meals. I started to make a coffin for him one night when I thought he couldn't possibly last till morning. I shall keep the pieces of wood till he is old enough to laugh about them. That's a touch of 'island life.' One has to be doctor, nurse, undertaker, sexton and parson to one's own babies.

Dysentery is a loathsome thing. You would scarcely believe the rate at which emaciation takes place. In three days the poor little chap's skin was literally hanging in folds on him, and one had to be awfully careful that he did not get ghastly sores. He has picked up nearly as quickly and is now actually getting firm again. I killed fowls and concentrated 'em to the last possible. It was a good job that there was no Food Controller in the islands. Now he is lapping down his milk and rice water as many times a day as I will let him. He sits on the table and takes a most solemn interest in the preparation of his kaikai and then arranges himself on my knee in the most approved 'feeding position.' I believe Topsy is really glad to hand over all this business to me, but the result is that he cares no more for her than for any other of his women and won't leave me for any of them. He has the temper and cunning of a ten-year-old fiend, but I have him as much under control as ever 'sportsman' had spaniel—a bit of the proverbial treatment too.

Topsy, of course, succumbed to his imperious will

before he was three months old. " 'Im 'e no want 'im " is quite sufficient explanation for her. Well, that is quite enough fond doting for the present. Mille excuses. But you see what it all leads to. I'm going to bring that kid up for better or worse. Here it will be for worse, because I couldn't take him away from his ma and he will soon be beginning to talk chi-chi and Biche-la-mar. Of course, he is too young to travel yet. . . . I don't see my way at all for the present, but must do the Micawber act. Something may. One thing I am quite decided upon (don't laugh) : I am not going to rot in the South Seas for good. The schemes and plans that I made for so doing were pleasant in the making. They will be charming some day in retrospect. Let them rest at that.

It has been the worst hot season that I have known. Prickly heat came upon me early in November—and prickly heat is a sore trial to even the most placid tempered. I have also had my worst dose of dhobie's itch. You can't imagine how nice that is. It is a fungoid eruption that itches like very hell, finally bleeding and suppurating. When in addition to heat, mildew everywhere—even on one's pillow—flies and mosquitoes, you add that for just on four months I have been treating dysentery amongst my Kanakas and finally my baby, it is a wonder that I have any temper left at all. If Fate and the war will that I must pass another hot season here, just remember that between November and April neither mind nor body is sane. Thank the Lord it is nearly over for this year. In another month the trade winds ought to begin.

But this is all jolly fine. I am hovering round what will have to be the main topic of this letter, because I rather funk the effort involved. About the ' super-normal ' then. Let me make two preliminary statements. (1) I hate philosophical jargon and the habit of imagining that words are turned into portmanteaux by spelling them with initial capital letters. No two ' schools ' agree about terminology, as far as I can see. On looking up the meaning of some word—*e.g.* transcendental, subjective, etc.—one finds that Kant uses it in one sense, Bergson in another sense, William James in another, and not one of them with any sense at all. I am convinced that I have neither brain nor stomach for philosophy. Metaphysics only convince me that there are idiots infinitely nimbler and more ingenious than I, and that with all their jarring disputes and profound jargon they have discovered absolutely nothing and have even done a vast amount towards obscuring the real issues.

(2) You ask for evidence without deduction therefrom. Where is such a thing to be found on such a subject ? Even a really scientific man like Crooks can't keep himself sane. One and all remind me of a Houndsditch Jew trying to discuss dispassionately the merits of a pair of second-hand trousers that he wishes to sell you. Sooner or later the raptures will come out. . . . I haven't got the infinite presumption to hope to succeed where Aristotle and Co. so conspicuously failed. The spook hunters will most certainly not find a way. They start convinced and find conviction in the silliest forms. There is also simple faith and the

'becoming as little children'; but that's not for me. Such an attitude when natural is as delightful as a baby's flaxen curls ; when forced it is as absurd as a cheap peroxide bleach.

No ; my quest is very modest. I simply want to keep myself au courant of the work that is being done in really sound experimental psychology. At the same time I can read plain statements of well-authenticated facts which tend to show that there is considerably more in heaven and earth than even P. Q. R. pretends to know. I do not for one moment assume that even when the problem of mundane man's brain and personality is finally solved, we shall be much nearer to the answer to the riddle of the Cosmos. But ' poco a poco va lejos '; and you can't deny that even our small problem is of interest. I don't deny that at one time I was very credulous. I swallowed all the 'Raymond' stuff and considered that I knew all that there was to know. I was very young then. Later on I fell in with a man who, though deeply interested in spooks, was a disciple and correspondent of Podmore. That put me on the right track. Very much later—in Montevideo—I came into contact with a quite modern psychologist in the person of one A. B. He was a hidebound materialist, but an experimenter of prodigious skill. He also had a very complete library which he placed at my disposal. I owe him many thanks.

Switch off here for a bit.

Topsy has just been in for a talk and has told me—to my horror—. . . . You would say, " We are in the family way again." It is abominable. Topsy will have to go back to Aoba to have that child au naturel and leave Bilbil with me.   One small métis may be ' mets delicieux,' but two would be a surfeit, an orgy, an impossibility, an Oxford breakfast. Bilbil the Bulbul is making frantic grabs at my pen, which disconcerts me. . . .

Just think of the ' free ' people, the people who love to exhibit their nakedness. Go for a dam good ride in the open country—and then think about them.   I am earnest enough in my detestation of harmful conventions ; I am not even very tolerant of the harmless unnecessary sort ; but conventions which are based on nature, necessary conventions, should be maintained most vigorously in these latter days.   I am afraid that I should be a most hopeless person in England just now.   In many ways I am a rank rebel ; and yet I hate the lengths to which most rebels wish to go—to say nothing of the rebels themselves.   I rather fancy that my real attitude is that of the (possibly fabulous) old-time yeoman who had no objection at all to being tyrannised by ' the gentry.'   As far as ruling goes, I am all in favour of a benevolent tyranny ; but I refuse to be governed by the mob and urged on by Harmsworth Bros.   But that will lead me into violent and forbidden thoughts.

June 11th, 1918.

. . .

YOUR letter was short and exceedingly unsatisfactory.   It acknowledged—with a bareness that amounted to indecency—two short letters and one long one from me.   It told me of an

eatanswill that you had done at the Café Royal.
Things like that do tempt me, so it is no use my
pretending to make a little virtue of my great
necessity. It was the fried salmon and the claret
upon which I hogged in imagination, plus the talk,
plus the beautiful lightness of head that one can only
enjoy—or permit to one's self—when feeding in
pubs. The first stage of the drunkenness that comes
from savoury food and good wine is, I believe,
almost religious. The crying pity is that the stage
is fleeting. . . .

. . . You see, the English polloi are in much
worse case than down-trodden moujiks and Prussian-
ised Germans. They have not only been exploited
quite as badly as their continental brethren ; they
have been grossly jested with as well. The huge
practical joke of ' Popular Government ' has been
played off on them as it has never been played
anywhere else, and, when once a Britisher realises
that he has been a simple fool and a laughing-stock,
he gets really angry. Of course, some super adroit
shuffler may manage to keep up the illusion a little
longer, but I fancy not. And when the mess once
begins, there will be some fun. Russia will be a
lotos land to which one will escape for calm,
Ireland a New Jerusalem. No; the really out-of-
the-way places will be the only possible ones for
living. The New Hebrides will be good enough.
It is highly probable that there will be fighting
about these islands, but not in them. There is not
a ten million to one chance of native trouble here
either. The good God has seen to that by giving
every little community a separate language, so that

each island is a Babel to itself and to all other islands. In some islands the natives are still truculent and cannibalistic, but—like the earnest, modern missionary, one avoids those islands. Australia will most certainly flame up before very long.

June 17th, 1918.

SO there I was with a Handbook of Obstetrics, howling directions to Topsy in Biche-la-mar, cursing the attendant midwives who wanted to kill the child, and generally enjoying myself. I fancy that I am in for another merry job about January 31st. I simply can't kick the poor little girl out for her ' trouble.' She places such implicit trust in me that it would be blackguardly to forsake her. If it were an ordinary sized native brat that she had to bear, things would doubtless pass off in the native fashion—work till sunset, bear the child at night, and up again next morning. But my colts— judging from Bilbil—are past all bearing. I hope, though, that this one will be a filly. Then Topsy shall have it all to her little self which she longs for. Bilbil, of course, is my child, not Topsy's. Topsy is quite resigned.

" Fashion b'long me feller, papa 'e look out piccaninny where 'e man, piccaninny where 'e woman 'e b'long mamma "—though papa snares the lion's share of the price paid for the prospective wife on the day following her birth.

Bilbil continues to progress in a very satisfactory fashion. He has now about six words to his vocabulary. One is 'toto,' which implies every-thing creepy, nasty, naughty or forbidden. Daddy's theodolite is toto, all insects are toto. One touch he has which pleases me muchly. If he knocks any portion of his anatomy against anything hard, he seeks me out to have the part kissed—it's usually his bum. But before seeking consolation he invariably hits the offending hard object a shrewd blow with his clenched fist. That means another kiss, but I like to see the determination to get his own back. He is very interested at present in his navel. He exhibits it to all and sundry, pointing it out with a tiny finger and ejaculating " Sammy." That is the name of his cat. He loves to ride with me and even backs a horse alone if I lead it. When one remembers that he is 17 months old, he strikes me as not too bad. Yes ; I wish with you that he was pure white. But it can't be helped now. I have never deserved a white baby. I did deserve this one ; and I am going to do my damndest to help him overcome the possible handicap of his mixed breed.

. . . I don't suggest that in these hard times you should buy the books which I have asked you to send me. You can borrow them from someone you don't know very well, or steal them from a railway bookstall if such things exist now. I daresay I could get them from Sid-nee, but an ordinary novel costs 10s. in the shops there, and at least 15s. by the time it reaches me. I hate encouraging robbery of that kind. Fancy taxing imported books. Is it to support home industry ?

July 10*th*, 1918.

IT is the spring of the year with us, just the short season when this climate is really delightful, and one reacts to it even here. There is nothing of the classical stereotyped spring about it, but the trade wind blows strong, the sea and sky are dazzling, one uses blankets at night and for a few short months gets rid of prickly heat and dhobie's itch. Consequently I feel very contented and gay. I just want to live, and don't want to probe at all. Everything seems to fit nicely into the scheme and the ' islands ' creep into one's blood.

The New Hebrideans are, I fancy, the most entirely artless people in the world. I started collecting war clubs and dancing masks once, and even packed up some with a view to sending to you. But the masks, besides being abominably ugly and decorated with human teeth, bones and hair (cannibalistic trophies), are too brittle to carry. The clubs are rather good, but scarcely small boys' treasures. For the rest, the natives make nothing. Their whole leisure is spent in making lap-lap (pudding) out of yams, taro, manioc and so forth, and in talking about it. Their huts are of the very rudest and barely last out the year. They have given up (as ' heathenish ') the making of beads and ornamental ' nambas ' and merely collect brummagen treasures from the stores. I sent you Topsy's gift,[1] because she had been so very downcast at not having acquired her proper status in my ' family.'

[1] A basket containing shells.

I invent messages from you to her by each mail, and you even sent her a lovely tortoiseshell (imitation) comb once, which she prizes enormously. It is very babyish, but rather pathetic and pleasing. H., of course, is ' piccaninny b'long brother b'long you, 'im 'ere where 'e good fellow,' which, being translated, is ' your fine nephew.'

Later.

Here we live on the edge of a volcano (not a geological one) nearly as threatening as your air raids. There has appeared—it is presumed from Australia—in the Group a peculiarly malignant variety of cerebro-spinal fever. Up till a month ago its ravages had been confined to two small islands off the south of ——. In one island 158 out of 200 inhabitants died, most of them within two days of infection. The good Government were petitioned and actually roused themselves to send H.M.Y. —— to impose quarantine on the two islands. The Government order was made known to the chief, but the bureaucrats forgot to take away the natives' boats. Naturally the survivors fled from the plague. Naturally the plague has broken out on ——. It is at present about 20 miles from here and gradually travelling northward. One waits. As the —— natives are dirtier than all other Kanakas, the spoil will be enormous. I don't see how I can prevent infection among my labour, as there is a constant intercourse between here and Mosquito Bay, and the latter place is the general emporium. I don't worry for myself, but I am a bit scary for the brat, because children seem to be the favourite victims. However, we shall see.

I had an unusual midwifery case at Mosquito Bay two weeks ago, where I was spending the week-end. I was summoned at 11 p.m. to the beach where a lady, wife of the engineer of an anchored recruiting vessel, had given birth to a seven months' infant. She had been taken ill aboard, and humanely packed into a dinghy and hurried ashore, which she just failed to reach. When I arrived mother and child were awash at the water's edge. I rescued and resuscitated them, and then had them transported to the nearest hut. With stimulants and hot water I got the pair all right; and they are 'both doing well.' Rather a rough way of being born, wasn't it? I very much fear that I am in for a private midwifery job again in about six months' time. You wouldn't believe the barbarities that are practised amongst these primitive folk to avoid the unwelcome child which spoils the value of a woman as a working beast. The favourite method is to get hubby and a few friends to dance on the recumbent mother. They have a special dance and music for it. Another way is to find a stump near a river—there is a specially consecrated one here in the stream—upon which the woman casts herself. . . . A coconut roasted in the fire and applied red-hot is also considered a very nice method of shirking maternity.

October 1st.

. . .

MY wretched mind simply will not be quiet about
Bilbil. I get him and his future nicely
settled—and then comes a shock. It is literally and
lamentably true that I love him now. But shall I
always do so? The " —— " was here yesterday
taking my cotton crop. I had a luncheon party of
three métis, one being the gentleman who wishes to
adopt Bilbil. They are all well educated (Pères
Jesuites), well behaved and well dressed in the
approved French colon style, which consists of
khaki uniform with a very high coat collar fastened
with three studs. (Naturally the colour does not
suit them and the high collar throttles their very
short necks. Bilbil has a neck like a bull calf.
That's how his name originated). I listened
abstractedly to their fluent talk of politics and
patriotism while I studied them. Mentally and in
their manners one could find very little fault with
them—as Frenchmen. It was physically that I
felt repelled. And what hope has my son of being
physically different from them? And, mind you,
after six years in the islands, I am perfectly accus-
tomed to treating half-castes on terms of equality.
They marry white women (French) and in all
respects are considered by the French as white.
But some lurking doubt in me refuses to be silenced.
I can't become French in that respect any more
than I could assume a Frenchman's inborn worship
of bureaucracy or his love of public tears. From
what I have seen of young half-castes Bilbil will be

very nice as a baby, as a little boy and even up to adolescence. It is after that, when they begin to grow pimples and generally become nasty-coloured hobble-de-hoys that I can't stand 'em.

You see I am absorbed in my little Kanaka world; I very rarely meet any whites and those only such people as are very little better than Kanakas. You don't know how the island blight eats into one. I do; but, while knowing, I don't like it. I tolerate the happy-go-lucky kind of life, but I am more than ever resolved not to give way to the soiled-lotos temptation. I am so afraid that, if I take Bilbil away and get him among whiter things, I shall straightaway begin to hate him. I know I should. Mrs. Cameron (my neighbour whose kiddies I doctor) brought her six months' old boy to me on a visit the other day. I had forgotten what really white babies smelt like and how their mothers talk to them. I simply couldn't leave that brat alone. I am quite sure that Mrs. Cameron brought the kid just to open my semi-blind eyes a bit.

Have you ever noticed during your bucolic spells that when a cow is about 6 months in calf she begins to neglect the earlier offspring? If the youngster is fastened up—(I have to rope them here so as to save any milk at all for myself: I hate calves brought up on the bucket: they are a dam nuisance)—she will feed placidly while he bellows for milk that she would have galloped a paddock's length to give him a month before. Well, Topsy is just like that now. Poor little Bilbil, who has just begun his season's crop of prickly heat and is consequently occasionally fretful, sits down

and mourns most pitifully for his mamma to no
effect whatsoever. He doesn't cry; he simply sits
down and repeats the word softly but insistently.
Topsy sees and hears him and takes absolutely no
notice at all. A month ago she would have shed
bitter tears. The neglect makes my blood boil.
Curious, isn't it? We are always yapping about
wanting to get back to nature and when we get
within smelling distance of it we are frightened and
angry. Fortunately Bilbil prefers his papa—I can't
teach him to say Daddy—to his Mamma, and Papa
is a child of craft rather than of nature. I shudder,
though, at what would happen to the poor little
chap were I not here to put some artificial joy into
his life beyond the natural joys of eating and sleep.
It does seem a blackguard shame that I should lose
the fruit of two years of thoughtful care and intelligent love. Perhaps it won't be really lost. I shall
have created something. And that will count. Bilbil
can never be the same as other men's half-castes.

Again ends a fragment. I have to go and weigh
my slaves' daily task of cotton.

October 27th, 1918.

I AM going to Mosquito Bay to meet Muller to
present my yearly report and weave new wild
schemes for fortune making. Muller is a lovely
man for scheming. Boccaccio would simply have
loved him—even as I do. He is about 6 feet 3
inches, weighs 20 stone, aged 35, and is covered
with hair like an Orang Outang. He enters with
terrific gusto into any scheme no matter how wild.

He is very shrewd, and manages to get home with a good many schemes too. Of course a lot fail, but that doesn't worry him in the least. The scheming is what he loves, the true artist. You would laugh to see the fuss and commotion among the niggers when it is known that Muller has arrived in the islands. The men love him because he is big and fat and masterful.

December 1st, 1918.

YOU talk about heat. The temperature here to-day is 109° F. in the shade. The humidity is close on 90%. There is not a breath of wind. There are mosquitoes and flies in black swarms. Very nice. Think of that lagoon and that palm tree and that coral reef and the stink of it. On November 9-11th we had the worst hurricane within memory of man. Over 20 braves colons went to glory with their recruiting vessels. Plantations were wiped out. Bush was wiped out. Here I escaped owing to the big hills all round me. My labourers' huts were blown into the sea, so was my galvanised iron kitchen. Otherwise very little damage to the plantation. So let the Lord be thankit.

... Why are old ladies so often described as charitable? Is it pure myth, or did one once exist?

1919

January 12*th*, 1919.

I HAVE always had an idea that pearl shell
fishing on the reefs here might be profitable.
It is at present carried out only by natives, who dive
au naturel. The New Hebridean is a rotten diver.
Three fathoms is the limit of the best of them, and
most can only do two. In any case to people who are
malarial, filarial, phthisic and syphilitic wrecks,
five or six immersions a day naked means a week's
rest for recuperation. No one here has tried the use
of a diving suit. No one here—it is hard to realise
that, but it's the simple truth—has had the intelligence and initiative. The reefs simply swarm with
trocas shell, which is worth even now £50 a ton.
A diver in a suit could easily pick up half to one
ton of shell a day. You see the possibilities ? Of
course the game can't last very long in its best
condition. The rotten Government will step in
and make export duties and put six months' taboo
on the reefs per year as a close season. It is done
in every other group in the Pacific, but not here yet.
Well, I am going to try the game. I have gone
partner with another man—two people are indispensable—who fortunately had a little saved cash.
He is one Collins, originally of Peckham, and
—— School, a proper cockney. At present he is

manager for Bernhardt and Muller at Mosquito Bay. We can only start in a small way, that is with a diving suit and a 16 foot dinghy; but if the thing pans out, we ought to get more dignified before very long.

You can realise what a lot depends upon the success of this venture. I honestly think that there is money—(there might easily be a hell of a lot, because I know (confidentially) of stray pearls also having been found here by natives; and the reefs have never even been tried by divers)—in the scheme. Even if it only came to successful trocas finding, there are thousands of pounds to be made. In a very short time that would mean a good schooner with you aboard it sharing in the work and experience. It beats me why no one has ever tried the game in the New Hebrides, whereas it is archiconnu and played out in most other parts of the Pacific. Knowing the traders here, however, very well, I am not really very surprised. They are all of the lower and quite unintelligent classes and have no more initiative than a cow. Also, the climate ashore very soon knocks all the go and all the white out of a man. I suppose I have been lucky and that my heritage of English games pays better in the long run than the French —— and O——n child labour. Anyhow, we'll see.

My partner is a rummy little bloke, a travelled, adventured cockney. He fought as a trooper in South Africa, sails a boat like any Kentish fisherman, and yet talks longingly of his ' boike,' ' beanoes ' that he and the other cheps used to have of a Saturday night and the gurls of the halls.

February 2nd, 1919.

.　.　.

AT present I am too stupid even to scheme. I have just had a somewhat trying week. Poor Topsy had a terrible time with a new attempt to add to the tinted population. Her pains began on Tuesday at 8 a.m. and on Saturday at 10 p.m. I removed with the aid of chloroform and ' the tongs ' my second son, fortunately very dead. I had diagnosed his death by the Wednesday night, but could not do anything. I had lent my chloroform and instruments to a missionary, who had promised faithfully to return them in time and had failed to do so. I had to send to Mosquito Bay and get a launch to go in chase of the swine, whom they found after three days' search. In the meanwhile poor Topsy had been suffering the torments of the damned. . . . I kept her doped with a chloral morphine mixture—I don't keep twilight sleep in my dispensary—but was afraid to press it too far, as I knew I should have to keep her strength up for the chloroform act. I got Ashby to come round as my assistant during the anæsthetising, but he started to vomit before the poor girl was quite unconscious ; so I had to kick him out and finish the job alone. I hadn't had a minute's rest day or night since the show began, so was not in the best trim for operative obstetrics. However, I kept to it by chewing cocaine lozenges and drinking whisky. I drank four bottles in the four days and didn't feel as if I had had a drop. Now, however, that it is all over, the reaction has come and I feel like a rat. Only

one definite idea obsesses me.   Never, never, never
again.   My neck is black and blue and extremely
painful and sore and stiff.   Topsy's one relief from
pain was to grip me round the neck and pull like
hell, and I must have done a good 72 hours of that
enjoyable form of exercise.   In spite of the present
horror and the tragic possibilities I couldn't help
smiling at Topsy's death-bed reflections.   She was
quite certain that she was going to die, but seemed
equally convinced that I was going with her where-
ever she went.

"By and by two feller 'e go where?   By and by
two feller 'e go same place?   'E where?   'E'long
England?   'E'long Nouméa?   Me think 'e stop
long way too much.   By and by two feller 'e go
'longa steamer? . . .   Bald 'ed, you sabby Koumala
(sweet potato) where me cook 'im long you me
burn 'im?   By God me sorry too much 'long that."

I had quite forgotten the incident.   She had done
even as Alfred the Great on one occasion and I had
cursed her heartily.   She had evidently been consumed with shame for the heinous offence and seized
the nearness of death as an opportunity for un-
burdening herself.   To-day she is as merry as a
cricket again and if I were out of earshot would be
up and off to the beloved sea for a swim.   She makes
no bones about her delight at the death of the ' pump-
kin,' and even apostrophised it as I was wrapping it
up for interment :   "Yes you bin make me sabby.
Now master he make you sabby time he plant you."

In the hurry and flurry of Topsy coming to from
the chloroform and the careful completion of my
job, I forgot about the poor corpse, and even sat on

it for some time. I got Topsy fixed up and comfy before I could turn my attention to it. Of course there had been no hope for it from the first, so I had no remissness to reproach myself with. It was extremely and urgently dead. . . . I made one rush down to the sea, discarded my garments under water and then remembered the sharks and so made a wild rush for shore again. But by that time I was clean and Ashby had fried me some sausages and opened a bottle of good red wine. I fairly hogged and then dropped asleep before I could get half-way through my first cigarette.

Do you think you would like a ' frankly Colonial ' life ? Most of the white men here manage to get their wives down to the missionary hospital at Vila for their accouchement ; but there are two cases on this island which will have to depend on my tender mercies in a month or two because the sweet missionary has gone away for his year's leave and calmly shut up his hospital during his absence. Personally I abominate obstetrics, and would refuse to help if I decently could. Just because I have a little common sense and am not an ignorant peasant I am looked upon as everybody's bloody doctor and get dragged out all over the place.

February 20*th*, 1919.

I SUPPOSE I shall have to pass through a six months' acclimatisation in Australia before going very slowly home, in order to get the malaria out of my blood and diminish the risk of haemoglobinurie. I think I have told you that several anciens colons neglecting that precaution have been buried at sea on their way home to France after years of longing. I don't want to be a mug of that sort. You don't know what seven years' malaria can do to even a strong constitution, so don't start wiring to me to come by the next tram or anything of that sort. I am not going to show myself in Europe as I am at present, neither do I want to patronise the hammock and case-shot method of interment. (Yes; I know, but it is too hot to think.)

Poor little Bilbil pays the price of his half whiteness by suffering badly from prickly heat which to a kiddie who doesn't know how to avoid sudden stoopings and other inducers of an attack of needles must be simple hell. He has had an awful lot of bad fever lately. The other day a temperature (axillary) of 108° F. made me scary of an accès pernicieux (which can finish off a strong healthy man in six hours—I have seen 'em), so I gave him 5 grs. intramuscularly injected. It broke my heart to ram that needle home, for I know from experience how hellishly painful a performance it is, but the injection brought his temperature down with a run and he was chewing navy biscuit two hours later.

He seems to suspect with a dog's instinct that I am going to leave him, for he hangs round my neck with " Darling Daddy, darling Daddy " until I have to cry like the neurotic I am fast becoming. Topsy, too, seems to smell desertion in the air. Her devotion to me in the cooking and mending line since her purification (' one pig-pig more one fowl where 'e man ' were sacrificed) is very touching. And two or three times I have caught her weeping quietly and have been refused explanation. I do feel an utterly damnable cad. It was very shallow of you to compare my case to ——'s. .... Topsy is the most faithful womanly woman and an insanely blind adorer of me. —— was injured ' socially.' I am not, at least not in that sense. —— hated his female. I couldn't hate Topsy, especially after what I have been through with her twice. —— kept his child. And that is the weakest point in the whole analogy. I can't pretend that I ' love ' Topsy in any ordinary sense of the word. Our parting will be a nice little regret stored up for times of sentiment or discontent. But if I do not love Bilbil, then I am incapable of understanding that sensation. By nature I am far more sloppily sentimental (that, I think, is the correct cliché) even than you are. The desire for a man child of my own has always been the one thing. .... At present no consideration of Bilbil's colour can stem the flow of my affection to him.

I saw a short time ago a review of a Spanish book *Novelas y Novelistas* over which I should like to have had a row with the reviewer. Amongst other curious (but presumably quite safe to English literary people) statements he gives, as not only his own opinion but as the general one, wholesale and contemptuous condemnation to Pio Baroja, and to that author's *La Ciudad de la Niebla* in particular. I believe I have actually singled out that work of Pio Baroja to you in a former letter as being in my opinion a literary gem. Tastes differ, but I don't think ' your reviewer ' has quite the weight of literary opinion behind him to which he pretends. At any rate he differs in opinion from the writer of the book under review, who, being a Spaniard and a literary one, presumably knew more about Pio Baroja's value than the journalist. The review talked very ignorantly too about Perez Galdós. I was glad to hear that you had an acquaintance who shared my admiration for the Spanish novel. I wonder whether he has dipped into either Gallego or Criollo literature or to the mixture of it that is found in Argentina and Uruguay. There is a fine field of discovery there either for someone who loves art or for someone who loves to boom it. I suppose the ' muy intelligentes ' of Buenos Aires and Montevideo are still so wrapped in admiration of their own quite unintelligent imitation of French literary art that they have not had time to appreciate the extraordinary local talent among their own Gauchos. It was a foreigner, a Frenchman, who put me on to the two or three modestly got up collections of stories and poems that I read. Of course the educated people in Uruguay are hopeless, silver gilt and stucco of the very worst ; but the Campos was bound to breed artistry in men of mixed Spanish and Indian blood. Do you think there would be any money or kudos in working up a boom in Criollo literature ? or must all finds in peasant literature deal with blood and guts ?

Prickly heat is really more damnable than fever. It keeps me awake at night and makes effort impossible. The worst ill for me is my Dhobie's itch. That catches me every hot season and itches like hell—much too painful and swollen to scratch.

I left off my last letter when my half caste father-remplaçant arrived. I have fixed up all details with him. Topsy and Bilbil are to go up to him in about three months' time. He is awfully keen and has mapped out a full programme of O——n school and French collège for the helpless Bilbil. I won't dwell on all that, because I am still very sore and very prone to relapses. It is enough to say that I consider honestly that what I propose to do is the absolute best for all parties concerned. Leave it at that. I know that I would rather die than do what I have got to do, but short of such a lucky deliverance I am going through with what I have decided.

You refer to me for a decision about Stevenson's 'sentimentality.' Honestly I can't tell you. As to the general climate of the Pacific Islands one cannot generalise. Naturally, being in the tropics they are extremely unsuitable as permanent living places for Englishmen. The climate probably hastened Stevenson's death. I am told that malaria is only found in Melanesia now. But dysentery scourges every group in the Pacific. Also that disease family, Filariasis, unknown practically in R. L. S.'s day, is quite general. Even Stevenson talks about elephantiasis. Well, elephantiasis is only one of about two score manifestations of Filariasis. I don't suppose that Stevenson stinted the colour when writing what he must have known would please millions. It is very hard for me in the savage, malarial New Hebrides to imagine what I should feel like in luxury in Samoa.

I wonder if anyone who really knows the South Seas will ever write about them. I fancy not.

Better not, too. Why upset if you can't replace
with better ?

. . . But I am going to part with my baby for all
that, while he is yet a baby. I have sinned against
nature—it is that, and there is no use in mincing
matters—and I am going to pay the price. There
will be no point in torturing myself and him—to say
nothing of Topsy—by trying to fight a battle
whereof the result is a foregone conclusion. Only
the payment of my debt is going to hurt damnably.

March 16*th*, 1919.

I AM sorry for the long gap between this letter
and the last. In some ways this long distance
exchange is annoying, but, Lord ! I shall miss it.
. . . Seven years of solitude have made me very
slow in the uptake. I know that, when an occasional
missionary visits me here and I want to shrivel the
worm without his even guessing at my idea, I find
myself at an awful loss for words—for the mot juste
rather—and I end up by exaggerating grossly.
It may simply be that the antagonism of the man's
presence paralyses me. Still, I know it would take
some little time before my mind flowed freely
through my tongue even to you. When I am writing
the affair is simple. If I don't feel the mood upon
me, I simply stop writing. Then again, when
talking to stray visitors here, I find it hard to curb
my temper. I feel my head begin to swim and I
contradict rudely everything that they say for the
sheer love of being rude to them. That, I fancy, is

almost entirely physical, because the condition
varies so markedly with my state of health. One
can't help being neurotic in a climate like this.
I despise the condition, but circumstances are too
strong. That is why I long so passionately for
bracing and appetite and physical strength. Now
every mouthful that I eat makes the sweat run in
streams off my chin and bare elbows. I used to
feel revolted when I saw people sweat. Now I
know that it is impossible to help it. Half an hour
after sunrise one begins and one is wet through
for the rest of the day. I used to change my clothes
and bathe about eight times a day. Now I don't
bathe (except a warm shower bath at sunset) for
fear of malaria, and I am too lazy to change when I
know that the fresh clothes will be just as wet in five
minutes' time. You know, that kind of existence
does not suit me. Most of the folk here are so
coarse fibred that they simply don't care. They
are of the Saturday night bath class (*i.e.* the Britishers)
and dirtiness is a pleasure to most of them. When
they feel 'low' they go on an almighty booze. They
don't worry, and therefore don't suffer. But they
die just the same. When I came here, there were
14 white men on the island. Of these 9 are dead,
3 have fled to Nouméa just in time, two besides
myself are left. I am the oldest man in the island.
Other islands are healthier. It all depends upon the
amount of stagnant water in the bush. Here there
are no rivers, but many brackish lagoons of which the
outlet is more or less permanently closed by sand.
These lagoons are the home of countless millions
of Anopheles mosquitoes besides their friends and

near relations of the Culex fatigans variety. The former, of course, spread malaria. The latter inject one with Filariasis, which is really more insidious and deadly in its innumerable manifestations than malaria. The commoner diseases due to Filariae sanguinis hominis, such as arthritis, chyluria, multiple abscess and so on, are what really play hell with the white population, and especially when their constitution is undermined by malaria and ' square face.' Dysentery, of course, takes its toll ; but more especially of the natives. Ten years ago there were seven flourishing native villages within a half mile radius of this house. To-day the villages do not exist. The same thing is happening all over the islands. Cheery sort of place to live in, eh ? And a cheery sort of patch I seem to have struck for your letter to-day.

In one of my compartments—I fancy it must be a good one and scantily furnished—I want to prefer sterling worth to polish. And yet, and yet—you know. Take an example : an O———n who will ride 50 miles to get a doctor for you, bring the doctor back to you, and then sneak away and sleep in a shed rather than come in and give the trouble of having bed and meal prepared for him—that man has the best of manners. And yet every time that he smirks out his " pleased to meet you " upon introduction to a stranger, I should feel angry with him and very superior. Incidentally, why is one not embarrassed by " Enchanté de faire votre connaissance, Monsieur," or other foreign equivalents, but quite speechless in face of " pleased to meet you ? " I always want to say " not at all." I don't know why. I suppose Miss Pinkerton would have replied " I trust that your present pleasure will never be diminished. May I add that the pleasure is mutual." But one has no time for such long speeches.

You might at some time or other like to know a few of the minor revisions that I have made of the lesser conventional ' manners.' For one thing I have radically altered Paragot's list of what may be eaten with the fingers. Asparagus, naturally was discarded first. That is a filthy habit. Of course, we are the only people who do it, but then we are the only people who know how to eat, so the sin is the more remarkable. You know that I have some little claim to being a polyglot cosmopolitan, although I have not been to many places, yet those places were centres of cosmopolitanism (Cairo, M'video and Sidnee). I maintain : the British are the only people who know how (1) to cook ; (2) to eat decently ; (3) to dress (of males) ; (4) to walk ; (5) to fight like gentlemen. I allow inclusion to Yanks in all those points except number 3. But let me return for a minute to Paragot. I agree with him about fried fish and kipper, although flying fish can only be eaten nicely when held in the fingers. But what about bacon ? I used to—I use that tense advisedly and with regret—like my bacon cooked very dry and overdone. I daresay you do too. But how annoyingly it chips up and flies about the plate ! When the whole dry curly rasher is seized delicately in the fingers, dipped deftly in the mustard and then eaten as a biscuit, one gets it all and is saved endless worry. Moreover the fingers are not made greasy. Why not then? A Frenchman considers our method of eating a boiled egg as very bad manners. He—ever a well bred he—will finish off a cutlet by taking the thing in his fingers. Then, drinking too hot tea out of a saucer. Why not? Of course one must be deft in order to avoid drops on the bottom of the cup which would soil the napery. But that art is acquirable. And one only gets the true fragrance of the tea thus. And, after all, that is what saucers were intended for. . . . Of course the retort to all this is obvious : never inflict yourself on others. But I am really dabbling a little in parable. And a little mission work in manners might be done tactfully by an elderly man of assured position.

By the way, thinking of ' plats,' one used to eat a very nice thing at Lanata's in Montevideo. It was called ' Bife a caballo con papas fritas.' It is a small and very nicely cooked and tender steak, surmounted by fried potatoes and crowned with a poached egg. Of course the Dagoes used to spoil it by putting a diadem of garlic on the egg unless the order was for an Englishman. You should try it. But the steak must be jelly-like in its tenderness. Cut right through the little mound and the blend of flavour is quite nice. I could get my living anywhere as a cook now. Sometimes I take a fit of eating here, and spend a lot of time in making myself nice dishes. More often I devour what Topsy cooks for me à l'indigène. These people may be crude savages, but they have very sound ideas on cooking. Everything is wrapped in banana leaves, moistened with coconut ' milk ' (not what you

think; it means the jelly-like meat of a young coconut
rasped over the food), and then cooked by placing
hot stones on top of the parcel. Thus flavour is
conserved in the most extraordinary way. I have
tried cooking white man's vegetables the same way,
and you would scarcely believe what potatoes taste
like. I don't know what one could substitute for
banana leaves in England : of course the rich man
could grow his bananas under glass—also his
coconuts. A laplap (universal Polynesian word for
made dishes cooked thus) of grated yam or manioc
with pig flesh inside has a taste that would make the
reputation of a restaurant. I have initiated Topsy
into the use of a few drops of Lee and Perrin or a
soupçon of curry powder in laplaps, and she has
gained thereby enormous kudos among her own
folk. Also, I taught her not to waste the blood of
a slain pigpig, but rather to make therefrom boudins
of the most delicious. That also has given Topsy
extraordinary renown. Perhaps you don't like
boudins ? Or, more probably you have never
tasted them. The English monstrosity—as also
the German bluth-wurst—is, I grant, disgusting ;
but boudins almost make me revise one of my above-
mentioned points. Only, an intelligent Britisher
makes them and cooks them better even than a
Frenchman. I first learned them on my voyage to
New Caledonia. The captain was an artist in
boudins.

I make no apologies to you for thus descending
from my pedestal. I do like my food when I can
get it. And I like cooking it. I specialise here in
fricasées and ragouts, particularly the latter. I

wonder whether you have ever tasted a good ragout ?
I learned a trick in South America from the ' carbonado Criollo,' which is a famous dish there.
They put peaches in their ragouts. I have no
peaches here, but pineapples are a pestiferous weed.
So I make my carbonado with pineapple—and
fresh-picked chillies, and pawpaws, and wild toma-
toes. Oh la la ! Mais c'est exquis ! Moreover,
I don't use common onions. I use eschalots. I
put them through the mincing machine and then
fry them lightly in cottonseed oil as a foundation
for the sauce of the ragout. That makes a great
deal of difference. Then the consistency of the
sauce (I can't call it gravy, because that is generally
so nasty) is attained with arrowroot—we grows it
wild—and never with flour. If you bruise one large
pigment with the arrowroot there is no earthly fear
of lumps. Then again, I use a proper utensil for
stewing—no beastly stewpan for me. Chez moi
nothing is ever allowed to boil, and I take great
trouble in sealing up my stew. Of course that
necessitated a certain number of spoiled experi-
ments before I arrived at the correct time and
temperature factors. Now I have them and would
not part with them for gold.

March 18*th*, 1919.

BADLY interrupted here and no time now even
to round off my treatise on the preparation of
food by heat. The filthy fall of volcanic ash which
fills one's house and mouth with an unimagin-
able beastliness arrived simultaneously with Bilbil's

prospective foster father, who has come down from
Aoba to see him and arrange business. For those
two reasons writing is no longer possible. So for the
present I crawl back into silence.

July 12*th*, 1919.

YOU can't understand fully because you haven't
lived without communication with human
beings for five years alone with your pride, your self
knowledge, your fear of madness. I suppose that
you do more talking in a day than I do in a year :
and talking—even if it is only the pettiest commonplace, is as vital a necessity to man as is oxygen.
That is one little point that has rankled badly during
these five years. You don't seem able to realise.
You write to me just as if I were in hourly communication with other people. Look—it is 17
days now since I saw a white man. That is about my
average. Even when I do see one, he is about as
much like me as, say, your postman is like you.
But I have sunk to longing even for the sight of
anyone to whom I can say a sentence that will be
understood. Probably you have some romantic
ideas about the kind of conversation that can
be carried on with Kanakas. All right. Go and
shut yourself up rigidly without books, papers,
windows for three solid weeks and amuse yourself
by talking to a dog. I fancy that it would pall after
about six hours. Try it for five years. Also try
the value of your dog when you are black in the face
with asthma and see how attentive and comforting
he will be to you when you are lying exhausted on

the floor for a day afterwards. Even the people at Mosquito Bay are in quite a different case. There are always four or five of them—and they are all about the same. Even the missionary with his wife and children is quite another case. He wakes up in the morning and straightway begins communicating with similars and continues to do so all day. I go round trying to find someone who will even answer my " Good morning." Usually one only gets a grunt, because the Kanaka does not understand social amenities. Now I am looked at askance, as one with the Evil Eye, because they think that I am " lib for die." That's like cows and fowls, you know. If they dared, they would butt me away from the food. Topsy despises me. She still serves me in her ludicrously incompetent way, but I am sure that it is only fear that keeps her from forsaking me. Oh, won't I waste a lot of time in yapping about ' beauty ' when I mean vile, crude nature. Hide it, paint it, gild it, stucco it ; only cover it up and keep it unsuspected. Uph— why didn't I ' reach ' psycho-analysis before I got here ? But that kind of leakage doesn't do me any good, or you either. Only let me get safely away. . . .

Later.

. . . I was interrupted by natives with cotton to sell and haven't been able to write since. I will just finish this off as the steamer is due. One little gem I must tell you. I have an acquaintance in these islands who is, I should say, unique—an entirely unspoiled literary critic. Brought up in the ' back blocks' and here, he only took to reading (self taught) very late in life. I don't suppose he has ever seen a ' literary ' paper or read a book review. I have amused myself in saving his time by doing a little selection for him, and his genuine exclusive appreciation of ' good ' literature would delight the heart of a Sir-John-Lubbock-Ruskin. Some time ago the gentleman was visiting me and we were talking books. I was trying to recall the plot of some novel or other. He was helping me by asking such questions as : " Was it about the man who . . . ? " Presently he thought he had run our quarry to earth : " Wasn't there an incident about an old chap getting drunk at a shooting party and trespassing on someone's land and then being wheeled off to jail in a wheel-barrow ? " Quite thoughtlessly I said : " That sounds to me like Pickwick plagiarised." Then I got : " Oh, yes ; now I come to think of it that comes in a book called Pickwick Papers. I was reading it a short time ago." There's freshness for you !

You will be glad to hear that teetotalism is doing me a vast amount of good. I haven't had a go of asthma for over four weeks now, and can walk about without feeling that I am going to burst. Fortunately the rains are on too, so that my galvanised iron prison doesn't get too roasting hot. Temperatures over 100° F. indoors are not really healthy when arterial tension is too high. Do you remember old Freeborn chucking me for the ' Novices ' in the year something ? Later Collier—a great authority on ' athletes' heart '—told me that I might have trouble in the forties. Well, I've got it all right,

but, although I must confess that some of it has
been earned, I think I know how to cope with it.
En tout cas I don't care overmuch. If I were only
assured about another chance, I think that I would
even speed up the exit of this one whose results
don't pass even my interested muster. But there
you are. You remember what Shakespeare puts
into the mouth of the introverted Prince of Den-
mark ? All right ; we'll leave it at that. Just at
present dust is thick on my Freud-Jung-Pfister
shelf. They ain't comforting—and it's comfort
that I want.

August 31*st,* 1919.

BY last mail I got a fairly definite and good offer
from the headmaster of the Sydney ——
School. If I am to usher, that would be a trifle
less beastly than Sydney board-schools. I fancy
that most of the staff are Oxford men, so one would
not be suffocated with the superiority of the O——ns.
I don't want to usher again for a single minute.
Neither do I want to write slush for O——n
cabbage leaves. I have a brand new idea in my head
now. I am going to get ' business introductions '
from Muller and offer myself and my European
languages and other brilliant accomplishments to
be used as a bagman. . . . I have got a nasty
interview to get through before I can be at all
definite. I am going to see a French doctor pal of
mine who is just back from the war. From him I
may go to Nouméa for consultation. The truth
is that my damned heart is getting worse and worse

every day, and I am getting nervous. I don't
grouse about having to pass out, but I want skilled
opinion as to whether bustle and worry and civilisation is going to be good or bad for me. I know that
there is serious mischief in my heart, but I don't
know whether the quacks can stop it from getting
worse. If they say that they can, I'll hie me quick
to Sydney and give 'em a chance. If they say that
they can't—well I don't know yet what I shall do.
So that's that. I feel beastly lonely. . . .

The South Seas,
November 12*th*, 1919.

YOUR letter arrived by the steamer 'Makambo'
on the 7th. When that steamer returns from
her two weeks of trading in the northern islands I
shall board her here, Mosquito Bay, and hope to
arrive in Sydney with her on or about the 17th.
Thus ends my experiences of seven and a half years
in the New Hebrides. My passage is booked ;
Mowbray will be my company. So it is all over.
At present I am loafing and lurking at Mosquito
Bay because I can't bear the sight of my Bilbil and
Topsy. Mr. and Missis Bernhardt are adopting
Bilbil ; Topsy will also find a home with them until
the spirit moves her to return to her beloved Aoba.
That is all doubtless for the best. I have no fixed
plans for my future. Too much depends on what
the Sydney doctors tell me. I can't say that I
greatly care. I suppose I shall take on a job at the
school for a bit, just to earn my keep and provide

a fund for new travels. Even if I remain for some time in Sydney our correspondence will take place on considerably easier terms. I believe that steamers leave Sydney at least once a week for England, so that we shall have shortened the time necessary for a reply by at least three months.

With rest and care I have restored myself to a fairly workable condition of health, without, however, making much effect on the origin of my trouble. At the last minute I funked going to Vila for opinion. I should only have contradicted the quack. So I await my final sentence in Sydney.

God's Own Country,
December 26th, 1919.

THIS letter will reach you some time before I do, because it will travel by mail steamer whereas I shall be content with sail. You see I have rather a sentimental longing to complete the earth-girdling in a wind-jammer. Actually, of course, the circuit will be finished shortly after I pass under Cape Horn, but the extra arc shall stand to my credit.

But how stupidly forgetful I am—and so un-methodical. I should have told you first of all that I had decided to pop across the degrees of longitude and see you. I decided yesterday. I have been in O——r exactly three weeks, exactly three weeks, bloody weeks. You got me? I have not yet found a sailing vessel, because I went to sleep last night very peacefully after my decision and it is yet very early in the morning of a ' doyeez nohrn.' But

to-morrow I begin my search. I don't fear that
the search will be a long one. Don't think that my
quest for employment here has been fruitless.
Plenty of jobs were willingly offered to me. I had,
however, to interview people. Each one was more
unutterable than other. Obviously only one course
was then open to me. How silly it was that such a
brilliant idea had not exploded upon me before.
I have just got about enough money to land me in
England and buy some tobacco. All right. I'll
land in England and buy the tobacco. Then I
will begin to think. I am sure I shall be able to
think by then. You see, the slow voyage round the
Horn in a hooker will acclimatise me decently and
land me in England when winter is over. A
steamer would be too quick. And I couldn't stand
much more of this ; certainly I could not stand two
more months. Also my scanty capital would be
dribbling away. Oh, isn't it fun ? I never even
dreamed in my wildest moments that I should
decide so casually and so absurdly.

1920

January 1*st*, 1920.

I HAVEN'T the remotest idea of what I am going to do for a living in England. . . .

February 2*nd*, 1920.

LIKE a fool I changed my mind in the New Year. Result—more disillusion, more nausea, nothing done. This time it is final. This very morning I go to seek a wind-jammer. As a matter of fact, I don't want to reach England till July or August—early July preferably. The trip should harden me up all right and then with a month or two of decent weather left (shall we go and tramp Dartmoor a bit ?) I can prepare to face the gloom and cold. I have an idea that, although cold will be uncomfortable at first, it is cold that I need. One gets some cold days even here in the middle of summer and I notice that on those days I am ten times as alert physically and mentally as on the warm days, which are really hotter than anything that I felt in the Islands.

Books, sympathy, understanding, my own language, a little living in the past—all these things I want. I must have them. Here all my desires are and would be for ever unfulfilled. Also, vulgarity, ignorance and blatency are the only assests in this country. I could sink, it would be easy. But it would be unspeakably obnoxious to me to do so. ... I won't waste time in cursing Sydney to you in this letter. That will be a treat for some evening round the fire. No ; I will now try and be faintly practical. I must obviously face the problem of a living in London. My own mind runs strongly towards a job of sorts in a bookshop. . . .

Last week the leading literary paper here reviewed *The Happy Hypocrite* as a new book, the reviewer being jocularly familiar in the O———n manner with many a bit of sound advice from an old hand to ' Max,' warning him that he was likely to become a cropper if he did not recognise his limitations. You may not believe that, but it is literal truth. What further need have we. . . .

I don't want to inflict doctors' opinions too much upon you. Bref, my heart is bad ; my liver is cirrhosed ; my kidneys are wavering ; my nerves are all to hell. I have fits of hysterical semi-fainting upon the slightest provocation. My own opinion— which alone convinces me—is that there is precious little the matter with my body, only enough to be explained as secondary reaction. But—and there's the vicious circle—my mental condition is horrid. I have days in which it is absolute agony to me to see or hear a living person. The periods end (at first they only last a few hours, lately they have been countable in days) in a crisis of tears and sleep, and then I am quite normal again. My idea of a cure is a long sea voyage towards definite work. . . . You

will agree that I have paid in hardish coin for my
dallying with the lotos plant. When I get to
England I don't suppose I shall be robust enough
to become a professional footballer, but the most
sensible of the quacks here promises me that, once
my nerves are right, the other things won't worry
me during a well-regulated life.

I have really no energy to discuss psanalysis in
this letter. I can't even think about it at present.
Honestly my last impression was one of disgust;
but I am anxious to analyse that disgust. You see,
I am fairer than you and less precipitate. But just
at present my brain is of putty. I am not sure that
my searches into psanalysis are not largely responsible for my present lamentable state, but I have not
even the energy to disentangle that one knot of
cause and effect. I crave feebly for the simple
faith of the Pelmanist, but know in advance that I
could not attain to it. Oh la la—cursed Scots
blood ! I know that it will drive me to ' the meta-
pheesics ' one day.

But I push that aside for the present. Since I
arrived in this malebolgian muck-pot I have devoured hundreds (almost literally) of modern
English novels. For one thing, I felt that I owed
it to you to do so ; for another, I was frankly
curious ; for another, the occupation kept me from
worse things. I sought out names that you had
mentioned and others that had intruded themselves
from six years of Lit. Sup. This was my first such
orgy for over ten years. Here are some bitten-
thumbnail sketches. . . .

It is all such a terrible labouring of the inessential.

It makes me think of two methods of dissecting an earthworm. One man who knows all that matters about earthworms lays the beast open with a skilful touch, demonstrates the important organs to a class of admiring students and the thing is over and done with in an hour. The other freezes his worm, cuts sections in a microtome across the entire length of the reptile, stains them, pores for days and weeks over each section mostly exactly alike. The study of the sections becomes a mania. Nothing is done, nothing is learned. And what do earthworms matter anyway except for broad notions of comparative anatomy ? —— devotes his obvious talent and energy to the apotheosis of the Paltry. I read (or rather, tried) ——. Marvellous, almost miraculous. I suppose there are still folk who will pay 3d. to go and see five-legged calves and double-headed chickens.

With great interest I got from my circulating library *Eminent Victorians*. I really can't see why that Blackwood man made such a pother unless it was for the reason that I suggested at the time of reading his angry stuff. I enjoyed the book immensely and thereby find myself for once in complete agreement with you. Oh fortunate you.

Mowbray and I spent two days ashore at Norfolk Id. So entirely captivated was I by this absolutely unique Paradise that he and I immediately made plans for retiring there from the world. I even got the matter on a business footing. I made plans for making my fortune by teaching the islanders how to prepare oil of lemon. The plan was quite sound. I got a certain market in Sydney, made samples and everything was ripe and ready. That was what occupied me after writing the first page of this letter. Mowbray left Sydney before the steamer got in again from Norfolk Id., but I kept him posted as far as Adelaide. The steamer arrived bringing certain influential islanders. Then my scheme fell to pieces, wrecked on the uniqueness of the Norfolk Islander. They were eager at first, but eventually backed out. Too much trouble. They only work when absolutely forced. They've got all they want now. Why bother about any more ? Back to the Garden of Eden. All right. I signed and acquiesced. Perhaps it is nicest. I shan't have done anything to spoil virginity. Mowbray doesn't know yet, as his boat had left Adelaide before I could get the news to him. He won't be in England till after this as he goes round the Cape. One day I shall retire to Norfolk Id. and marry one of their dream-like wenches. I don't think Mowbray will. His old pa is bound to die soon and then he will inherit and take seriously to hypochondria and hyacinths. It's a pity, because I have known him to be very nice.

February 27*th*, 1920.

ALL above this has been fooling and unreal. I am very very ill—mentally—I have cabled to —— to send me money to come home. I tried to pull myself together by writing to you in a normal way. It has taken me nearly three months to write what I have done and I can't go on any more. . . . Make enquiries about bookshop jobs. I am hoping

that the voyage will cure me. Then I shall want
to start work right away

G. O. C.
March 16*th*, 1920.

I HOPE that this will be the very last letter that I
shall write to you, at any rate for a very decent
number of years. It should reach you about the
same time as the lugubrious epistle that I sent by
the 'Niagara.'

I will state briefly my actual position and forecast
my probable movements. . . . If the money arrives
I shall immediately start trying to find a craft in
which to make my voyage. I hanker after 'sails';
but it is not so easily found as I thought. I may
have to go to Melbourne or Adelaide in order to get
one of the various French sailing-vessels which are
at present loading grain. There seems to be nothing
available in Sydney.

If —— for some reason or another fails to send
me money, I am absolutely done. My own stock
of money will be exhausted this week. I can't get
employment here, except as a 'teacher,' and that
will be practically a sentence of death. My other
letter will have hinted to you that my condition of
mind and nerves is not such that I could take on
the job of teaching O——ns. I need not enlarge
upon that subject. By law and everything else all
jobs are reserved for returned soldiers. You jeered
at that difficulty arising in England. Here it is a
very real one. I have found it so to my cost.

I think I should prefer a French hooker to a
British. From the British seaman's point of view

they are ' bloody 'ungry ships,' but not so from mine. Moreover, after hearing nothing but the O——n language spoken for three months it would be a relief to hear and talk French again for a bit. Moy bleedin' owth, it will ; fair dinkum chainge, cobber. (Say that to your artisticule,—and notice the far-away longing look in his eyes. His very name with its horrid reminiscence of Sid, Lez, Gus, Alf, Tib, etc., robs him in my opinion of all claim to artistry. The nicest O——n abbreviated given-name is their short for Hubert. Of course we all know 'Erb, but 'Ewb. What ?)

I have the haziest idea of what I am going to do for a living in London. I refuse to usher. My body may have to be enslaved ; I am damned if my mind and soul shall. You may be able to find out whether employment in a bookshop or publishing factory is possible. I don't care how menial is the work or how small the pay. I only want a means of livelihood that will be mechanical and will not demand surrender. . . . Well, we shall see. Is it possible to live cheaply in London at post-bellum prices ? The price of living here is awful, and the manner of living unspeakably beastly. Lodgings as we understand the term do not exist. You live in a ' residential,' *i.e.* a furnished room in a house, but can get no meals. Feeding is all done at cafés, chop suey houses, sundae shops and such-like abominations. The commonest of badly cooked meals in a café costs at least 3s. 6d., and if you take more than 10 minutes to devour it you are practically kicked out. There are 17 theatres which are advertised in the papers. Of these 16 are cinema, and the other some sort of revue. During the three months that I have been in Sydney there has been one concert advertised ; that was Mr. Handel's ' Messiah.' You may then guess what a comforting refuge Sydney is for me. The art gallery here is divided into three portions, the first containing reproductions (real ones, done by hand, in oil paint) of old masters, the second consists of a few works purchased at the Royal Academy (two Marcus Stone, three Alma Tadema, very choice and typical), the third—and it has a merit all its own—is a collection of pictures and frames by O———n artists. I have already indicated to you O———n literary style, knowledge and criticism. Oh, but why go on ? I told you that I would save all that till we meet. By the way, in my confession of the modern English novelists that I have devoured lately, I forgot one item. I promptly secured *The Hill of Dreams* by Arthur Machen. I can't possibly explain my feeling about that man ; perhaps after talking with you I may get to understanding. He seized me and held me this time exactly as he did God knows how many years ago. I didn't feel that I was reading, that it was fiction, a ' yarn ' at all. I simply entered into the book and lived in it. I seemed to know all that he was going to say. I don't know. . . . I am more than usually inarticulate just now, but perhaps you can see a glimmer of what I mean. I shall want to hear quite a lot about this. And how does that hypothetical ' novel-reading ' public receive Mr. Arthur Machen ?

One more confession about novels and novelists. I must make it ; it is due to you. Shortly before leaving the New Hebrides I tried, being badly in need of solace, to read again the *Newcomes* and *Pendennis*. I couldn't read them. I simply couldn't stand what seemed to me mere verbiage, long-winded jocularity, and patronage of the reader. Have I caught a disease, or lost one ?

[A healthy Island]
20*th July*, 1920.

.   .   .

I WANT to wipe all that horror out of at least my conscious mind. I will just give you the shortest of résumés. About three weeks after my last letter came a remittance from ———. I did my best to get a passage home. Pas moyen. Nothing but 1st class available till September. That meant months more of horror in O———r and an arrival in England in winter. Quite out of the question. I was in despair again. Then came a cable from Muller in Nouméa telling me to apply by cable for the job of secretary to the Compagnie Française des ———. I did so ; was referred to Sydney agents and immediately booked. The pay is good. I was assured by a Sydney specialist that my only chance of regaining health was to go to a warm non-malarial climate. So here I am. I left Sydney on May 20th, got to Auckland in 4 days, waited there a fortnight (bloody cold, 2 doses of bad fever in consequence), and then left by the U.S.S. Co.'s 'Talune' for Papeete via the Cook Ids. You will understand that I was not a little excited about seeing those promised lands. I was also prepared for a bad disillusionment—

and got it. We spent two days at Rarotonga. I spent half an hour ashore. The first thing I saw ashore was an ' automobile ' marked R73. Merci. Even scenically, viewed from the steamer, Rarotonga is not within a million miles of the New Hebrides. In fact it is ugly. The inhabitants are cheeky niggers who talk a mixture of American and Australian, keep motor cars, have Trade Unions and look like Jack Johnson. Aitutaki was very much better. I wandered about there quite a lot, dreaming old dreams. But I am afraid it can't be very long before the Kerlonial blight attacks it. Thence to Raiatea (Society Ids.). Not too bad, but spoiled by swarms of Chows with their filthiness. Also the scenery is distinctly sub-tropical, great bare hills and jagged peaks. But there were no motor cars. On again to Papeete, which we reached just at dusk on Saturday, June 19th. Of course I was prepared to find Papeete up-to-date. There are swarms of motor cars. The streets are lit by electricity. But in spite of that the impression that I got in about 48 hours is that it is really a charming little place. The streets are shaded thick with acacia and flamboyant trees. The houses are pretty. The gardens are a wealth of lovely colour. I was prepared to find (and had carefully refrained from asking questions in Papeete) that this island was the proverbial ' phosphate rock,' à la Ocean Island, where life is a dreary horror only made possible by hard work. I had not allowed myself to think, but was prepared for the worst. I found the best. I have found—as far as scenery goes—the real S. Sea Island. There is no ' bush.' The only vegetation is coconuts, pawpaws, breadfruit, and gorgeous flowering shrubs—hibiscus of all sorts, Bougainvillea and many others. The reason of this is that there is practically no soil here. There is bare coral and in the crevices a sprinkling of soil. The phosphate does the rest. The result is more lovely than I could ever have pictured. Of course the buildings, works, elevators, shoots, etc., necessary to phosphate exploitation might be expected to befoul everything. But they don't. They are practically unnoticeable. The island, which is in the Tuamotu (Paumotu) Group, is 5 miles long by 2½ wide and is one perfect little dream. There are two native villages, very up-to-date, but clean and pleasant. There are about 30 whites here, all Frenchmen except myself and the Chemist. The labour is performed by about 400 indentured Chows. No expense has been spared for our comfort. I have a charming little 5-roomed bungalow to myself with a good Japanese servant. We célibataires feed at a Mess, and dam well too. There is a Club, with billiards, bridge, and a good library. We have a doctor and a hospital, church and a priest, telephones and electric light, train to and from the office. Once a week our own steamer arrives from Papeete with ice, fresh vegetables, sheep, bullocks, etc. We have our own T.S.F. which connects at Papeete with the world. This all sounds very unlike the S. Seas ; and yet it is all very charming and more like the S. Seas than anything I have yet struck. I don't wish to appear too unpatriotic, but really the French are superior to us as artists. The British impose their own brutal, competent Philistinism everywhere. The Frenchman makes himself more comfortable and doesn't spoil things.

25th August, 1920.

I HAVE not yet stopped shuddering at Sydney. I fear very much that London would displease me also. I look at illustrated papers and see pictures of the smug crowds, particularly the crowds. I feel them pushing and jostling as I felt it in Sydney, the enormous earnestness of the effort to catch the 8.11, the frenzied rush (I apologise for all clichés) for the beastly train when it comes in and the mad scramble to get out of it and catch the tram. I could be very happy perhaps in Devonshire as long as it didn't rain, but unfortunately I could not spend the rest of my life in summer time in Devonshire. I too should have to take an interest in the 8.11 and relearn to want a morning paper. You see ? It is no use composing a wonderful theme for a cracked instrument. However, I have got four years in which to make up my mind. You might think that I am in danger of becoming a bureaucrate here. I thought so just at first. I was wonderfully regular in my attendance at my office and fully prepared to take my varied duties quite seriously. In the short space of two months I have discovered that this show, from top to bottom, although superficially very business-like, is run entirely on ' Island ' principles. You couldn't understand what that means. I didn't really see very much of it in the Nlles. Hebrides because of the large number of

British and O——n people who very rarely manage
to rise to the ' Island ' outlook on life. A Frenchman makes the ascent quite naturally. The big
boss man of this Cie., although outwardly of the
keen Pelman-Hoover type, is really married to a
Tahitienne and a thorough ' Islander.' When I
first interviewed him on the subject of my duties,
he impressed upon me the enormous importance
of a dozen or so monthly reports for Paris, Ren-
seignements Statistiques, Rapport de l'Exploitation,
etc. As I rather like statistics and figure-juggling
generally I wanted to get to work at once on this
job. No earthly hope. They hadn't been made up
for over six months.

Years ago in Uruguay—I was spending a holiday
in the Colonia Siuza—I registered a vow to a star
which seemed to point directly to Tahiti that I
would get there. The way has been long and hard
and the turnings have been quite unforeseen.
What does that matter ? Cogito ergo sum.

When I first came here I thought that life would
be exceedingly humdrum. As a matter of fact, we
have had an armed revolt of Chinese labourers, a
disastrous fire, and are at present under Martial
Law with a man-of-war in port, sailors and machine
guns ashore. We have 400 odd Chows newly
arrived and there has been trouble. I dam near
got done in last Sunday through volunteering to
go and try to pacify them, but managed to bluff
my way out. The next day the swine broke into
one of the stores, armed themselves with 18″ knives
and axes, hoisted a Chinese flag and defied us for a
week. Fortunately a man-of-war turned up at

Papeete and got our wireless and hurried over.
Twenty of the ringleaders have been arrested and
sentenced to jail and deportation and for the moment
there is calm. They set fire to the Laboratory the
other night and it disappeared in about $\frac{1}{2}$ an hour.
Doubtless they will repeat that ' coup ' before long
with other buildings. I hope they won't choose
my house. So, man is vile even here and the
wicked trouble.

   . . . I don't remember a dam word of anything
I read in Sydney—and don't want to. At present
I am reading Anatole France, which is far better.
Try his *Jardin d'Epicure* and *La Rôtisserie de la
Reine Pedauque* if you want to know what pleasant-
ness he can give to a jaded mind.

August 29*th*, 1920.

. . .

I AM finally and firmly resolved that this island
shall be the final stage of my wanderings in the
Pacific. I have had to fight rather a hard battle
during the past week in order to arrive at that
decision. When I dallied in the New Hebrides
the question was not, at all events at first, so serious.
I never really saw myself settled in these islands for
ever. My scheme was always to transport my
impedimenta to some more accessible and more
benign spot. Now and here dalliance is no longer
possible. The question resolves itself very clearly
into two quite exclusive alternatives which I need
not detail. The ' stay ' alternative is, I must
confess, tempting. But the attendant sacrifices are

more than I can make. I am feeling new health rushing into me every day and that combined with the attractiveness of the place and its inhabitants leads to dreams. Fortunately I have many reminders before' my eyes of the results of ' going native.' It is a funny thing. Although I pine for that savage simplicity which, as you may remember, I once agreed spelt degeneration, I simply can't stand the sight of it in other white men. You must remember that at the plantation I was always the Pasha, the Sahib. I never in any way tried to adopt native manners or customs. It was not hard to keep oneself above the level of the Melanesian Kanaka. Here the matter is quite different. For one thing, these Tahitians have a language which is very easy to learn and which is very expressive. For another, in this as in all French colonies the ' colour question ' does not exist. The natives live more or less like Europeans and are received everywhere. Here, as I have already told you, it is very strongly expected of you to take a native woman. Unfortunately I am no Don Juan, and know it to my cost. Temporary little love affairs are out of the question for me and I refuse the other. Voilà. I said above that I could not stand the sight of a white man gone native. By that I do not refer to ' beach-combers ' of the Whish[1] variety. I mean men who earn their living honestly and support a wife and very large family of snuff and butter bastards. There are plenty here, both British and French. They are quite decent folk—but they have gone native. They wear a wreath of tiaré round

---

[1] *The Ebb Tide* (Stevenson and Osborne).

a native-made straw hat. They go bare-footed except on Sundays, when they have to undergo hell to re-wear boots. They sit more easily on their ' hunkers ' than on a chair. They expectorate when and where the fancy dictates. When they are frightened they say so. That is the complete gone native. You may say that such folk were not very favourable specimens of ' whites ' originally. That is quite true in the large majority of cases.

September 11*th*.

. . .

I HAVE finally and formally renounced all interest in Psanalysis. I tried it again upon my arrival here because there chances to be a Frenchman here who is very keen. You should see him and smell him. Any way I have no more stomach for that particular kind of befouling of all that tends to make this wretched life bearably amusing. It may be that I am getting lazy in my old age. I seem to long now simply for simple pleasures and no questions asked, to live in pleasant charity with agreeable folk and even with disagreeable ones. So we will talk no more of Jung and go no more a-Pfestering.

... I am assured that it is comparatively easy to get free from the ordinary even in Tahiti, and that in several of the other Society Islands things are in much the state described by Stevenson and Loti. The poor Marquises are sadly depopulated, but are full of charm still. I am very keen on seeing some of the Tuamotus, the real atolls. We have a good number of the natives working here, and I like their manners very much. Also the Austral Ids, attract me in spite of their name, which, incidentally. no one here seems to have heard. They are always called the Tubai Group. The natives are much sturdier and rougher than the real Tahitian, but I like the look of them very much. There are plenty of quite nice schooners going to the various groups every week or so.

I will now give you a rough idea of a day here. Firstly I rise at 5 o'clock. Without performing any toilet I make my way to the Observatory, about ten minutes' walk from my house, I being in charge of the Meteorological Service and having quite a battery of instruments to attend to 3 times a day. From there I go to the mess, where I take my bol of very excellent coffee. Thence back to my house for a shower bath, shave and dress. By the time I am dressed it is about 6 o'clock and time to go to the office. The offices are at the very edge of the cliff and again about ten minutes' walk from my house. On my way to work I meet a crowd of natives coming back from the night's fishing. I am greeted by every man of them either by a really ' nice ' salute and Bon jour, M'sieu, or else with a friendly smile and Io rana, which means the same thing. That always puts me in a good temper for the day. The offices I really like. In front a scene of quite conventional ' South Sea Island ' scenery. Behind the sea, gorgeous and dazzling. The buildings of the offices are the standard tropical business house type. Built of wood, painted white, wide verandah all round. The trade wind blows through my office so strongly that I have had to contrive an arrangement to keep the door one third open. All the doors and windows are fitted with gauze screens to keep flies and mosquitoes out. I very rarely bother to shut my screens, there being no flies and these mosquitoes being unable to pierce a hide well tanned by eight years of the New Hebrides. Once at my office my day varies very considerably, according as to whether there is a boat in, whether our own steamer is in and taking a mail to Papeete, whether it is the end of the month and therefore time for a dose of monthly reports, etc. For the last two weeks, for example, I have scarcely had time to breathe. When none of these three contingencies, or only one, is on hand, I have just about enough to do to keep me from getting bored, but not enough to prevent me from passing from office to office to have a friendly chat or a comfortable curse at the Company. I personally have no grievance against the Company, but it seems to be the proper thing to do. There are 9 offices all in a row along the verandah. I am Sécrétariat et Bureau des Expeditions and nearly everybody has to pass through my hands at least once a day. I always find that the morning passes very quickly and that I arrive at 11 o'clock with a good appetite. We all go to lunch by train, a funny little affair about 2 feet gauge. I like the train because one gets some lovely peeps of scenery when rounding the curves. At the Mess one sees almost the only sign of non-égalité in that there are two rooms for the all-white and superior persons, and the other for the really remarkable collection of shades that

there are. The food is what I have got used to by
now and missed very badly in Sydney ; you know,
all those messy little dishes so dear to the Frenchman.
I like the French way of eating, at least in hot
climates. Some of the muck that used to be served
up in Sydney when the temperature was well over
80 could only have been imagined by an O——n.
We are ten at our mess, when there are no visitors.
It would take a very long time to describe properly
the members of this mess. One day when I am
feeling spiteful. . . . The only one that I really
object strongly to is the Psanalyst. He is very
scorbutic. I don't mind his views except when he
shouts them too loudly. But he eats very lightly
boiled eggs, and this is the manner of his eating.
He holds the egg lightly between the finger and
thumb of his left hand, cuts the top neatly off, helps
himself to the contents of the top, with the point of
his knife, and then drinks the rest of the egg out
of the shell with most horrid sounds of appreciation.
This performance is repeated at every meal. Can
you wonder that I have lost my enthusiasm for
Freud ? To get back to my daily round. Lunch,
coffee and cigarettes at the Club next door, and then
up to my Observatory for the mid-day readings.
At 12.45 train back to the office. From one till
five occupation much the same as the morning.
At five I walk home, bathe, change and read for an
indefinite time. More often than not I don't go to
dinner at the mess, but content myself with a bit of
bread and cheese chez moi. For one thing I find
that I keep much better on only one meal a day in
the tropics, for another I like the twilight hours to

myself. Very often I stroll into the Club in the evening for a game of Bridge. I find that both brain and temper keep better by allowing myself that little social relaxation. I have a horror of getting into the misanthropic state that I wallowed in for so long in the New Hebrides. At nine o'clock I mount to the Observatory for the last time, make my readings and then home to bed. And so the week, and I suppose there won't be much variety, passes. Just at first I spent a few Sundays in exploring the island. There are one or two quite good footpaths, but they are soon exhausted. Walking off the roads is quite impossible, not on account of the bush but because the island consists of nothing but cruel coral, sharp as a razor. The phosphate fills up the pockets and valleys in between the points and ridges of coral. The roads have been made by the Company at a vast expense. One in particular which crosses the island is quite a masterpiece. It ends at the edge of a 300 ft. coral cliff on the weather side, and from the top of the cliff there has been hacked a Cyclopean stairway down to the water's edge. There one finds the native village of Moumou, quite a charming little place. The houses are all European little wooden bungalows, the village road is grass. The shade is coconut trees. There grows Tiaré in abundance scenting the whole village. The trade wind and the surf on the reef do all that the most ardent sentimentalists could expect of them. Needless to say, I at once made plans for finishing my days at Moumou. By chance there was a house for sale, 300 fr., the whole caboodle, two rooms, kitchen, wide verandah

all round, nice little garden full of tiaré and hibiscus,
in front the blue Pacific beating itself into snow on
the reef and stretching on till where, with faithful
eye, one sees the atolls of the Tuamotus some 50
miles distant ! The little house is remote—some
100 yards from the village, rather an advantage
when one wants to sleep, because the Tahitian has
no fixed time for sleep ; he sleeps when he is sleepy,
and that is usually in the daytime after a night spent
in either fishing, singing or mere talking. In the
heat of the afternoon, the time chosen by the
European for walking and otherwise being energetic,
one will not meet a single Tahitian abroad. Every
verandah will be full of profoundly sleeping forms ;
the coolest and breeziest verandah being the fullest
quite irrespective of any wish of the owner to keep
his verandah for his own use. What is good is for
the common weal. What is bad is left alone. Could
the early Christians have evolved a better code ?
The code of manners is not strictly insisted upon ;
it is taken for granted as among all well-bred folk.
For example just at present there is a shortage of
water owing to lack of rain (of course there is nothing
but rain water in the island), and I being the fortunate possessor of large tanks do not suffer the
dearth of the rest. I was a little surprised when I
first found no less than four native ladies in my shower
bath room at once, while a few families were gathered
round another of my tanks engaged in the weekly
blanchissage. However, they showed no em-
barrassment, so I had to be as well mannered as they.
There you have a good text for a sermon on manners.
Only don't preach it. Morals, I grieve to say, do not

exist in our sense of the word. There have never been any damn Presbyterians here with their substitute of dreariness for godliness. The only rivals of the Pères here are the Mormons ! At Moumou, for example, half the village is Mormon, the other half Catholics. So you can imagine that promiscuity is regarded as at worst a form of supererogation. And there are not many who do not indulge in that form of religious overtime. I believe the Mormons do indulge in worship about once a month, when they have no other way of killing time. The Romans, although there is quite a nice little chapel at —— owned by the Company, do their job only once a year. We have a priest affected to our needs, but he very rarely feels energetic enough to say Mass. He has been here three times in two months, but only to be witty at the mess, never even dreaming of going near the chapel. He told me that the Europeans here were all anti-clerical, and that he did not believe in too much sacrament for Tahitians. I quite agree with him.

I am already a thousand miles better than I was. I really shudder when I think of my escape. However, we will leave that alone for the present. It's a bit too soon yet. I do bless Muller for sending along this job. Nothing else would have been a little bit of good. I simply had to get work and plenty of it, but I was in no condition for city life. Besides, my qualifications, although many and varied, scarcely appeal to commercial pigs such as inhabit big cities. I could not go back to fever. I could not go straight to a cold climate. Here I have nearly all that I want, plenty of work not too dull and not fatiguing physically, a lovely climate where I can comfortably lose my fever, the first real chance in my life of saving money, absurdly cheap living, and the ' Islands ' again.

September 16th.

I AM sure that if one could have dipped beneath the surface of the New Hebrides there was a gold mine. There, however, the language-difficulty was too terrible. Also the Presbies had been too energetic. The heathen in his blindness had forgotten his wood and stone. The more fortunate Tahitian has been spared the Protestant Dissenter, and, in consequence, there still lingers, particularly in the Marquesas, much of the old priestly caste who preserve tradition. It is an awful pity that the real Tahitian language is practically extinct. No one speaks it, and only the old people of very noble blood understand it. It is an awful bastard tongue that is spoken now ; it has lost all the lovely old words, for example, descriptive of the different kinds of fear that come by night. Fortunately an old French priest has taken the trouble to write a grammar and dictionary of the ancient tongue. More fortunately I have got a copy of it from the Mission in Papeete.

September 18th.

I HAVE been thinking a lot lately about what I shall do when my time here is finished. Of course I do not forget about man and his propositions, but still it is wise to make a few plans. My mind runs very strongly on my original idea of a caravan life. I don't see at all why it should not be perfectly practicable and extremely pleasant. Of course I shall have to earn my living as I go, but that ought not to be hard. I think that the itinerant photographer line offers most inducements. There are always fairs and so on where one can earn enough to last quite a long time. The job is clean, not arduous and quite interesting in itself. I am quite certain that I shall never be able to settle down to a life of confinement in a town after so many years of vagabondage. I find that even the comparative respectability of this island is very hard to bear. I must have my bits of things always with me. I must be my own master. I don't see any other way out of the difficulty. I am hankering already after a cooler climate, where one can expend some of the energy that with returning health I feel fair rushing into me. People told me that the climate here was wonderful for recovery from malarial cachexia, and I am proving to my great satisfaction that the saying is perfectly true. I can scarcely believe that I am the same person who crawled about at the plantation, and in Sydney with the melancholy idée fixe that his days were numbered. I have at any rate learned for certain what I always believed before, to wit, that most doctors are arrant idiots. Two of the asses in Sydney confirmed all my most gloomy fears about myself. Then I had to go and undergo examination for this job, and fortunately fell into the hands of a man with tropical experience who knew what the combined effects of malaria and drink could be on a subject inclined to be hypochondriacal. He told me what the effects of a few months of the real island climate would be. I am glad to say that he has proved himself a true prophet. Of course I am not robust yet. I had gone too far down the hill to hope to regain pefect health in a few months. But I am beginning to enjoy life again. Good night. Anatole France shall lull me to a pleasant and profitable sleep.

. . . It is a most delightful morning. The wind is full trade, which does not often happen here. I was up with the dawn to make my meteorological observations and it is only seven now. The world is very clean and very sunlit. I feel strongly tempted to stroll over to Moumou, but am rather too lazy to dress. In the Nlles. Hebrides I never bothered to dress if the fancy seized me to go for a walk at any odd time. Here one has to consider the queer tastes of the petits bourgeois. They sleep in their shirts and never dream of bathing, but going out of doors in pyjamas would be considered an indecency, an insult by an Englishman to their national pride. I fear that I shall not be popular here for very long. The froggies are horribly jealous of me, and I am not always careful of their susceptibilities. That does not worry me over much, but I don't want to precipitate an open rupture, because I want to stay here, and I prefer peace to war. I foresee the time not very far distant when I shall have to retire within my own works and live without much converse with the mob. That does not worry me either. I am not sociable by nature in the way of being dependent upon much intercourse with many. As long as I have my letters to write and a few books, I can jog along quite well. Especially can I do that now that I have got renewed hope and very little to worry about. The time rushes along and that is all that matters. I do not expect very much from these four years here. I am not going to try to be serious, to stuff my poor head with a lot of difficult and useless lumber. That is a very wise decision.

. . . Bilbil. Cold logic can't cure that wound. I fear that it is incurable. Another case of the great wisdom of keeping well away from one's ideals. I cherish only the reality that I knew and that was charming. The ideal that could never, never have been realised exists with me. The actual wound hurts, but I am sure that the hurt is nothing to what I must have suffered. As for him, poor little man, he has forgotten me, and has gained a pair of very kind parents who will leave him very well off materially and will never disturb his poor little spirit as I must have done. I dream about him, see him with reproachful face and even suffer his spoken accusations, but Freud has done that much for me that I know how little there is to worry about in those dreams. I thought that when I came here I should find it easy to set up a mixed ménage once again, but I see now that it is quite impossible. I might, perhaps, manage to fall utterly. But there can be no half-way for me. For that reason the sooner I am out of the S. Seas the better. In my quality of white man, and educated white man at that, these Tahitian women do not appeal to me at all. I should have to give free play to the savage that is in me. And, as I have remarked above, that game does not seem worth the candle. I certainly could not do as some of these Europeans—let a Kanaka woman boss me and my house. My Topsy was my very slave, and enjoyed the condition. These Tahitian women have only left the slave condition behind a few years, and are as objectionable as all other liberated slaves. In reality I am sure that they would welcome a return to slavery. If I were alone on a plantation I could try the experiment, but here there are too many bad examples and too many restrictions. I have no use for a semi-civilised savage. For one thing, all these women have learned to drink. You can imagine the result. I hate a drunken white woman, or even one who drinks. I am afraid I am very primitive.

. . . In Sydney I refused two good jobs in the ushering line. But how dam glad I am now that I had the sabby to do so. I don't suppose for a moment that I could have kept on either of the jobs for a week. I was in the habit of bursting into tears without any warning two or three times a day. Imagine the joy of a class of young O——ns when ' teacher ' gave them such a chance. The head of the —— School was a very decent chap. He quite sympathised with me when I told him what was necessary of my reason for refusing one day what I had accepted the day before. Further, the pay was not equivalent to half what I was getting here. And here I have absolutely nothing to worry me as far as work is concerned. I do it when I feel inclined. If it tickles my fancy to stay away from the office for a day or two, nobody would dream of saying anything. As long as the work is done, that is all that matters. I can smoke all day, and, in short, am practically my own master.

October 17*th.*

· · ·

I DON'T think one is going to be bored so much here by the heat and damp as in the New Hebrides. You see, we are three hundred feet above sea-level, and there are no hills, so we catch every sort of breeze. At the plantation I was shut in by high hills and dense bush. Also there was the lovely fever. The natives of these parts seem an unhealthy lot of animals, elephantiasis is their speciality ; it is quite rare to see an adult native who is not in some stage of the disease. They are really suffering from civilisation quite as badly as the over-godly Melanesian. They can get as much drink as ever they like—and that is a lot :—they have learned to smoke opium, and there is no limit there except the price ; they are fuller of venereal disease than even the natives of Pimlico. The Marquesas have been absolutely emptied of people through opium and syphilis. The British have some good points after all when compared with the French. . . . A little self-control will not hurt me at all. I was in rather bad need of a little practice in it. You see, at the plantation I had been God for so long that I had lost all idea of keeping myself in hand. What pleased me, I did. When I ran up against something that was really greater than me, I had to fly to artificial means of preserving my sovereignty. That led to a lot of regrettable habits.

It was a jolly good job for all parties that I did not come straight home from the New Hebrides.

October 27th, 1920.

. . .

THE very nature of my employment here forces me to habits of more or less diligence and regularity, concentration and observation. Let me make my profit out of that. That reflection and the consequent resolutions have caused me to alter my mode of life here—which, incidentally, was not particularly agreeable to me—in various respects. Firstly, at the end of this month I am going to forsake this over-crowded village of —— and betake myself to Moumou, the village on the weather side of which I have already spoken to you. By great good luck there chances to be vacant quite a nice cottage belonging to the French Government. ... I shall be living in quite an ideal spot. I have tried to give you an idea of Moumou before. I shall leave my office at 3 o'clock every day. The walk will take me about 40 minutes—that in itself will be an excellent thing for me—and I shall be in an atmosphere far removed from all the little banalities of the life here which could only end by driving me into a dreary misanthropy. Then again, the Moumou natives speak no French. Therefore am I forced to learn the Tahitian tongue. That will be very useful to me later on. I can foresee, when my four years' hard labour are over, a very useful trip round the Marquises and Tuamotus, in which having really soaked myself in the language and

methods of thinking of the Polynesian Maori I
shall be able to gather material that escaped him
of Samoa by a million miles. (Really he only
wrote as a rather amiable tripper, when all's said
and done.)

Moumou,
October 31*st*, 1920.

PROBABLY the first words that have ever been
typewritten at Moumou. I am sitting just
inside a wire-gauze door. It keeps out the mosquitoes, but does not stop the breeze, which is
coming gently off the sea from the north-east.
North-east is not really a good quarter, but one is
thankful for breeze of any kind, and any breeze
that comes even partially off the sea is kind. Sitting
out of doors would be quite impossible because of
the swarms of mosquitoes which seem to have
appeared from nowhere during the last day or two.
Wire-gauze is a thing to be thankful for. Perhaps
it stops a little air, but very little. At least it does
not stop the view. That is wonderful, simply wonderful. I am right at the water's edge. I suppose 100
yards would take me to the end of the steeply sloping
reef, and into 200 fathoms of water. The Pacific-
blue water simply hammers and thunders on the edge
of the reef, beats itself into snow-white foam, and goes
on with the performance all day and all night. Last
night I got up at midnight—I'll tell you why later—
and found the sea busy by the light of the three-
quarters moon. For several hours sleep was quite
impossible. Any fool can sleep at any time. It is

not every night and everywhere that there is enjoyment such as was here last night. Moumou is in
a medium-sized bay on the weather side of this island.
The bay is rather shallow and the two points of the
horn-crescent are two huge cliffs, the highest points
in the island. In the centre of the bay there is a
flat stretch, back to the cliffs, of about 250 yards.
The flat tapers out to the extreme points where it
vanishes, the cliffs being real sea-cliffs, perpendicular drop of 300 feet to the water. All the flat
land is covered densely with coconut palms. Among
the palms straggle the houses of the village. Along
the water's edge runs a grass road among the palms
and tiaré. My house is at the far end of the village.
Fully a hundred yards separates me from my
nearest and only neighbour. The rest of the
village is too far away to count. From my verandah,
or better, from where I am sitting writing now, I
get a view of the whole sweep of the bay, that and
countless palms, and the smell of tiaré which is like
nothing that you know. No sound could be heard
above the din of the surf, like a very large organ
booming something in the very very bass. Last
night I stood and watched the palm trees and tried
to find a reason for the fascination exerted by the
coconut palm. For after all these years I love it
just as much as I did in those years when Kew was
my tropical island. So I began to wonder. Jevons
came to my aid ; and I found an explanation which
at least pleases me. I reasoned thus : I must confess
that I do not always like coconut palms. At times
even they have struck me as being of a grotesque
hideousness. Now where in particular have I

had that impression ? Answer obvious : in a coconut plantation. Why there ? What is the difference between Cocos Nucifera in its wild state and as cultivated by man ? Answer again obvious : man plants his palms in dead straight lines and— what is the real answer—takes care that his palm *grows perpendicular*. Of course that is it. Then I began to observe these leaning palms in quite another way. They lean towards the trade wind. The stronger blows the wind, the more the palms incline. And it is just that inclination that gives them their charm. As I watched them last night they were swaying in the light breeze and looked for all the world like dancing girls. In their dance was every degree of voluptuous grace ; some only leaned a very little, swayed in rather a condescending way—obviously well born and brought up ;—others were frankly given up to pleasure, they leaned as much as they dared and swayed in the arms of the wind in a style that admitted of no double entendre, why should they care ? they didn't know that a white man—even a sympathetic one—was watching their natural expression of natural feeling. Why should it not be as I say ? Here in the islands there are no pollen-bearing insects. The trade wind is absolutely indispensable for the propagation and fertilisation of the palm. Why should they not dance and lean comfortably on their fertiliser just as much as a Jazzing human does, only gracefully instead of grotesquely ?

Ognissanti, 1920.

Di donne io vidi una gentile schiera
Quest' Ognissanti prossimo passato. . . .

THAT is not strictly true, but I did see what
pleased me quite as much as Dante's band
of females would have done. I rose at 5 o'clock
and watched the sun rise out of the sea—a
thing I had not done for some time—'all hoar
and red.' Directly he rises here he is swallowed up again for about half an hour in mist
of his own making. That gives one time to
enjoy the pearly freshness of everything before the
obvious sets in and after it the heat. I bathed,
dressed myself nicely in silk and grey flannel (you
grant the influence of clothes ?), and went for my
first early morning impression of Moumou. I
wish you had been with me. In vain had I tried to
find the realisation of my ideal of a South Sea
island. This morning I must have been as close to
finding it as I can ever be in this wicked world.
The savage, even the quite untouched and unvisited
though beautiful in itself, has very little charm for
me. There must be these human interests of people,
their houses, their gardens and so on. Of course
these human interests must be quite free from
surburbia or colony. That was the impossible
that I was seeking. Here have I found it. I am
the only white man in the village ; I am the only
white man who has ever lived here. My pre-
decessor for whom this Government house was
built was a native though Agent Spécial, Juge de
Paix, etc., etc. The post was too badly paid even

for a native, so he resigned and no successor has been found. That was five years ago. The houses of the village are all in the European style. You might regret that until you had seen them. They are all of the chalet variety, built up on piles, verandah all round, and seem to fit the picture admirably. Then they are so smothered in flowers that they could not be hideous even if they had been perpetrated in ' art nouveau,' which, thank God, they are not. The village road is grass. Everywhere is there perfect shade, palms and the flamboyant which is just in flower ; everywhere is the heavy scent of frangi-pani and tiaré. The sea this morning was startlingly blue inshore ; further out it was stained crimson by the sunrise. Fortunately the two mentioned colours separated by the band of white foam did not make me think of—you know what.

The colours, the smell, the surf-song, and the peace made me a pleasant walk. The village was not stirring, except the two chow stores where Mrs. Chow was in each case roasting coffee for the breakfast of her lord. All the inhabitants of Moumou sleep out on the verandah on the sea side of the house, which is also the street side. As they are not used to mosquitoes and have no means of protecting themselves, all the sleepers were wrapped up tight in their sleeping-mats, to me (used to Melanesian burial customs) rather a gruesome sight. There had been a great religious festival at the village on the other side of the island (Temao) to celebrate the opening of a new tabernacle ; and all Moumou had been there to drink, dance and praise the Lord, hence the lateness of the village. In each garden was picketed a horse, or rather what passes as horse here. All along the street was a little colony of pigs out scavenging. I walked along and praised the lord that I had had the good sense to get away from —— with its dam Frenchmen and pseudo-parisian surburban, petit bourgeois, bloody-awfulness. Here I am quite remote and safe, although it only takes me ¾ hour to walk to the office. The French cockney is no walker at all, and there is always the great staircase up the cliff to mount. They—the frogs—think I am quite mad. That leaves me a bit cold, as you may imagine.

The manner of my moving here on Saturday was quite amusing in its way. It is very difficult to get these Moumou natives to do anything. They are spoiled by the French for one thing, and have very little use for money for another. The only temptation is alcohol. With the promise of alcohol I had managed to get a carpenter to make and fit mosquito-doors to the house. With the promise of much grog I had persuaded an ancient bird, possessor of a cart, to come to —— and get all my effects, including the stock of food and utensils that I had purchased at the Company's store. Of course the cart only begins at the top of the cliff, down the staircase and along the flat at the bottom things have to be carried—no small joke. Well, my ancient turned up all right at —— at about two o'clock; between us we got everything on the cart, leaving only the store goods to be called for en passant. I thought I would push on on foot leaving the carter to load up at the store and catch me up.

Then I made a fool's mistake. I gave him the bottle that was to be his wage. I did not want to carry it with me. I ought to have known my Kanaka better. Result, at about six o'clock arrived my carter triumphantly drunk with two pals ditto, safely carrying all my luggage, furniture, etc., but —having quite forgotten to call at the store. So there I was at dusk without a bite, no chance of getting any in Moumou as all the world was going over to the other side and going to stay there till Monday morning. My stock of Tahitian is exceedingly limited. Obviously it was no good trusting to any of the drunken brigade. I managed to tempt an old boy who looked trustworthy and thirsty, by the promise of a bottle of whisky, to repair at once to —— before the store shut and bring back my rather heavy and numerous packages—including two largish cases of tinned potatoes, one bundle of Chinese mats filled up with odds and ends—no mean load for two strong men considering the conditions. The old thing, however, refused help and set off. I waited for him, foodless and lightless, till nine o'clock. Then, being dog tired, I turned in on my deck chair. The house has been unhabited for years and was only lived in by natives even then. You can perhaps imagine its condition, not a nice one for sleeping in. However, I slept. At midnight I was awakened by my faithful old porter. He had had to wait for the moon to rise and had then made three journeys up and down that terrible staircase and had triumphantly done the job on his own—no one to share the bottle with. He had got all the things as far as his own house. Did I want them to-night ? Rather than lose the drink he would have turned to and brought them along, but I had mercy on him and produced the bottle. With profuse thanks he hugged it to his ancient but stalwart chest and bade me good-bye. Five minutes later he was back to reshake hands and ask " Comment t'appeler toi ? " He insisted on learning my name thoroughly before leaving, being afraid doubtless that I was only a vision and would perhaps vanish in the night. He came round about seven next morning looking much the worse for wear but faithful to his trust. I shall like that old man. And that is how I came to see the Moumou palms dancing in the moonlight.

Sunday, except for a brief interval in which to tap a few words to you, I spent in cleaning the house and arranging my few sticks. I have got a kerosene stove from Papeete to do my little bit of cooking. I never eat more than once a day, so I shall reserve my feeding till I get back here and thus escape the ' mess,' which was quite the worst trial I had to endure—not on account of the food, which was good, but because of the manners and flatulent conversation of my mess-mates. So here I am again, in solitude, but nearer far to my ideal South Sea existence than ever I had expected to be. The regular work at the office, the regular going to and fro, will prevent me getting into the melancholy state that the last year of the plantation brought me. I am very nearly fit in health. The walking will do me a lot of good. I have given up alcohol and feel all the better for so doing. In short I am beginning to enjoy life once again. All the same, I don't feel in the least tempted to think of a permanent dwelling in the islands any more.

November 3rd.

I WAS too lazy to write last night; or rather I was too tired. It will take me a few days to get used to the walk and the strong sea air. At present I am full of sleep, a luxury I have had to do without very largely at ———, as my house was in easy ear shot of the cercle where the French proletariat made night hideous with their howls, to say nothing of their beastly mongrel dogs, of which each human mongrel possessed at least three. When master at last went to bed about two a.m. his even fouler dog began to yap in French. When you add that to bands of prowling Chows raking over heaps of empty tins in search of scavenger crabs, you can imagine how I, still rather nervy and irritable, used to pass my nights. Here there is no noise but the surf, and I could wish that that were ten times more loud, for every note of its music is healing and delight to me. After my frugal meal to-night I went and sat on the edge of the reef for an hour and a half. I am just back, and then only because it was all so wonderful that I could not bear it any longer alone. I can't describe my sensations now. It would seem too much like sacrilege. You will perhaps get it one of these days when the memory has to come out. Even the mere telling you that I have been enjoying myself seems to do me good. I am sure that if I were to begin to try and express my sensations of the last hour, I should quickly have to resort to the French sentimental writer's " Ah ! . . . " à la Pierre Loti, which (and whom) I loathe. I feel my limitations very much and am sad.

One thing I must tell you, and you must not laugh. When sitting at the water's edge I can see a very, very bright star—I know its name and its Right Ascension, etc., but I refuse to think about such things—and it shines exactly over my house. Now it is the very self-same star to which I prayed in Uruguay when vowing to get to Tahiti sooner or later. Of course Moumou is not Tahiti, but the difference of longitude and latitude is very small, an error that even an experienced navigator might be excused. I feel that I have done very well. I fear that I can't delude myself that my star will continue to point out my South Sea home, but it does at the exact date of my finding this refuge, which is quite curious enough chance to please me very much. Tell me that you too would be pleased at such a childish game.

I have been called on by all the best people of the village—which means the whole lot. They come in batches and sit on the verandah and chat pleasantly while weaving their invariable Tiaré garlands. Most of their talk I can't yet understand, but I smile and make the most of my few phrases. They think that I was born knowing Tahitian. Perhaps I was. Anyway it is very amusing, much more so than talking Biche-la-mar. This is really a wonderful language. Their stock of separate words to express the soul, its attributes, after-death conditions, night fears, joys and sorrows is perfectly bewildering.

Then the number of separate words for describing wind, sunset, states of the sea and other pleasant South Sea matters bespeaks a people who must have been artists in quite a Greek way, although their self-expression only reached the oral stage. Shame to these French who only teach French in the schools—and make attendance compulsory : the present generation know none of these words. Instead of their own magnificent stock of words for appraising nature's wonders, the modern Tahitian child says that something is ' épatante,' ' rigolo ' or ' moche,' just like any vulgar Parisian, and, like the vulgar Parisian, has no further choice. If you knew how I loathed those three adjectives.

November 4th.

WESTERLY weather to-night. No need to explain that to an islander. Besides the general mugginess the West wind here brings swarms of mosquitoes. I tried sitting out this evening, but even down on the reef the brutes found me out. I was very sad at having to come in. Besides a more than unbelievable sky—green and purple—there was a very pleasant addition to the picture in the shape of a big native schooner on the skyline trying to beat up from the Tuamotus. I had spotted it from the top of the cliff at four o'clock, and at six it was if anything a little further off— strong tide and light head breeze—they will, perhaps, make the island some time to-morrow, if they don't get tired of beating and make a fair wind of it fetching up any old where. That is how natives navigate, why shouldn't they? It's much more interesting than having a fixed time table and sticking to it. Many white men, however, never reach that happy condition. That wretched ' fifty years of Europe' seems mapped out into minutes from their cradle to t'other place. I am sending you this time a map of the island roughly drawn by myself so that you may follow my perhaps bewildering repetition of names that convey nothing to you.

. . . By the way, I have mentioned several times, and you have doubtless seen mentioned elsewhere, the Tiaré. It would be hard to talk about the Eastern Pacific without talking about Tiaré. As a matter of dull fact, Tiaré simply means flower; but even the natives always mean the particular Tiaré whose full native name is ' tiaré Tahiti.' I find that it is known to botanists as Gardenia Tahitensis ; that may give you an idea of what it is like, though it does not remind me of Gardenia at all. It is really only found wild on one or two islands, Tahiti, Raiatea and here—and here only will it grow at Moumou. It does not seem to like either Frenchmen or phosphate dust, another point in its favour in my eyes. It really is a most entrancing shrub. It grows on quite low bushes which are simply smothered in flowers. It has no season, but is everlasting and ever delightful. Here at Moumou it is strongly rivalled by the Frangi Pani (I don't know what language that is or how to write it) which, though more strongly scented and a more pretentious tree, does not please me as much as

Tiaré. I think that is because I have unpleasant memories of Frangi Pani in the garden at Mosquito Bay.

. . . I have got so used to roughing it that I can be quite content with the excessively plain and strictly necessary. I can't stand the ornate, the badly made, or the sham. I can stand packing cases, faut de mieux though. Of course if I had the money I should love to have a nicely furnished house and a well considered garden. I don't think that either my house or garden would be either vulgar or precious. The money value and the historical of furniture leave me more than cold. I hate museums except in so far as they are collections of beautiful objects. I should loathe my house to be any sort of museum. As for antique hideousness, I hate it every bit as much as modern hideousness. Why not ? The man ———, you know whom I mean, was a very ardent collector of ' lustre ' and ' Toby mugs ' and ' sailor jugs.' I am certain he did not really consider them beautiful. He certainly was keen on collecting them. That mania I can understand and despise. But that man used to jargon by the hour on the ' beauty ' of his grotesque chunks of ill-made, unserviceable pottery. That is the sort of snobbery that makes me rave. I used to affect it myself once on a time. Then again you know my overstrained—perhaps—notion of fitness. If I had to inhabit a new house, and there is no reason why I should inhabit an old one of someone else's, I should seek out a really good cabinetmaker —I should go to Hong Kong for him—and have my furniture made under my eye of the very best wood that I could get. I guarantee that my house would not be unbeautiful. And once again I should thank God that I am not. . . . Mind you, I can get enormous pleasure out of merely looking at really good furniture, but my pleasure is almost inarticulate on account of my ignorance and is not at all joined to a lust of possession. I have quite definitely renounced any waste of time in trying either to be or to appear to be cultured. Being pleased with a thing of beauty I no longer want to know the date of the death of the maker, nor yet his name, nor yet the name of his mistress, nor any one at all of the data so essential to real culture, to hack journalists and secretaries of Improvement Guilds. I like that. All right, finish. I don't like that. Then your taste is bad ! Tant pis. Oh, ye Antinomians, praise ye the lord ! Oh, ye daring men of sense magnify his name with me ! Please forgive my savagery. Remember where I am and what I can see through my doors and windows.

November 7th.

.   .   .

THERE are a few Yankees who have come for the simple life, living on coconuts and dressing in a pareu. The mosquitoes soon cure most of them in a few weeks, those that manage to hold out against mosquitoes are the ones who provide later the few cases of Europeans suffering from elephantiasis. I saw one on the wharf at Papeete, mad as a hatter. The only people who manage to go native properly, I mean to live a real simple life with

natives without becoming vicious, are the Germans.
I knew several in the Hebrides, and travelled from
Auckland with some who had had to clear out of
the French islands during the war, and were then
on their way to the Cook group. They slept on
deck in their clothes, sat about in the scuppers, wore
native clothes, ate like natives at any odd time, and
yet seemed very decent hard-working people.
Perhaps the German is not so far along the de-
scensus of Civilisation as we are. I believe that the
Scandinavian races also make good white natives.
I knew several Petersens and Simonsens in the
Hebrides, and they all had good plantations and
dozens of half-caste children.

. . . I sat at my evening meal an hour or so ago
and could scarcely eat because my eyes would turn
to the window. I do not believe that any man could
describe at all adequately the view from that window.
Certainly no painter could paint it. The very
thought of photography on it makes me laugh. . . .
At one instant to-night I was marvelling at the
curve of the bay, the stretch of pure white sand in
the distance under the dreadful black of the cliffs,
the sea which is quite rough and of the palest
Cambridge blue—and then I turned my head slightly
and looked out of one of the three doors which open
to the front (the window in question faces south,
the house east). To my great surprise the sea on
that side was of the richest purple that I have ever
seen in these tropic seas. I could scarcely believe
my eyes. I got up to look and there sure enough
was a distinct line of demarcation on the water
between the pale blue and the purple. Cause?

Unknown and immaterial. Effect ? Almost unbelievable when added to the bay and the palms
and the general idea that here is the S. Sea as dreamed
of by you and me. Is it more lovely than the
famous beauty-spots of Europe ? I am perfectly
certain that it is. There is an ' atmosphere ' (cliché
and ignotum per ignotius at that, but what would
you call it ?) that could not exist in civilisation which
makes a tremendous difference in the values of what
is intrinsically wonderful. The sum total is the
S. Seas. Here is a little difference. My neighbour
has been making copra all day—he had already
started when I passed at five-thirty—and this
evening he is burning the husks and shells of his
coconuts in little heaps scattered about the area
that he has worked to-day. The bright red flame
of the burning shells and the blue smoke make an
addition to the colour scheme that the good man
should be paid for at the price of many tons of
copra. Then after eating I strolled down the
village street. On every verandah was a party with
a guitar and a flaring kerosene lamp. The soft
(really) twang of the guitar and the gentle humming
song, mixed with the smell of the tiaré which one
could no longer see but knew surrounded every
head on every verandah, take one thousands of miles
above the finest thing in Europe, spoiled as it would
most undoubtedly be by hotels and crowds ! Then
where in Europe could you get sea music as one
gets it on the reefs in the Pacific ? I have heard
surf beating in Europe and elsewhere, and the sound
to me was always cruel. Here it is only music.
One is apt to forget that surf and underestimate

its influence, so perpetual is it. But since I came to Moumou I seem to have begun to realise what an awful lot there is to be thankful for. I really feel ashamed sometimes when I catch myself standing still with hat off and arms outstretched as if to embrace the beauty of it all. A very little more and I shall be on my knees. Most un-English, what? And to think that during the twelve years that this company has worked here I am the first of its ' agents' that has discovered Moumou. I am perfectly certain that Moumou would bore them all heartily except for the chance of an adventure with a native woman. So much the better for me. I don't suppose that these French are more Philistinic than the same sort of Englishmen would be, but for a nation that openly labels itself as the only artistic one in Europe and is always ready to go into ecstasies, such neglect is curious—not really though, only if one did not realise that France is living on its past.

November 19*th.*

. . .

THIS is really a most extraordinary life that I am living, even for me who have not been exactly humdrum. It is the unique combination that is pleasing me so much. Just think. I get up each day at five o'clock, all alone in my house. I bathe and so on and then have quite the most wonderful walk that any man could have to any office. Such a walk for a planter might not be strange, but to an office! Arrived at the said office I work for eight hours really hard at a job which keeps my brain harder at work than it has ever been in its life. This week, for example, I have been preparing a truly colossal mail. Up to date I have written over seventy letters to say nothing of fifteen monthly reports, two complete dossiers of the loading of two steamers and various odds and ends of orders for things ranging from railway sleepers to tinned jam. The letters include Paris, London, Sydney, Melbourne, Auckland, Frisco, Hong Kong, Tokyo and Singapore. That in itself is not banal. All those letters are written in seven-fold and each of the six copies has its own separate classification and destination : so one needs to keep one's head pretty clear.

At three o'clock I have had enough. I walk back to Moumou reaching my house about four. Then household matters keep me busy for about an hour, cooking, washing and so forth. At five I bathe and change. Feeding being finished I take my pipe and enjoy myself on the beach till seven. At seven I come in, light up and write a few pages. At about nine I go out again. Just at present the moon is between first quarter and full, giving enough light to read by, and the palms and surf would make me cry if they did not make me feel so gorgeously happy. I think I am just beginning to know what happiness beauty can give. . . .

APPENDIX.

THE ACTUAL DOCUMENT WHICH IS THE BASIS OF THE FOLLOWING STORY

Declaration made at —— on April 1st, 1916, at 7 p.m., by a native named Jack of Léhili, being seriously wounded and likely to die.

" A. and B. had been quarrelling for some time. On Friday (yesterday) A. came to Tahi to trade. B. went down to the shore and called out to A. (who was in his dinghey) to come ashore. A. replied: ' All right, I will come ashore to-morrow.' He and B. blackguarded one another, and A. went back to Léhili.

" A. came back on Saturday morning (this morning). B. and his wife went down to meet him. A. came ashore, and he and B. started to fight. I was some distance away looking on. A. and B. both fell down and then Mrs. B. tried to pull A. away from B. Mrs. A. then hit Mrs. B. and all four fought. B. fell down in the water. A. took a stone to hit B. I came down and called out: ' finish ' and pulled B. out of the water. I caught hold of Mr. A. and said: ' Finish now.' I then let him go. A. then went to his dinghey (which was pulled ashore) and took a revolver out of a case. I called out: ' Oh, Mr. A., stop.' A. then shot me and afterwards shot B. A. got into his dinghey and went away."

Signed : JACKSON.

Witness : (The author).

HARRY C. his mark.

ON THE BEACH.

SCENE.

A white sandy beach at Léhili, Pauma. About a quarter of a mile out at sea is the barrier reef with big surf breaking. Half a mile inland, up a steep hill, can be seen a galvanised-iron store. White man's launch is at anchor close to the shore. He wades ashore and accosts ABOH, *who is walking about with a bow and arrows looking for fish which he could not hit. The two shake hands.*

CHARACTERS.

WHITE Man (*dressed in dungaree trousers, white singlet and broad-brimmed felt hat. Very dirty. Looks like a third-class stoker on a tramp steamer*).

ABOH, *a native of Pauma.*

DJEMALAOS, *a Seychelle Island nigger.*

VARIOUS PAUMA NATIVES.

Aboh. Goudé, Master.

White Man. Goudé, Aboh. You go where?

A. No. Me walk 'bout no more. You, you go where?

W. M. Me come long Ambrym longa lannitch. Me want pay 'im some somethin' longa store longa Mis Collins.

A. Oright. Gooby. Me, me stop. (*They shake hands. Exit* W. M. *along bush-track. Thirty minutes later* W. M. *reappears.*)

W. M. 'Ere. Which way longa Mis Collins? 'Im ' e no stop?

A. Yiss.

W. M. Missis b'long 'im 'e no stop?

A. Yiss.

W. M. Two feller 'e go where ?

A. Two feller 'e go Vila finish.

W. M. (*angrily*). Which way you no bin tell 'im out ?   Me, me bin go longa store.   Me sing out, me sing out.   No. (Авон *laughs merrily.   W. M. enraged forgets his biche-la-mar.*)   You . . . you.

A. (*frightened*).   Me no sabby.

W. M. (*anxious for information, recollects himself*).   Two feller 'e go Vila finish long time ?

A. No.   'Im 'e go yissterdi no more.

W. M. Two feller 'e go longa what ?

A. Me no sabby.

W. M. Two feller 'e go longa lannitch ?   No, two feller 'e go longa boat long all boy ?   Which way ?

A. No.   Two feller 'e go long *picnini man-war.*[2]

W. M. *Capman*[1] 'e bin take 'im 'e go.

A. Yiss.

W. M. Longa what ?

A. (*brightens up*).   You no bin haar 'im ?

W. M. Yiss.   Me no haara nothin.   Me come now 'ere no more.   Mis Collins 'e bin make wha'name ?

A. 'Im 'e bin killa one boy.

W. M. 'Im 'e *kill 'im dead finish* ?[5]

A. No.   'Im 'e no dead no more.   'Im 'e no dead finish.

W. M. 'oo 'ere boy where Mis Collins 'e bin kill 'im ?

A. Jack.   Me haar 'im all 'e tell 'im all same.

W. M. Wha'name Jack ?   Jack long Liro ?

A. No.

W. M. Jack longa Tapolai ?

A. No.

W. M. 'oo Jack ?   You tell 'im out.

A. You no sabby ?   Jack longa Tahi.

W. M. Brother b'long you ?

A. Yiss.   How much you pay longa copperah ?

W. M. Mis Collins 'e bin kill 'im longa what?

A. Me no sabby.

W. M. Mis Collins 'e bin kill 'im long hand b'long him? No, 'e bin kill 'im longa one wood?

A. Me no sabby.

W. M. Yiss; you sabby. You tell 'im out you . . .

A. (*frightened*). Me no sabby. (W. M. *sees a whale-boat pulling for the passage.*)

W. M. Wha'name boat 'ere?

A. (*with his back to the sea*). Me no sabby.

W. M. Me tink 'e one boat long all boy.

A. (*braver at the thought of approaching help turns round and looks at the boat which is still almost indistinguishable*). No; 'im 'e boat long *Harry*? [6]

W. M. 'Oo 'ere Harry?

A. White man where 'e look out store long Liro. 'Im 'e come longa pay 'im copperah. 'Im 'e pay good-feller price longa copperah.

W. M. Wha' name white man? 'E no got white man longa Liro.

A. No. 'E got. 'Im 'e no white man all same you-feller. 'Im 'e black. 'Im 'e no boy.

W. M. (*enlightened*). Oh yiss. Name long 'im Djemalaos?

A. (*brightly*). Yiss. Me haar 'im all 'e tell 'im all same. (*The two then solemnly watch the approach of the whale-boat which after about ten minutes anchors close ashore.* Mr. Djemalaos, *fashionably dressed in pyjamas and boots, is carried ashore. On landing he dusts his boots with a red silk handkerchief, rolls a cigarette and then advances. He first shakes hands with* Aboh *in Kanaka fashion, i.e. with averted face and without salutation, then salutes* W. M. *with an elegant bow.* Aboh *then shakes hands all round with the dozen or so of the boat's crew. They are from his village and he only left them about two hours ago; but it is the proper thing to do. The "boys" then sit down and begin to smoke as if they had come for that purpose and had no other interest in life. Mr. D. rolls another cigarette which he stores in the pierced lobe of his ear and then addresses W. M. very politely.)*

D. B'jour, m'sieu, vous allez bien ?

W. M. Me no sabby talk Frennich. Me no *man oui-oui.*[7]

D. Oright. Me sabby talk Ingerlish. Me gotta " éducation " Me no all same all boy. All boy 'e " sauvage."

W. M. You stop long time longa Liro ?

D. Yiss ; 'e long time little bit. Four moon 'e go finish now.

W. M. You you stop where beefore ?

D. Me me stop Vila beefore. Me bin work two *yam*[8] longa Ballande. Beefore me work long time longa ――.* Me look out coal longa machine. Me me " matelot." Beefore me stop――

W. M. (*losing interest when the history looks like leaving "the Islands"*). Wha' name 'ere longa Mis Collins ?

D. Yiss. 'Im 'e bin killa one boy. Capman 'e take 'im 'e go calaboosh.

W. M. Mis Collins 'e bin kill 'im boy longa what ?

D. 'Im 'e bin shoot 'im longa small feller musket.

W. M. Longa one 22 ?

D. No ; longa small-feller musket where you fire him off long hand.

W. M. Longa revolver ?

D. Yiss ; 'im 'ere―" révolver."

W. M. Jack 'e bin make wha' name longa Mis Collins ?

D. No. Mis Collins more Harry two feller 'e bin row.

W. M. 'Oo 'ere Harry ?

D. Harry Two-Flags longa Tahi.

W. M. " B." ?

* Name of a steamer.

D. Yiss; 'im' e name b'long 'im.

W. M. You you stop time Mis Collins 'e bin shoot 'im Jack?

D. Yiss; me bin stop long house long Harry.

W. M. Oright; you tell 'im out; you storyan.

D. You, you capman?

W. M. Wha' name, capman? Me no capman nothin'.

D. Oright. More better you me two-feller sit down. (*They sit down on a coral boulder. The " boys " move and make a ring round them and hawk and spit with gusto.*)

D. (*after much circumlocution gets into his stride*). Mis Collins more Harry two-feller 'e row all time all time.

W. M. Two-feller 'e row longa what?

D. Two-feller 'e row longa Mis Collins 'e speak " Frennich money 'e no good." All boy 'e no want 'im Frennich money. Mis Collins 'e pay 'im copperah long Ingerlish money. Harry 'e no got. 'Im 'e no sabby pay copperah. 'Im 'e cross.

W. M. Two-feller 'e row where?

D. Longa Friday Mis Collins 'e come longa Tahi longa dinghey. 'Im 'e want come ashore. Harry 'e stop long house. 'Im 'e derronk. 'Im 'e look Mis Collins. Allez; 'im 'e races 'e go down longa salt-water. 'Im 'e sing out no good longa Mis Collins. 'Im 'e sing out " You come ashore; me fight 'im bloody face b'long you. You one——"

W. M. Mis Collins 'e come ashore?

D. No.

W. M. Which way no? 'Im 'e fright long Harry?

D. No; 'im 'e no fright. 'E got big-feller sea longa beach. 'Im 'e no sabby come ashore. 'Im 'e sing out " You wait. Byumby to-morrer me come talk long you back again. You one —— too."

W. M. Mis Collins 'e bin come ashore longa Saturday?

D. Yiss. Me more Harry two-feller me stop long house. Harry 'e derronk. Missis b'long 'im 'e derronk too.

W. M. 'Oo 'ere Missis b'long Harry ?

D. 'Im 'e one woman Maré.

W. M. Harry 'e marry long 'im ?

D. No. 'Im 'e look out long 'im no more.

W. M. Time you more Harry two-feller you stop long house you look Mis Collins 'e come ?

D. Yiss. Mis Collins more missis b'long him two-feller 'e come longa dinghey. Dinghey 'e come ashore. Allez ; Harry 'e races 'e go down long salt-water.

W. M. You you go ?

D. No. Me more missis two-feller me stop long house.

W. M. Harry 'e make wha' name ?

D. 'Im 'e fight 'im face long Mis Collins. Mis Collins 'e pull 'im up dinghey. 'Im 'e no look Harry.

W. M. Mis Collins 'e fight 'im Harry ?

D. Yiss. Mis Collins 'e pull 'im up dinghey finish. 'Im 'e fight 'im face b'long Harry. All blood b'long 'im 'e fall down. Mis Collins 'e catch 'im Harry longa neck b'long 'im. Two feller 'e fall down longa salt-water. Salt-water 'e wash 'im Harry.

W. M. Miss Collins 'e stop on top ?

D. Yiss. 'Im 'e sit down longa belly b'long Harry. 'Im 'e fight 'im face b'long Harry long one piece corail. Salt-water 'e go inside longa mouth b'long Harry. Close up 'im 'e derrown.

W. M. You, you no give hand long Harry ?

D. No. Me me fright long Mis Collins. Me stop long house. You gotta matches ?

W. M. (*who is smoking " trade " tobacco in a silver-mounted briar*). No. (D. *then takes a lighted pipe from a boy's mouth, lights a cigarette and replaces the pipe without a word.*)

W. M. Jack' e bin give hand long Harry ?

D. No. Jack 'e stop no more. 'Im 'e no give hand. Missis b'long Harry yiss ; 'im 'e give hand. 'Im 'e races 'e go down longa salt-water. 'Im 'e want pull 'im out heye belong Mis Collins longa finger b'long 'im. Byumby Missis b'long Mis Collins 'im 'e cross too. 'Im 'e *take 'im out all calico b'long 'im.*[3] *'Im 'e stop nothin.*[4] 'Im 'e kaikai (bite) b'long Missis b'long Harry. Dog b'long Harry 'e come. 'Im 'e kaikai —— b'long Missis b'long Mis Collins. Four-feller more dog b'long Harry 'e fight. (*Laughs heartily at the recollection of the " bagarre."*)

W. M. All time Harry 'im 'e stop down longa salt-water ?

D. Yiss. All time salt-water 'e wash 'im Harry. All time Mis Collins 'e fight 'im face b'long Harry longa one piece corail. Four-feller more dog 'e fight. (*Laughs heartily again and ends with a good hawk.*)

W. M. All time Jack 'e no makea nothin' ?

D. No. Time Jack 'e look Harry close up 'e dead-finish 'im 'e sing out " Finish now Mis Collins." Jack 'e pull 'im Harry longa make 'im salt-water 'e no wash him.

W. M. Harry 'e sabby walk about ?

D. No. 'Im 'e dead. All blood b'long 'im 'e fall down. 'Im 'e good now. Face b'long 'im 'e broke no more.

W. M. Jack 'e no bin fight Mis Collins ?

D. Yiss ; 'e no fight 'im. Mis Collins 'e races 'e go longa dinghey. 'Im 'e take 'im musket b'long 'im. Allez ; 'im 'e fire 'im off quick-feller. Bullet 'e catch 'im Jack longa belly b'long 'im. I'm 'e fall down.

W. M. Mis Collins 'e want shoot Harry ?

D. Yiss. 'Im 'e want shoot Harry ? 'Im 'e no bin shoot good. Bullet 'e catch 'im salt-water no more.

W. M. Mis Collins 'e no want shoot Missis b'long Harry ?

D. Yiss. Me tink Mis Collins 'im 'e no sabby look good. All

blood 'e fall down longa heye b'long 'im where Missis
b'long Harry 'e break 'im longa finger.

W. M. Missis b'long Mis Collins 'e make wha' name ?

D. 'Im more Missis b'long Harry two feller 'e fight. All time
all time. Dog b'long Harry 'e fight too. 'Im 'e kaikai
—— b'long Missis b'long Mis Collins. (*Laughs merrily,
and spits.*)

W. M. Jack 'e stop long ground ?

D. Yiss. 'Im 'e dead. All blood 'e fall down longa belly
b'long 'im.

W. M. You, you stop long house all time ?

D. Yiss. Me fright long Mis Collins.

W. M. Which way ? You no shame you . . . coward
you ?

D. Yiss. Me fright long Mis Collins. You gotta matches ?

W. M. No. (*Same business as before with pipe.*)

W. M. Harry 'e dead all time ?

D. No. Byumby 'im 'e get up. Allez ; 'im 'e go long house
longa takea Winchester.

W. M. Harry 'e fire 'im off Winchester ?

D. No. (*Laughs heartily.*) 'Im' e no gotta cartouche.

W. M. All time Mis Collins 'e stop ?

D. No. 'Im 'e pull 'im Missis b'long 'im. Two-feller 'e go
longa dinghey. Missis b'long 'im, 'im 'e no want 'im.
'Im 'e want fight back again longa Missis b'long Harry.
No. Mis Collins 'e no want 'im. 'Im 'e pull 'im Missis
b'long 'im. Two-feller 'e go finish longa dinghey.

W. M. Jack all time 'im 'e dead ?

D. Me tink. Me no bin go look. Byumby all boy Tahi 'e
come down longa salt-water. 'E look Jack.
Allez ; all 'e take 'im longa boat long altogether.

W. M. All 'e take 'im 'e go where ?

D. Me haar 'im all 'e tak 'im 'e go long one white man longa
Mapuna.

Aboh (*re-awakening*). Yiss. Me-feller take 'im 'e go longa white man longa Mapuna.

W. M. White man 'e speak wha' name ?

A. 'Im 'e bin makea one paper long capman. Finish, 'im 'e send 'im Jack 'e go Vila longa Dokkitor longa lannitch b'long Lizzy.

W. M. You bin haar 'im news long Jack ?

A. Yiss. 'Im 'e dead finish. All 'e bin put 'im long ground. How much you pay longa copperah ?

D. Me tink byumby Capman 'e cut 'im off head b'long Mis Collins. You tink ?

W. M. Me no sabby. Might Capman 'e make ' im all same.

D. Me tink Mis Collins 'im 'e no good. 'Im 'e sabby fighta boy all time all time. You gotta matches ?

W. M. (*lighting his pipe*). No.

D. Oright. Gooby. Me me go pay 'im copperah.

W. M. Gooby. Me me go Ambrym.

(*General handshaking.* *Exeunt* OMNES.)

NOTES.

(1) Capman = " government " as pronounced by natives.

(2) Picnini man-war = H.M.Y. ——.

(3) Take 'im out all calico b'long 'im = strip.

(4) Stop nothin' = be naked, be neglected, be a widow, etc.

(5) To kill = to hit.

    ,, ,, dead = unconscious.

    ,, ,, dead-finish = dead.

Aboh says that Jack was ' dead ' but not ' dead finish ' although at the time of speaking he knew that Jack was buried. The Kanaka only connects cause and effect when they are immediate.

(6) ' Harry ' is a generic term for all 'store-keepers ' whose names are hard to pronounce.

(7) Man-oui oui = Frenchman. Compare Malay ' ourang-didong = a man dites donc = Frenchman.

(8) Yam = year, *i.e.* the time between planting and digging the yams, approximately twelve lunar months.